A Different Drummer

E.J. Banfield, 1886, aged thirty-four, about the time of his marriage, after having his eye removed. In almost all photographs he is shown in profile, favouring the left side of his face.
(A.H. Chisholm Papers, courtesy of Mitchell Library.)

A Different Drummer

the story of E.J. Banfield,
the Beachcomber of Dunk Island

by
Michael Noonan

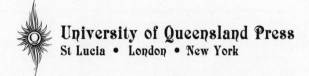
University of Queensland Press
St Lucia • London • New York

University of Queensland Press, St Lucia, Queensland 1983

Typeset by University of Queensland Press
Printed and bound by The Dominion Press—Hedges & Bell, Melbourne

Distributed in the United Kingdom, Europe, the Middle East, Africa, and the Caribbean by Prentice-Hall International, International Book Distributors Ltd, 66 Wood Lane End, Hemel Hempstead, Herts., England.

Published with the assistance of the Literature Board of the Australia Council.

National Library of Australia
Cataloguing-in-Publication data

Noonan, Michael, 1921–
  A different drummer.

Bibliography.
  Includes index.
  ISBN 0 7022 1764 6.

  1. Banfield, E.J. (Edmund James), 1852–1923.
  2. Authors, Australian — Biography, I. Title.

A828'.209

Library of Congress Cataloging in Publication Data

Noonan, Michael.
  A different drummer.

  Bibliography: p.
  Includes index.
  1. Banfield, E.J. (Edmund James), 1852–1923.
2. Dunk Island (Qld.) — Biography. 3. Dunk Island
(Qld.) — Description and travel. I. Banfield, E.J.
(Edmund James), 1852–1923. II. Title.
DU280.D7B466   1984   994.3'6 [B]   83-16765
ISBN 0-7022-1764-6

This book is dedicated to
ANN MOLONEY
who passed away as gently and gracefully as she had lived about the time it was completed. Without her initial help and continuing encouragement over many, many years, I would not have been able to complete this or any other book.

Contents

Contents

Illustrations

Introductory Note

It is said that the Beachcomber still roams the strands, the paths and the forests of his old domain.

Someone has even claimed to have seen a barefooted, straw-hatted figure lingering pensively in the moonlight on the verandah of a tourist chalet, a man of seventy or thereabouts with a white moustache and steel-rimmed spectacles.

It would not be surprising if the Beachcomber were still on his beloved Isle, even if only in spirit. After all, to him it was utterly paradisial, everything a man could wish for in this or any other life.

It has not been the author's good fortune when on Dunk Island to glimpse the Beachcomber, let alone to have had the opportunity to waylay him. Had it been possible to interrupt him on his ghostly strolls, and to ask him to do a little beachcombing from the past, certain gaps in his story might have been filled, some of the shadowy spaces illuminated.

When *The Times* praised his first book, *The Confessions of a Beachcomber*, it stated that throughout what he called confessions he carefully kept his own personality in the background. In *My Tropic Isle*, which followed, the Beachcomber undertook to fill in some of the blanks in his island career.

This he did, but blanks remained — not only in his island career, but also in the years before he made Dunk his home. Some blanks still remain, even though there is an apparent abundance of material, including semi-autobiographical books; hundreds of articles on a multitude of subjects; his own letters and those of his wife and others; almost twenty-five years of day-to-day diary entries covering his occupation of the island;

many accounts and reminiscences by those who knew him, some of whom were still living at the time of the writing of this book.

Despite all this, there are occasions when the Beachcomber withdraws into the forest and jungle, like the birds and butterflies whose haunts he knew so well.

Therefore, while the greater part of his career can be accounted for, he would not have been brought to life as fully had some attempt not been made to fill those blanks. There are not many, and there is always some fact to provide a basis of truth for conjecture, in line with the Beachcomber's own approach, as in "The Death Bone" in *My Tropic Isle*, a story about an Aboriginal artist, which he described as "fact cemented with fiction".

It is also relevant to remember that the Beachcomber used two quotations at the start of *The Confessions*. The first is from Thoreau: "If a man does not keep pace with his companions, perhaps it is because he hears a different drummer. Let him step to the music which he hears." The second, which does not appear in all editions, is from Longfellow: "Trust in yourself and what the world calls your illusions."

Prologue

The floating palace glided into the bay, watched by a man half hidden under an umbrella tree just behind the beach. Its anchor splashed into its own reflection and sent growing rings of light towards the long curve of the sands. At the stern of the motor yacht, the blue stars and red stripes of its flag hung motionless.

An officer in uniform and white cap stepped out from behind the storm glass of the bridge to the deck. The owner, in a lightweight dressing gown, and then his wife in a silk wrap, also appeared and looked towards the shore. In an otherwise virgin setting they saw a flagstaff and grass hut on the sand-spit, a thatched boatshed among flame trees and coconut palms nearer the other end of the beach, and up on a rise a white bungalow which commanded a sweeping view from its verandahs. The three became aware of having been enveloped in a cool cloud of fragrances that came from the same source as a medley of birds calls — all from within tiered bowers of forest and jungle rising behind the inner end of the strand.

The watcher presently stepped out barefooted and sauntered down the beach, laying the first human imprints of the day on the sand. His dog followed, adding paw prints to the scrawls of crabs and scribblings of sea birds. The man revealed himself to be slight and wiry. He wore dark dungaree trousers rolled up to the knees, a short-sleeved white singlet unbuttoned at the throat, and a straw hat with a long forward brim that shaded his features but did not conceal a thick snowy moustache and small steel-rimmed spectacles which caught the light reflected off the water. He stopped in what appeared to be, from the practised way he adopted it, a characteristic pose — head craned forward a little, hands clasped behind his back.

Thus the islander and his dog and those on the motor yacht appraised one another across two hundred metres of silver-surfaced water, while further out in the bay, from a solitary islet plumed with trees, sea birds rose and dipped as they limbered themselves for the day's foraging.

Raising an arm in greeting, the man in the dressing gown called, identifying himself as a visitor from the United States of America.

"Say there, Beachcomber — we're comin' ashore!"

He waved his hand, and then he and his wife returned to their cabin while deck hands at the stern of the yacht set about lowering a small tender with an inboard motor into the water. The islander made no reply — other than to assume a more proprietorial pose by unclasping his hands from behind his back and placing them on his hips. The dog, of a predominantly Airedale strain, caught on to its master's attitude, standing more alertly, its slightly floppy ears sharpening.

The tender was brought to the side of the yacht, where steps were lowered from the deck, and the owner and his wife emerged again, having donned casual tropical attire, each wearing a sun helmet of the type made famous by explorers in Africa and big-game hunters in India. Once they were in the tender, the boatman started the engine, and with a low growl — to which the dog responded with a yelp — they headed towards the animal and its master, Ted Banfield. The voice of the female passenger carried forward, revealing the speaker to be an American also.

"This has got to be just the cutest island we've struck so far!"

Even though the choice of adjective grated, Ted Banfield took the remark as a compliment to his Isle, his misgivings melting away as his hands slipped from his hips to hang in a relaxed fashion. The dog concurred with a friendly flicker of its stubby tail.

As Ted prepared to accord the uninvited travellers an unstinted welcome, he was oblivious to what a number of crew men were doing on the yacht, and so it came with the force of a totally unexpected blow when a gun was fired from the deck. Other shots followed in quick succession, all somehow magnified by the amphitheatrical shape of the bay and made even more monstrous by the echoes that overlapped and buffeted one another like tangled cross-currents.

The rifles were aimed at the birds above the islet; terns, pigeons and other species, all startled by the reports, took to the wing in their hundreds.

Ted Banfield was so seized up with fury that at first he was incapable of speech. But the dog was instantly vocal, barking furiously, aiming its hostility at the occupants of the oncoming tender as if holding them responsible for the explosive shots.

In the same angry yet anguished breath, Ted shouted at the men on the yacht and those in the tender.

"Stop! Go back!" And when the shots continued and the tender kept approaching, he went on, "You can't land here! Put down those guns!"

At a quick instruction from the American, the boatman threw the engine into reverse, and it roared as the propellers churned, bringing the small craft to a stop forty metres from the strand. As it did so, the American turned back to the yacht and hollered through cupped hands.

"Boys! Quit that shooting!"

On the deck of the yacht, the rifles were lowered, but the birds kept milling above the islet, filling the air with shrieks and screeches of alarm and distress.

Grinning sheepishly towards the islander, the American called, "Sorry about that Beachcomber! Sincerest apologies!"

"Too late, too late!" Ted cried with a dismissive sweep of his hand. "It's against the law to shoot birds here. This is a sanctuary."

In his fever of outrage, he turned to point to a tree near the boatshed, with a calico notice tacked to its trunk. The white cloth had weathered to grey, and it was too far away for those in the tender to be able to read its black lettering; but it stated that the island had been proclaimed a reserve for the protection of native birds and animals and that anyone who killed or interfered with them was liable to a penalty.

Facing the tender again, he fumed on, jerking his head to get the words out with greater scorn. "By rights, I should report you to the authorities and have you prosecuted!"

After having so recently rhapsodized, the American woman decided to be petulant.

"Who the hell does this little pip-squeak think he is!"

"Who am I?" the islander cried, digging into his trousers pocket and bringing out a metal badge and holding it up. "This is who I am. The Ranger of this island — and that islet — and of all the neighbouring islands and islets!" He thrust the badge to the north, then swept it to the west and to the south.

"Don't tell," said the American woman, unfortunately too quickly for her husband to forestall further provocation.

The dog continued to take offence on its master's behalf; and to quell its strident barking, Ted had to grasp it by the ear. Meanwhile, an alarm had been sounded up at the bungalow, and Bertha Banfield and Essie the housekeeper appeared in aprons through the trees backing the beach. A glimpse of Ted's attitude was enough to tell Bertha that he was riding on a high horse, whether with good reason or without.

After pausing by the trees, the two ladies hurried down the beach, Bertha with her petite way of crossing sand and Essie, with her slightly splayed Irish feet, making untidy going of it and kicking up spurts with every step.

As they came to his side, Ted was announcing, "I am afraid I must forbid you to land on this island."

The American looked genuinely apologetic. He could only give a sad shrug and tell the boatman to return to the yacht; but before the engine roared up there was just enough time for his wife's voice to be heard again.

"He's a nut, all right — just like that lugger captain warned you."

Ted began to raise a tightly-clenched fist in protest and indignation, only to find his arm grasped by Bertha and firmly lowered. Being deaf, and not having brought any form of hearing aid with her, she had not heard what the American woman had said; but the peeved pout on that lady's face and her husband's visible embarrassment had enabled Bertha to gather very swiftly that Ted was reacting to some unfair or inflammatory statement.

Bertha, Essie and the dog waited and watched with Ted as the tender returned to the yacht, where it was winched back on board. The anchor was raised. The air shimmered about the stylish squat funnel as the engines below moved the floating palace slow astern out of the bay. Once clear, it headed into the inner passage between the island and the mainland, resuming a southbound route.

Ted slumped, exhausted. The birds out on the islet were already settling down after having been so savagely disturbed, but the Beachcomber would suffer inner turmoil for days to come. Bertha and Essie realized this. Such was the finely-balanced temperament of the man who had turned his back on "all the bother and contradictions, the vanities and absurdities of the toilful, wayward human world", after having "pondered upon the destructive instinct which prevails in mankind".[1]

On this island, dubbed Dunk by the then Lieutenant James Cook, Ted Banfield continued his morning strolls on his "promenade" facing Brammo Bay, which he himself had named by adapting an Aboriginal word for butterfly. It was his favourite "strip of the tropics", a crescent-shaped strand ten minutes' stroll from the sand-spit, which lay five kilometres from the mainland, to the inner corner where, on his first visit here, he had found the air teeming with many varieties of butterfly — creatures which brought "the art of inconsequent revelling to the acme of perfection" as they "cut delirious scrolls against the unsullied sky". Among them were the brilliant blue Ulysses and the green and gold Cassandra.[2]

He had finally thrown off the affects of the intrusion by the floating palace when there came another vessel carrying uninvited visitors. An open launch from Townsville, some 160 kilometres to the south, with a party on a weekend camping expedition — three young men in their early twenties and a fourth some years their senior.

With his dog spotting shells ahead of him, Ted was collecting what had been brought in overnight by the tide, when the launch puttered into the bay. He recognized all four; they had been here before and had come ashore without seeking permission, so he gave them no chance to drop their anchor.

Gesturing them to be gone, he called, "You can't land here!"

As the launch was brought to a stop, the oldest of the four stood up. Ted saw that he held a sheet of paper in his hands as he proceeded to take a stand.

"You have no authority to turn us away."

"No authority?" cried Ted. "This is *my* island!"

The dog at Ted's side barked, as if to assert that this was as much his island too.

"That may well be so," granted the upstanding spokesman, "but you still cannot impede us from coming ashore."

Hands on hips, Ted stood astonished at what followed. A long legal rigmarole, quoting parliamentary acts of the state of Queensland, referring to clauses, paragraphs and amendments. It was not so much a matter of Ted hearing him out as waiting until he had finished. Legal jargon he could not abide. An abomination. An insult to English prose.

Brushing it all aside with a gesture of disgust, Ted turned and started to walk away. They could do as they darn well pleased! And so the four interlopers held their breaths — only to brace themselves as Ted halted, and swung back towards them.

"I won't have you bringing any noxious grass seeds with you. See that you all give your trousers a good brushing down — and walk ashore through the water."

With this said, Ted withdrew. It had been easier than the four had expected. Even the dog shared the Beachcomber's surrender, slinking behind its master to disappear with him through the trees behind the beach. The four again held their breaths to allow the pair to get further away; and then, grinning at one another in victorious delight, they burst out laughing.

After swimming and fishing, and then cooking their catches over the camp fire built on the sand-spit, they were still laughing at the success of their legal triumph. Beer to wash down their food made them all the merrier. The senior member of the party was encouraged to repeat his legal address — and he did so, embellishing it by quoting even more acts and edicts — all from a blank sheet of paper, improvising as he had done from the open boat.

His three younger companions rolled about on the grass.

Unknown to them, Ted had come within hearing distance. It was not that he had intended creeping up on them, but after so many years of observing the fauna of the island, especially the birds, he had developed a silent, stealthy walk and could approach without giving away his presence.

A blank sheet of paper, eh! He automatically delved into his trousers pocket to arm himself with his badge of authority as the officially-gazetted ranger; but even as he did so the humorous side of the situation struck him. Perhaps he would have done the same thing had he been a member of the camping party. And so he left the badge in his pocket and trod on some fallen foliage, announcing his arrival with the crackle and splintering of dry debris.

The four campers shot to their feet, fully expecting a dressing down. Ted eyed them in turn through his spectacles, making it a disturbing scrutiny. All four knew that one eye was sound and the other glass, but it was difficult to decide which was which. Ted did not prolong their discomfort; nor did he let on he had overheard anything, and so they hastened to accept with much relief when he said, "I'm sure you'd like some fresh Jersey milk and fruit. Come along up to the bungalow."

The walk to the bungalow was a conducted tour, with Ted pointing out the presence of insects, patting trees as if they were old friends, and halting everyone so that they could listen to a particular bird call. All four were under the spell of his enthusiasm by the time they climbed the steps on to the verandah, where Bertha came out to welcome them. Neither she nor Essie was the least surprised that Ted, having gone out ready to send the intruders packing, now returned with them as guests.

Essie brought out glasses of cool fresh milk from the herd of dainty little yellow and fawn Jersey cows up behind the back sheds, while Ted himself selected choice bananas, papaws and mangoes, ripened to perfection. All round introductions had been made and presently each of the four revealed what work he did in Townsville, and so it came out that the oldest was a solicitor.

Ted appreciated the humour of the legal argument all the more, even though the perpetrator and his companions remained somewhat abashed. At the same time, Ted seized upon the fact that the main culprit was a solicitor. Here was someone whose advice he could seek, whose help he could try to enlist, in his crusade to maintain Dunk and its neighbouring islands and islets as the sanctuaries they were supposed to be. They had been proclaimed areas where all wild life was protected, but he seemed to be fighting an impossible battle to enforce this. Parties in pleasure craft hove to just off islands and islets while their passengers fired at random at such protected but vulnerable species as the beautiful white nutmeg pigeons.

Even the great Lord Northcliffe on a recent trip from Britain had taken part in the wanton killing.

What was Ted to do?

He brought out his metal badge of office.

What help was this in the face of man's inhumanity to the feathered species?

Chapter 1
World of Change

Edmund James (Ted) Banfield was born in Liverpool, Lancashire, England, on 4 September 1852, two and a half years before his father, Jabez, saw him for the first time.

Ted Banfield was the second son. Had he been the first it is almost certain that he would have lived out his days in Ararat, Victoria, as did his elder brother Harry, by taking over the running of the newspaper his father had established. Had that been Ted's destiny, a marvellous adventure in living, one which was to begin in almost total seclusion and then come to be played out under world-wide scrutiny, would never have gone beyond an escapist's dream. Ted's innate loyalty and sense of duty would have kept him firmly on deck at home.

Considering the times and his origins, Ted's father, Jabez Walter Banfield, was a remarkable man. He was born in Chatham, Kent, on 16 August 1820, the second son of a pierhead master who moved to Liverpool when Jabez was six years old.[1]

Jabez escaped the horrific life of so many other children, working up to sixteen hours a day in the gloom and darkness of factories and mines. On his thirteenth birthday he was apprenticed to a Liverpool printer and stationer, Robert Dickinson — although his indenture read more like a committal to penal servitude than a binding contract. For a period of seven years he promised faithfully to serve his master, whose secrets he would keep and lawful commands gladly obey; for the first year he would receive three shillings a week, and then a rise of one shilling a year until in his fifth, sixth and seventh years he would be paid seven. In return, Robert Dickinson promised to teach, inform and instruct his apprentice in the "Art, Trade, Mystery of the Occupation of a Printer, and Stationer".[2]

Shortly after completing his apprenticeship, Jabez Banfield was engaged by another Liverpool printer and stationer, John Rose. A year later he became foreman of the printing shop; and a year after that, two days before his twenty-second birthday, he married Sarah Ann Smith, daughter of a book-keeper, at St Bride's Church.[3]

Jabez remained with John Rose for twelve years until he left this position to be free to journey abroad. On 12 June 1852, John Rose gave him a reference in which he wrote: "I part with him reluctantly under a strong conviction of his superior moral worth — having ever found him a person of persevering modesty and strict sobriety, integrity and honesty."

To Jabez personally, he wrote: "I deeply regret as you know your departure and wish you all happiness in your new enterprise and that you may long be spared in the land of your adoption. May God grant that you and I, and all in whom we are interested, may learn to live in this world of change."[4]

The changes Jabez had been seeing had filled him with concern for his wife and young family. Outrageous profits were being made by the owners of mines and factories, but at the cost of misery for men, women and children. Jabez had become well aware that there were places in the world where the gaps between the privileged and others were not so wide. As far back as when he still lived with his parents at Queen's Pier on the River Mersey, he had seen men returning to their homeland after living in America and Australia. Penniless when setting out, they had come back prosperous. The mouth of the river was the gateway to parts of the world where there were space and opportunity for the common man — and unlimited fresh air and sunshine. Jabez needed more of both, for the long hours of work and his conscientious attitude to it had found out a weakness in his lungs, making his winters wheezy and leaving him run down.[5] Such spells were accompanied by depression and despair about the future — although Sarah might well have wondered to what extent his state of mind contributed to his physical ailments.

Jabez had a special friend, James Gearing, to whom he referred throughout his life as his best mate. They had much in common: both were the same age, born in Chatham, Kent, and came to Liverpool with their parents about the same time; both were apprenticed for seven years to Robert Dickinson, and both found employment in the same area; both had been married at St Bride's Church; their wives were friends, and their children played together; and both had been looking into prospects abroad.[6]

Pierhead master James Banfield was now a widower. Reading

was a great consolation to him, and he was always on the lookout for discarded journals and newspapers from incoming ships from the colonies and America. These he passed on to Jabez, who shared them with his mate. All confirmed that experienced printers were in demand almost everywhere.

The two mates had also shared the monthly numbers of Charles Dickens' recent *Personal History and Experience of David Copperfield*, in which all had been solved for the impecunious Micawber by emigrating to Australia, where he had found security and respectability. More recently they had been sharing that mouthpiece of reform *Household Words* which was edited by Dickens, who also wrote for it. His readers were left in little doubt that the nation was in a sorry state, with the prospects of the common man decidedly bleak.

For the two mates, those lands beyond the horizon beckoned with greater allure, although it remained a dream of distant green fields. This changed when the discovery of gold in New South Wales was made public. Jabez and Gearing were not men to take a gamble, not when their wives and children had to be involved; but as shipping companies offered special passages to the Australian diggings and men set sail in droves, it was difficult to restrain themselves from joining the exodus. More and more discoveries were reported and the first successful diggers returned with tales of how they had literally scooped up nuggets from under their feet. Ships began to berth with huge consignments of bullion, which were taken from the docks under escort. A plaster cast of a mammoth nugget weighing over a hundred pounds (forty-five kilograms) was painted gilt and put on display, a sort of image of the Great God Gold, an icon that exerted an overpowering influence on those who came to pay court to it — even over the most cautious and sober of men.

In the summer of 1852 there were still more discoveries in the colony of Victoria. Jabez and Gearing came closer to a decision to take the risk and leave, praying for guidance at church in the morning. At the tea table at the Banfield house, the two mates talked it over with their wives. If they decided to go, it would not be a total risk. Some who had gone, but had so far failed to make fortunes, had still managed to find enough gold to send home money to provide for their families. Besides, they knew there was work to be had in the printing trade, so they would always have something to fall back on.

All agreed to think about it overnight. Jabez had great cause for misgivings: Sarah was seven months pregnant, so how could he even think about leaving her now? But she was concerned that if he was to go, he should get away before another winter started. She and the children would manage — they had relatives and friends. The next evening Gearing came by ferry from Birkenhead, and in the long twilight the two mates took up the previous day's subject as they strolled around the docks and looked over ships fitting out and taking on stores for the voyage to Australia. By the time they left the docks, they had made up their minds — and the first person to know was Jabez's elder brother James whom they found fishing off Queen's Pier. He promptly decided to join them.

The following day the three men booked their passages and began to assemble their gear. From those who had come back they had learnt what equipment to take with them and what to buy once they reached Australia. They picked up a valuable piece of advice: take your own hand cart and make sure it is strong enough to stand up to rough roads and bush tracks. So they had one built to order and fitted with wide metal tyres.

James Banfield, who was forty and a warehouseman, took his wife Elizabeth and their eleven year-old son Jabez;[7] but the two mates had not altered their plan: their wives and children would wait until such times as they had tried their luck.

Jabez's first two children — Eliza who was six and Harry who was four — were old enough to remember the slow departure of the *Serampore* from the dock. With them, as they waved their father on his way, were their Banfield grandfather and other relatives. Also many friends of the two mates. The third child, Sarah Wake, was still only two and in her mother's arms. As for the fourth baby due to come into the world, Jabez and Sarah had decided that if this child were a girl, her name would be Eva; if a boy, Edmund.

The *Serampore*, 873 tons, carried 206 steerage passengers — 223 in all — under Captain Hope Smith, who was to note that on this voyage there was an unusually high proportion of men of a markedly good type, and that attendances at church services were excellent throughout the passage, which turned out to be longer than average. Jabez occupied much of his time reading, and he and Gearing kept their hands in by helping the editor print the ship's news-sheet. After leaving Liverpool on 7 July 1852, they arrived in Port Phillip, Melbourne, on 11 October.[8] By this time, back in Liverpool, Sarah's fourth baby had arrived, a boy — Edmund James.

A year later Jabez included a special letter to "Miss Eliza and Master Harry Banfield" in the envelope when writing to Sarah. It was from Three Mile Creek, Ovens Gold Field, Victoria, and was written on 9 October 1853 in a delicate copperplate hand, every letter and word meticulously executed. What Jabez had to say to his children brimmed over with affection and longing for them:

> You still remember me, and often talk of me I dare say; not a day but I think of you both, and also Sarah and Edmund. I hope

you love your little sister and brother and that you are very kind to them. And your dear ma also . . . Your Grandpa has been very kind to you, and you will still love him dearly. Mrs Golding has been very kind to you also, and I hope you are very grateful to that lady, please give my love to her, and my best thanks for her kindness to you. This is a very nice country that I am in, and I think you will like it.

The Mrs Golding to whom Jabez sent his love was to be the mother of a daughter who would one day be married to Edmund, the son Jabez had yet to see.

Chapter 2
Black and White Gold

The cart Jabez and Gearing had built in Liverpool proved to be a boon. With its wide metal tyres it handled better than most other such conveyances which were loaded, like theirs, with tents, provisions, blankets, iron pots; machetes and axes to remove scrub and trees; picks and shovels to break into the ground; and tin dishes for panning.

A picture of the cavalcade they joined was contained in a dispatch sent about this time by the Lieutenant Governor of Victoria, Charles Joseph Latrobe, to the British Secretary for War and the Colonies, Earl Grey:

> Not only have the idlers to be found in every community, and day labourers in town and adjacent country, shopmen, artisans, and mechanics of every description thrown up their employment — and in most cases leaving their employers and their wives and families to take care of themselves — and run off to the workings, but responsible tradesmen, farmers, clerks of every grade, and not a few of the superior classes have followed: some, unable to withstand the mania and force of the stream, but others because they were, as employers of labor, left in the lurch, and had no other alternative. Cottages are deserted, houses to let, business is at a standstill, and even schools are closed ... The ships in the harbour are in great measure deserted, and masters of vessels, like farmers, have made up parties with their men to go shares at the diggings.[1]

In this year, 1852, there was an enormous rise in the numbers of immigrants to Victoria — a total of 63,719 — ten times as many as in the previous year.[2]

On the way to the gold fields, as the weather grew warmer, Jabez found himself for once at this time of the year facing summer rather than winter, and was free of the threat of cold and its rigours. He and Gearing were constantly aware of the presence of forms of flora and fauna entirely different to those of England. How their children would delight in the wallabies, the wild flowers, the massive gum trees, the flocks of exotic parakeets.

Once they reached the diggings, a carnival atmosphere greeted them — townships of tents and bark huts in valleys and on hillsides where the big timber had been hacked away. Interspersed among the makeshift abodes were little hillocks of red, yellow and white earth marking where diggers had turned virgin land into what in the opinion of one eye-witness had the appearance of a "fresh and rudely made burial ground".[3]

The two mates staked their first claim at Spring Creek, but they had arrived too late to secure a prime position. They were forced to decide that there was little prospect here, and thus they began a series of forays in various directions, blown from place to place by the winds of rumour.

It was not that they failed to find gold, which they carried in pickle jars. As a precaution against thieves skilled at silently slitting the side of a tent, they buried the jars in the earth floors and slept on top of them. The trouble was they did not find enough of the yellow stuff. Although he remained outwardly optimistic, Jabez became down-hearted and depressed, and an attack of his old trouble confined him to the tent when the cold of the Victorian winter struck. Gearing knew his mate well enough to recognize the significance of his ailment. He himself had begun to have doubts whether they would make that rich strike. And so the two mates found themselves being frank with each other.

"There's still tons of the stuff waiting to be found," Gearing said, "but we're just not fated to be lucky."

The gold fields already had hordes of disillusioned derelicts and destitutes. It was just not in the natures of Gearing or Jabez to risk such a fate any longer, so they decided to sell up their equipment and to head back to Melbourne to find steady employment. Besides, they had something to show for all their foraging — enough money for immediate needs.

On 16 July 1854, in one of his regular letters to Sarah, Jabez included another specially written for Eliza and Harry:

> Once more, my dear children, I write a note to you, and I hope it will be the last one. Oh! how I long to see you again, and I am sure you will be glad to see your dear papa again. I have sent your mama the means of bringing you to me; and, my dear children never in your petitions to your Heavenly Father forget to pray that He will guide you and your dear mama in safety over the mighty deep and that He will spare me to receive you. You will like the country I am sure, we have plenty of green green grass for you to ramble and romp on . . . I hope you will pay attention to what is said to you on board the ship, and be as

little trouble as possible. Kiss Sarah and Edmund for me, and love one another.[4]

Four months later, on 12 November 1854, Sarah Banfield and Mary Gearing, with seven children between them, were farewelled by a gathering of parents, brothers, sisters and friends as they set sail from Liverpool on the *Indian Queen*.[5]

They had qualms about leaving, about the long voyage ahead, about the future that lay in store for them; but the spectacle of tall smoking chimneys and the pall hanging over the city, and the early winter chill, combined to dismiss such qualms. It would be high summer when they reached Melbourne and the air there was sweet and uncontaminated.

The *Indian Queen* was a bigger ship than the one on which their husbands had travelled, and it carried more immigrants. Built in Canada in 1852, registered tonnage 1,041, she had already proved herself a fast sailer. Now, with 353 passengers on board including children, under the command of Captain Robert McKirdy, she lived up to her reputation and shaved nearly a fortnight off the *Serampore*'s time by reaching Williamstown near Melbourne in eighty days on 31 January 1855. There was still a huge inflow of immigrants — 51,291 in 1854. In the year Sarah, Mary and their children added nine souls to the sum total there were still over twenty thousand.[6]

Despite the swift passage, it was an arduous one, through latitudes of cold and heat, through storms and stifling calms. However, like their husbands, Sarah and Mary were well advised by previous voyagers. They took furniture, cooking utensils, blankets, linen and other household goods, together with something they were forewarned would be most essential to safeguard the health of their children — extra food — since the daily fare from the ship's galley, especially on such a vessel carrying migrants at low cost, was notoriously meagre. After the slow grind down to the Cape of Good Hope and a speedy leg across the Southern Ocean, all nine arrived sound and well.

For the children it was a great adventure. Albatrosses and castles of ice. Giant birds and towering white castles with grottoes of green, blue and pink in their sides; castles that growled when they ground into one another, and boomed when battlements cracked off and crashed into the sea, creating waves which rocked the *Indian Queen* up and down, and from side to side.

The Sunday church services were also highlights of the voyage. They were conducted by an emigrating Congregational minister in the first-class saloon, a rich roomy world to the children after their gloomy cramped quarters between narrow decks. Seats of polished mahogany and crimson velvet; overhead a gabled skylight, making it seem as if they were in a church with a glass roof. But what really made these occasions

In the early hours, 1 April 1859, half way from Melbourne to Cape Horn, the *Indian Queen* collided with an iceberg and suffered serious damage, but managed to reach Valparaiso, Chile, ten days later.
(*The Illustrated London News*, 27 August 1859.)

so exciting were the painted wall panels showing a captured English army officer about to be scalped by fierce braves, with stern chiefs watching, and a beautiful Indian maiden begging them to spare the young officer's life.[7] These panels, with their romantic tale, made such an impression on the children that they brought them to life by acting out the scenes, Eliza taking the part of the Indian maiden and Harry that of the young English officer.

They were soon able to act out this little drama for their father. Jabez was overjoyed to be reunited with his wife and family. He took his second son into his arms for the first time, and Edmund looked up into the warm eyes of the bearded man his mother had keep assuring him he would meet once the tiresome voyage was at an end. From that day, Edmund, who was soon to be called Ted, worshipped his father and was ever striving to give Jabez cause for pride in him.

Jabez and Gearing had been very busy since leaving the gold fields. They sold their cart to police in Benalla, and it was there that they left Jabez's brother, who was also to give up chasing the gold.[8]

The Mount Ararat Advertiser.

No. 1. ARARAT, SATURDAY, AUGUST 1, 1857. Published every Wednesday and Saturday. Gratis.

The Mount Ararat Advertiser
Published
Every Wednesday and Saturday,
Distributed gratuitously throughout the Diggings.

TERMS FOR ADVERTISING.
All Advertisements to be paid for in advance

Thirty words and under — —	2	6
For every twelve words beyond thirty	1	0
Half a column and upwards, per inch	5	0
Displayed Advertisements, per inch	5	0

LIST OF UNCLAIMED LETTERS
Lying at the Post Office,
CATHCART.
For the week ending, July 27, 1857.

A—Edwin Amail.
B—J Bayle, storekeeper, J Brookes, D F Bruce, or McBeath, G H Barrert, Mrs Burden, Mr Butler, Alex. Baillie, Jno Busban, A Waaytsbell, T Alx Brown, W J Barnes, W Byron, Rich Boroyer, Walter Bramby, Thos Butler, Thos Bartin.
C—Jno Calder, Jno Chapman, W Coyle, Luke Callen, Jos Cooks, Chas Croaker, Joil Campbell, Jas Caitness, Francis Chambers.
D—Jas Dunbar, Henry Dodd, J Lolsey Drury.
E—Ed Eccles, Herman Ehlbeck, Jno Ede, T-s Edwards, James Edwards, D S Espay.
F—Ed Ford, Jas Farley, Miss Anne Flynne, Jas A Forbes, Pat Fogarty 2, Mr Forbes, Ed Finey, Stephen Finey, Rob Filgate, Alex Forbes, Foake Beacsa.
G—Henry Gibbs, T C Goetchens, Thos Guest, Jno Greenhough, Thomas Greenhough, Daniel Greenhouse, Wm Gilmore.
H—Jno Hill, Geo Howard, Henry Henderson, Jos Hardy, W T Holmes.
J—Hy Jonas, Johnson, P, G W Jones, T Jell.
K—H Keoks, 7, E & S Kenworthy, S J Knight, Thos McQuarter Kerr, Jas King.
L—Flea Laparge and Meyers, Thos Lithgow, Matienville Tnoboth, Te Peake, Laid, 2 Laid, Jas Latch 2.
M—McSheehan or McPherson, H E Mitchell, Geo Morgan, Robt Muir, Walt Morgan, Jas McGil-… Duncan Mathieson, George McGowen Frank Moar, Duncan McDonald 2, Wm Millaie Robt. Milne, Wm McKerney, Ronald McDonald 2, Arch. McShannon, Terence McCauly, M, McDermott, McDonald, Inverness Store, Jermb. Murphy, Geo. Minton, T C Martin, Ben. Michell, Robt. M Millar.
N—J Notley
O—Henry Ovens, S J S de Oliveira.
R—Daniel Recklebeen, Wm Rees, Cath Reily, Jno Robertson, T P Richmund, S Rutter, Fanny Redd,
S—Jas Schofield, Jas Storer, Mrs Sullivan 2, Thos Simpson, Dan Sinclair, Wm Spears, Jeremiah Sullivan, Margaret Stuart, Wm Sinclair, A Slattery, Oliver S Stock, Robt Settle 2, Wm Snell, J J Spears, W Souting.
T—A J Taylor, Martin Tierney, Jno Towgood, Geo Tracy, at Wilkie Brothers, F. T. Post office. B Tysall, David Tindedie, Jas Thompson, Robt. Thomson, T H Townsend.
P—Wm Pearce or Pat Irvine, Isaack Parker, Job Price, Jno Potter, Fred Pervis.
S—S J Williams, Hy Whale, Bistol Store 2, Thos Thomas Wheeler, Warnambool, C T White, Ellen Welsh, at Jonathan Smiths, Thomas Waiton, A J R Wallace, Francis Watkins 2, W P Wiles, Ed Wtters, Edmund Wells.
Mails made up every Tuesday and Sunday, at 4 p.m.
JONES & LOWE,
Postmasters.
Cathcart.

V. R.

Notice.
CERTAIN evil disposed persons having

Meyer & Wolfe,
Wholesale and Retail
Ironmongers,
Main Street, Government Road, Ararat.

HAVE on sale, at the lowest market rates :—
Iron—bar, rod, sheet, &c.
Steel—shear, octagon, blister, &c.
Blacksmith's tools of all descriptions.
Manilla rope assorted.
Holloware of every description.
American hardware in variety.
Ewbank's patent nails assorted.
White lead, linseed oil, &c.
And a large assortment of general hardware.

ON SALE, by the undersigned :
American cooking stoves, assorted sizes.
Lamp oil, best quality.
Grindstones.
Buckets—galvanized, tinn'd japan'd, tin-wood.
Shovels, spades, brooms, &c.
Meyer & Wolfe,

The Mount Ararat Advertiser.

SATURDAY, AUGUST 1, 1857.

MOUNT ARARAT DIGGINGS.

THE prospects of Ararat are now assuming a form which would not alone stamp it as one of the greatest rushes which have ever taken place in the colony, but show every appearance of stability as a settled diggings, spread over a very large extent of country. A general feeling of satisfaction seems to exist amongst the miners, which bodes well for such recently opened ground, the more so as it certainly has not as yet shown evidence of any extraordinary richness, at all equal to such a gold field as Bendigo was. The experience of many, however, leads them to prefer a payable ground to the vicissitudes of a richer field for their labours, where although the results may be brilliant to a few, to the many they only end in disappointment or a bare existence. Most of the sinkings are dry, at a depth varying from 40 to 70 feet from the surface, and in some places through very hard cement. 16 to 18 ozs. to the load have been taken out of a few claims, and numbers have averaged from 6 to 8 ozs. The gold is rough, and of a fine quality, most of it "shotty."

Ararat is splendidly situated for a township, can boast of many streets, the Main-street, Commercial-street, Victoria Crescent, Market Square, Union-street, Argyle-street, View Point, Ludgate Hill, Regent street, Bond-street, and several others. As yet the appearance of the stores is not very handsome, people seeming rather inclined to feel their way: business, however, appears to be pretty good, and no doubt those who are spirited enough to erect handsome buildings, and lay in a good stock will find it a profita-

---

THE WANTS OF ARARAT.

To the Editor of the Mt. Ararat Advertiser.

SIR,

After spending some months at the Dunolly diggings, I arrived here a few days ago, hoping and believing that the Government of the day, instructed by past experience, would have prepared for such an occasion, and provided for the wants and requirements of such an assemblage of persons as are now here. I naturally expected to find, 1st, a resident magistrate. 2nd. an efficient police force. 3rd, a police court 4th, a gold receiver, a gold office and escort, and 5th, a post office. These are actual and positive necessities in all large communities on the gold diggings, but what do I find here?

1st. No resident magistrate, and no local magistrates. It is true, I believe, that the police magistrate of Fiery Creek, thirty miles distant, does occasionally once a fortnight, attend at a police station among the ranges, some five miles off, for the purpose of hearing cases, but this so far from being an advantage is simply an absurdity, and an injustice.

2nd. There is not an efficient police, there being only a force of ten men to a population of nearly 50,000! [and several of those men are stationed some miles off for the sake, I presume, of the healthiness and quietude of the retreat.

3rd. There is no police court. At a remote creek, five miles off among the mountains there is a tattered calico shed, where justice is now and then administered. The only suitors are the Kangaroos, for there is not a house or human habitation near, except the police tents, and the inhabitants of Ararat, no doubt, prefer suffering a wrong to the labor of attending the same court for redress. When I was there on Tuesday last, I found that no court had been held for several days, and that six individuals were then in the lock up, and likely to be so for some days. In consequence of no magistrate being in attendance, the Court stood adjourned till yesterday. That number has been since increased, and there they must be until the Court sits, or until the police magistrate of Fiery Creek finds it convenient to ride over and dispose of them.

4th. There is no Gold Receiver, no gold office, and no gold Escort provided for one of the largest and most important diggings yet known in the colony. This certainly speaks volumes for the paternal care of our responsible ministers.

5th. There is no Post-Office. Fifty thousand people contributors to the revenue of the country, have been left without a post-office. I enquired for the post-office, and was coolly told to place my back to the sun and cross the nearest range of mountains, and so on from range to range until I should find some one to point me out the place of my enquiry. I did so, and after travelling over several miles of bush and moor and mountain, I did at last find a woodcutter who directed me to the post-office at Cathcart, which I at last reached, and

---

DR. CURRIE,
Surgeon and Accoucheur,
Licentiate of the Royal College of Surgeons, Edinburgh; and late Surgeon to the Salford Eye and Ear Institution, may be consulted daily at his residence, Victoria Crescent, corner of Main-street.

SILAS E. CRAIN, M.D.
Surgeon and Accoucheur,
Office, Main Street, opposite the Manchester Drapery Store, Ararat.
N. B.—Children Vaccinated at the Office between the hours of 9 and 12 a.m.
And the Medical Certificate given.

DR. FLATTERY,
Surgeon and Accoucheur,
Main-street, Government Road.

DIVINE SERVICE (Church of England) is held every Sabbath, in the School, Regent-street, at 11 o'clock, a.m., and at Church-hill, 3 o'clock p.m. Sunday school in both places at the hours of 10 a.m. and 2 p.m.
For Marriages and Baptisms, enquire at the Schoolmaster's Tent.

WHEELER and HAYMAN,
Watchmakers and Goldsmiths,
Main-street, Government-road.

Oxley's Fancy Bazaar,
Crescent-street, Facing Main-street.
CUTLERY, Boxing Gloves
Music, Looking Glasses
Baskets, Books
Playing Cards Dolls
N. B.—Masquerade Dresses.

Earl & Walton,
WINE & SPIRIT & GENERAL MERCHANTS
"View Point," next to the Police Reserve.
GOLD PURCHASED :
Bank drafts on Melbourne.

Kentish Store,
CRESCENT STREET,
G. W. PHILLPOTT,
Draper, Clothier, and General Storekeeper.
A varied assortment of Fancy Goods Haberdashery, &c.

GEMMILL & CURRIE,
Drapers & Outfitters,
Crescent-street, Ararat.

Rose's Circulating Library,
Crescent-street, opposite Richardson's Crescent Hotel.
J. ROSE begs to inform the public that he has the largest and best selected Library on Ararat diggings.

Jonathan Smith
CALLS the attention of his friends and the public to the first-class Hotel he has just erected on View Point, adjoining Gilbert's Auction Mart, affording good bed-rooms, an excellent table, with best liquors in stock, and stabling for a dozen

---

EDWARD GILBERT,
AUCTIONEER,
Late of "Tattersall's," Melbourne,
REQUESTS the attention of Horse and Cattle Dealers to the extensive premises erected by him for the purpose of Selling by Public Auction, or Private Sale.
The Cattle Yards are now completed, and ready for the reception of Cattle
of every description. E. Gilbert will exercise every legitimate means in his power to further the sale of Stock to the best advantage, and will be prepared at all times to advise as to the state of the market.
Tattersall's Horse Repository, View Point, Mount Ararat.

KERR, SMITH & CO.,
Of the Iron Store, Fiery Creek,
BEG to solicit from Storekeepers, Hotelkeepers, and Others, a continuance of the liberal support that has been hitherto granted them in this District, and shall always keep in stock such goods as are suitable for this market, consisting of—

Flour	Coffee	Brandy, bulk and case
Rice	Sugar, Mauritius	Old Tom, do. do
Butter	Do. Cossipore	Whiskey, do. do
Cheese	Oilmen's stores	Port Wine, dr. do
Biscuits	Hams and Bacon	Sherry, do. do
Tea	Porter and Ale	

NOAH'S ARK.
Commercial St., Ararat.
J. W. WILDER begs to inform his friends and the public, that he has fitted up the above premises, where gentlemen will meet with every comfort. A Billiard Table, and the best band on the diggings will be found at this establishment.
A first-class Table will be laid. Good Beds, with every accommodation.

Dunolly Rifle Gallery and Bagatelle Saloon,
Commercial-street, Araarat.
THREE SHOTS, 1s.
THE above commodious Establishment is now opened with a first-class assortment of English and Swiss Rifles by the first makers.
HENRY J. WALTER.

J. Marriott,
From the Harmonic Hall and Star Bowling Saloon, Dunolly.
HAS opened his splendid Alleys next to Foo's, Golden Age, Main-street, Ararat.
The £5 weekly prize will be given as usual, on Monday evenings, at 11 o'clock, for the highest number bowled on the half string during the week.

MR. GREVILLE,
(From the People's, Chinaman's)
BEGS to inform his friends and the public that he has opened in Commercial Street, Ararat, where he will be glad to see his old friends.
Bagatelle, &c.

Nightingale Billiard and
Bagatelle Saloon.
The Largest and best Board on the Diggings, Main-street, Government Road.

J. Jones,
EATING HOUSE, ARGYLE-STREET.
Ararat,
Board 25s. per week, payable in advance.
Meals 2s.

Hussey & Co.
HAIR-CUTTING SHAVING AND
Shampooing Saloons,
LUDGATE HILL, ARARAT.
H. & CO. beg to inform their Friends and the public generally that every comfort has been provided for their accommodation, clean towels, hair brushes, &c. to each person.
N. B.—A private room for Ladies and Childrens Hair Dressing.
A large assortment of Perfumery.

F. A. WALLIS,
Haircutting, Shaving,
And Shampooing Saloon, Main Street, Ararat,
Opposite the London Store.

Shamrock Restaurant,
(From Dunolly)
T. MANDERVILLE begs to notify to his friends and the Public that he has opened in Argyle-street, Ararat, where he hopes to merit a continuance of the patronage so liberally bestowed on him.

AMERICAN RESTAURANT.
Main-street, Ararat.
MR. & MRS. NALDER beg to ...

The first issue of *The Mount Ararat Advertiser*, 1 August 1857. (Courtesy of La Trobe Library, Melbourne.)

The two mates started work together on *The Argus* in Melbourne, already well established as a responsible newspaper. Then Gearing joined an older printer, E.H. Nuthall, while Jabez took another job, too, where he handled printing work in connection with the Australian version of the magazine *Punch*. Sarah and the children lived in a canvas hut in a mushroom migrant settlement near Richmond. The green green grass that Jabez promised was all about them, but their home was below the standard of the one they had vacated in Liverpool.[9]

Gearing's new employer realized that there were great opportunities for printers on the gold fields, so when the Maryborough (Victoria) field opened at the start of 1855, the master printer sent Gearing there with part of his plant to print an advertising sheet. Nuthall himself followed shortly after. This operation prospered from the start, so Gearing suggested that his mate Jabez Banfield should join them. Soon after this, Nuthall made the two younger men his partners.

It was a shrewd and fortuitous move. As rush followed rush, Nuthall's colleagues were on the scene with press and type to print and distribute advertising sheets free of charge. Storekeepers and tradespeople found this a most effective way of bringing their services to the attention of the miners. As he took orders for space, and advised on content and layout, Jabez was back doing the rounds of the same part of the land he had adopted, but instead of involving himself along with a crowd of others in a series of wild gambles — something not only alien to one of his sober and thrifty upbringing but also immoral to the point of tempting Providence — he was consolidating an occupation for himself and protecting the future of his family.

As he used to say in later years, the strike at Fiery Creek was a gold mine for advertising. As well as the free sheet, he printed notices, leaflets, pamphlets, menus for eating houses and posters. One of his largest and most profitable orders came from a brewer for posters printed boldly in black on white calico squares to be tacked to tree trunks around the diggings to entice thirsty prospectors.

Much of the history of the period was written in these news-sheets which proliferated in the early days, some undergoing bewildering changes of title and ownership, some coming out overnight and vanishing as swiftly. It would appear that the free sheet called *The Dunolly Advertiser* went under this title from September 1856, with Jabez in charge. At this point, Sarah and the children joined him again — and there were now five of them as a third boy, Walter Gearing Banfield, had been born in April.

In November of the same year the free sheet became a fully-fledged weekly newspaper, *The Maryborough and Dunolly Advertiser*, which sold well at sixpence (5 cents) a copy.

Then, when the gold seemed to be running out, there came the Ararat rush of the winter of 1857 in an area about eight kilometres from the peak which had been named Mount Ararat in 1840 by a pioneer sheep farmer because, after battling his way through flood waters, he had come to rest there, like the biblical ark on the mount in Armenia.[10] Flocks of sheep had invaded the preserves of wallabies, possums and other native animals; now there was another invasion, with a township constructed mainly of the material which had brought the eager diggers from the other side of the world — the canvas which had harnessed the winds.

Gearing stayed in Maryborough to print *The Maryborough and Dunolly Advertiser*, which had the young Julius Vogel — later Sir Julius and Prime Minister of New Zealand — as one of its first editors. Vogel also wrote for *The Mount Ararat Advertiser* early in its existence, not long after Jabez set up his press in a tent, between the tents of the local police and the Bank of New South Wales.

Issue No. 1 of this one-page news-sheet was published on Saturday, 1 August 1857 — Gratis.[11] From then on it also came out on Wednesdays. Despite the primitive conditions under which it was produced, it was a fine example of the printer's art, reflecting in its spacing, choice of type and general layout all of Jabez Banfield's pride in his craft. Those who had purchased space could consider themselves done proud — drapers and outfitters, doctors, a circulating library, an ironmonger, an auctioneer, a rifle gallery and a bagatelle saloon, restaurants, a dispensary, stores supplying groceries and provisions. The

Advertiser Office, during Jabez Banfield's partnership with Thomas Merfield.
(Courtesy of Irene L. and Zoe Banfield, Ararat.)

news-sheet also listed unclaimed letters, and the arrival and departure times of Cobb & Co. coaches.

The master printer E.H. Nuthall now had two prospering newspapers; but on a visit to Queensland in October 1860, he died. In March of the following year, Jabez Banfield took the coach to Melbourne to attend the executor's sale of the Nuthall estate and secured the newspaper with type, presses and other machinery for the round sum of £1,000. In the issue of 26 March 1861 he announced that he was the sole proprietor. Two months later he changed the name to *The Ararat and Pleasant Creek Advertiser*.[12]

The sum paid, the equivalent of $2,000, was most substantial in those days — such was the extent to which Jabez had seized the opportunities offered in the land of his adoption to ensure a better life for his family, to which on 6 March 1860 was added a sixth and final child, a daughter Eva.

Two years prior to this, Sarah Banfield had set out from Dunolly with her five children: Eliza, twelve; Harry, ten; Sarah, eight; Edmund, five; and Walter, two. They had reached Dunolly by coach and bullock dray, and now they headed for Ararat in a wagon loaded not only with their furniture and other goods and belongings, but also heavy cases of type for Jabez's paper. Harry walked beside his father while Sarah and the other children rode in the wagon. Even at this early stage, there was a special bond between Jabez and his eldest son.

The roads were rough all the way from Dunolly to Ararat. After several days of heat and dust, the Banfields saw their new home from a hill on the Maryborough Road. Darkness was falling, so they camped here for the night. Across from them the camp fires of the diggers twinkled like a carpet of stars; and in the morning, below columns of blue smoke, Sarah and the children saw the clustered tents surrounded by what looked like big mud pies. They had come to the short last leg of a long journey which had begun in Liverpool three years earlier.

After a few weeks in tents, the family moved to a cottage with slab timber walls and a canvas roof, later replaced with shingles. The kitchen was a shed at the back containing a camp oven over an open fire. It was still all very basic, but progress was being made. The paper which had depended for its existence on gold now began to find its true role as a source of news within a law-abiding community. At the end of the family's first year here, the rate book of the recently-declared Municipality of Ararat showed Jabez Banfield as a rate-payer. They had moved to a dwelling in Ligar Street between Chadwick's former horse and auction mart, now occupied by the plant of the newspaper, and the home of Judge Clarke, uncle of the author of the Australian classic *For the Term of His*

Natural Life. In fact, Marcus Clarke wrote part of his book here in his uncle's house.[13]

It cannot be said that this novel or its author played any part in the literary career of Edmund James Banfield. However, it was in this street that literary influences were to play a major role in his life.

The green green grass was all around; also, bush, forest, hills, creeks and a river; virgin countryside to be explored, and for a start little Ted Banfield did so in the care of Harry, learning to identify shrubs, flowers and trees, and the creatures who lived among them — especially those which came in clutches and flocks, cooing, whistling, belling — birds of brilliant plumage flashing all the colours of the rainbow. While not as exotic as species he was to see later in life, it was around Ararat that they first captured him with their wonder and magic, and started to play a major role in shaping his destiny.

Chapter 3
The Bone-Shaker

To turn the pages of early issues of *The Ararat and Pleasant Creek Advertiser* is to see the growth of an orderly community based on a social system and institutions transplanted from the country which people referred to as "Home" or "The Old Country" — counterparts of the seeds and seedlings of the flowers, shrubs, vegetables, fruits and trees which were also transplanted in Australia.

In the issue of 3 November 1857 the paper announced that a township was shortly to be declared; and on 28 February of the following year that the township was to be thoroughly surveyed. There was a steady stream of developments: municipality suggested and inaugurated; sale of township blocks to residents; clearing of tree stumps from the main street; formation of a fire brigade; tenders for a gaol and hospital; formation of a cricket club, a choral society, a dramatic society; laying out of botanic gardens; a circulating library, and a private library with a news room holding English, Scottish, Irish, German, Italian, French and American newspapers and periodicals; hospital opening and suggestion for an asylum.[1]

Mid all this, the outside world was not entirely forgotten, although the Crimean War, the Indian Mutiny and the American Civil War rated less space than highway robberies and attempts on the mail and gold escorts by bushrangers, including the notorious Frank Gardiner.

The newspaper also chronicled the range of Jabez Banfield's participation in community affairs. In 1859 he helped to form a local branch of the Mechanics' Institute; he became a trustee, then president. He was present at the laying of the foundation stone of the hospital, at its opening, and became a member of its governing committee. There was scarcely an issue in which his name did not appear.

Sarah also took part in civic activities, and these were also recorded in the newspaper. She was one of a small group of ladies who banded together to form a Benevolent Society, its object being "to relieve cases of actual distress with pecuniary and otherwise assistance".[2]

For fifteen years from the wooden house in Ligar Street, Jabez went next door to the former auction and horse mart to supervise the editing and printing of his paper and its distribution to the many parts of the widespread district it now covered. Whether taking one of his dogs for a walk around the town, or going no further than his place of work, it was his habit to wear a buttonhole, invariably something from Sarah's garden — a rose, a carnation, a sprig of may or myrtle from the plants, shrubs and trees of her native England.[3]

Even though Sarah and Jabez each acknowledged modest backgrounds, they took a certain pride in their origins, and had grounds for doing so. Sarah's mother was the daughter of a parson, Thomas Wake, who claimed descent from the legendary Hereward the Wake who had led a rebellion against the Norman conquerors.[4] However, all she knew of her ancestor was contained in the novel by Charles Kingsley. She had brought a copy of this book from England, and whenever she took it down from the shelf to read aloud, how eagerly her brood must have gathered around to listen and envisage the gallant Hereward, son of none other than the legendary Lady Godiva:

> His face was of extraordinary beauty, save that his eyes wore a strange and almost sinister expression, from the fact that one of them was grey, and the other blue. He was short, but of immense breath of chest and strength of limb; while his delicate hands and feet and long locks of golden hair marked him of most noble, and even, as he really was, of ancient royal race.[5]

As for his side of the family, Jabez believed its roots were in Devon where there were many records of "Bamphyles" having lived there and some memorials to them in churches. He also had a book with a family link, one that had been published in the middle of the eighteenth century: *The History and Curious Adventures of Bamphylde Moore-Carew*, who had lived with a band of gypsies and was elected King of the Beggars. He was a master of the arts of disguise and the hard-luck story, one of his best dodges being to pass himself off as a shipwrecked sailor — and there was no shortage of genuine survivors of this kind in those days on the Devon coast. He also kept his ears open for word of fires and floods and other disasters, and would then masquerade as a victim in need of a helping hand.[6]

It was all fun, neither to be believed nor approved, yet it was a story of an individual's escape from the regimes of his day, and could well have had an effect on the boy who was himself later in life to adopt a certain pose, one not entirely unrelated to that of a shipwrecked sailor, by styling himself as a beachcomber and furnishing himself with the perfect background for such a role by acquiring a remote tropical island on which to live.

It was part of the histrionic streak in Jabez coming out, as when he bought a magic lantern with long hand-painted slides on each of which were four or five "scenes". He provided his own commentaries, linking these highlights in the lives of Cinderella, Red Riding Hood and Robinson Crusoe, embellishing and improvising, but without realizing that through the island castaway he might be implanting a wildly romantic desire in the mind of his second son.

The magic lantern showings were so successful that Jabez went on to stage them in a local hall to a wider audience of children and adults. Present at one of these performances was a former convict who had gained his freedom by volunteering for a party to erect a beacon on a remote far northern part of the Great Barrier Reef. He was now fossicking near Ararat. At the end of the showing of Robinson Crusoe, he loudly informed the audience that there were long strings of tropical islands along that coast, all there waiting for the taking.

The Banfield children received their education at the Church of England Denominational School in the High Street — one of the town's two schools — where they were taught by the Reverend William Brown and his wife, the tuition fee being one shilling a week for each child.[7]

Parallel to this, Ted Banfield gained further education in the surrounding countryside with his big brother Harry as guide and protector. They learnt to swim and fish in dams and in the Hopkins River, sometimes going out with their father, who had returned from a business trip to advertisers and newsprint suppliers in Melbourne with a symbol of success in the form of an imported fishing rod.

The two boys also learnt to hunt and shoot, but this was something they concealed from their father. Jabez had a phobia about firearms — and not without reason. When he arrived in the colony with James Gearing, the carrying of weapons was commonplace, and Jabez had a pistol in his belt. On the first day out from Melbourne on the road to the diggings with their cart, the pistol went off suddenly of its own accord. Jabez looked behind him and was horrified to see smoke coming from Gearing's guernsey. His first reaction was that he had killed his best and closest friend; but in his pocket Gearing had a thick pair of woollen gloves which had been found on the wharf while they waited for their luggage and the cart to be unloaded from the *Serampore*. The rolled-up gloves had cushioned the impact of the bullet: when they were opened out, one of them nestled the hot bullet in its palm.[8]

Following the example of men such as the former convict who still panned around the old diggings and tailings, the two boys collected enough gold to buy a gun and cartridges from a local dealer. They kept them wrapped in canvas and hidden in the bush under a dry rock ledge. It must have troubled them to go to such lengths behind their father's back; but seeing other lads out hunting and shooting was a temptation they could not resist. And the strength of their father's phobia somehow justified them in keeping the matter secret.

When they read about a new type of bicycle in *The Illustrated London News*, to which their father subscribed, the two boys wanted to have one. Jabez believed that they would be much better off using the motive power of their own legs; as far as he was concerned "bone-shaker" seemed a most apt name for the contraptions. But he did not forbid the boys to have one. The drawings in the periodical were in great detail, almost blue prints, so they enlisted the help of the friendly local undertaker.[9] In his workshop, timber that usually went into the making of coffins was shaped into parts of a home-made bone-shaker, a design which preceded the penny-farthing, motive power being applied through pedals attached to the front wheel.

To propel and control the bicycle required much practice and involved many spills; but once the boys mastered the knack of riding it, they began to extend the range of their explorations of the countryside. One would start off by walking. The other would follow on the bicycle, overtake and ride on, then leave the bone-shaker by the side of the track and keep going by foot. Alternating in this way, Harry and Ted managed to cover much more ground, reaching across the southern plains and west towards the Grampian Mountains.[10] They saw more of the wild life of the area, and brought back native orchids and wild flowers for their mother — and the odd unusual buttonhole for their father, who could not help but be intrigued by their ingenuity and expeditions, even though his reservations about their vehicle remained.

While in their early teens, each of the two boys started work in their father's business, firstly in the composing room. Tuition in journalism followed from Nathaniel Swan, their father's editor. Harry, of course, was trained ahead of Ted, although Ted was so eager to keep up with his elder brother that he managed to reduce the age gap between them. Each began by reporting local events, functions and meetings, at some of which their father presided or spoke. They also reported evenings at which Jabez "performed".

Jabez had succumbed to histrionic aspirations. At home, when Sarah began reading to her children, Jabez would often want to take over, so she would leave it to him, especially as he read with such relish, such gusto, such command of dialect. He was even able to render *Paradise Lost* dramatic and exciting when reading from the volume of Milton's works which he had brought with him from Liverpool, so that to his younger audience the great epic poem became as much a story of goodies versus baddies as a conflict between the powers of light and darkness.

He began to find a wider outlet for his talents, as issues of the newspaper indicate. In the latter half of 1860 he was reported as having been the speaker at a dinner, of giving a Dickens reading at the Mechanics' Institute and of acting in scenes from Shakespeare's *Hamlet*. Two years later, after being elected president of the Mechanics' Institute, he delivered a series of lectures there on poetry, drama and literature, and he gave a reading of Dickens' *A Christmas Carol* at the neighbouring town of Moyston.[11] Thus began something which he was to keep up for many years, with recitals in Ararat and at various places in the district known as the Wimmera, including scenes from the works of Sir Walter Scott and others in his repertoire.

Harry became part of the act behind the scenes. In the wings of town and church halls, he would sit on a stool, copies of the master works in his lap in readiness to prompt his father,[12] although he didn't need the texts as he had heard the selections so often that he knew everything by heart.

Ted was in the same position. He had made it his business to be word-perfect, just in case he might have a turn in the wings. But as eldest son, and his father's right-hand man, so to speak, this remained Harry's prerogative. Not that Ted — or any of the other children, for that matter — stood any the less in their father's regard. As his heir, Harry occupied a special place in his father's affection, and Ted was forced to accept that by the simple accident of order of birth he had been relegated to second place. It was this situation that made him anxious to distinguish himself in some way in his father's eyes.

Much of Ted's love of Shakespeare, Dickens and other great and classic writers was instilled in him by Jabez; but there was another strong influence. Having alleged ancestors such as Hereward the Wake and the King of the Beggars had conditioned him to be able to accept bizarre or wayward real-life characters — and one in this category turned up at the newspaper office in the person of Henry Jerrold.[13] With his mellifluous voice, his flourishes, his graciousness and his disreputable and impecunious air, he might have stepped out of the pages of one of Dickens' extravaganzas. Henry was a brother of the English dramatist and humorist, Douglas Jerrold, one of the leading contributors to the London *Punch* in its early days. He had been trained as a printer and had been a journalist, and was looking for work. Jabez was amused by the rascal and commissioned some freelance articles.

Henry promptly got to work on the premises, actually composing and writing as he went along, producing a good readable article direct in type, something which held young Ted Banfield totally fascinated. At the same time he went on to disrupt the normal routine of the newspaper office even more by quoting chunks of Shakespeare, whom he referred to as his "friend William", and scenes from Dickens who was alluded to as his "dear friend Charles". There was little likelihood of his ever having had a friendship with the former, but Dickens and his brother Douglas had worked together. Dickens had gone out of his way to be present at Douglas Jerrold's funeral and had organized stage performances to provide for Jerrold's widow.[14] So when Henry claimed to have accompanied brother Douglas and friend Charles to haunts which appeared in Dickens' novels, he had grounds for being taken seriously.

The upshot of all this for Ted was that thereafter, when reading Dickens — and he was to be a lifetime devotee — he kept seeing facets of the incorrigible Henry in many of the characters.

Ted and Harry used Dickens' works when teaching themselves Pitman's shorthand, taking turns to dictate and transcribe from *Great Expectations* and parts of the monthly numbers of *Our Mutual Friend*, which were then just reaching Australia. Also excerpts from Blair's *Lectures*, discourses on composition by the eighteenth century Scottish minister whose chief claim to distinction was to rest on his four volumes, *Sermons*, which Jabez was to consult when he had been licensed as a lay preacher.

These shorthand exercises, which their father was pleased to see as evidence of his sons' determination to succeed, took place mainly when Harry was back at Ararat from Melbourne where he was gaining journalistic experience on *The Age*, first as a copy boy and then as a junior reporter, under editor David Syme whom Jabez had met on the gold fields.

Harry's absences in Melbourne gave Ted the chance he had long craved to go along as prompter when his father staged evening recitals. And he had the bone-shaker and the gun entirely to himself, even if he was starting to have qualms about shooting wild life just for sport.

Jabez had remained disapproving of the bicycle and still knew nothing about the gun. In terms of what emanated from the local pulpits, if there was to be any retribution for this underhandedness, it should have involved the gun. On the other hand, something called a bone-shaker, and built with the help of an undertaker, might have been expected to bring trouble to its user; and, alas, it was from this machine, rather than the secret firearm, that Ted sustained an injury which was to impair one of his most precious faculties and so greatly influence the course of his life.

Freewheeling down an incline and dodging around tree stumps, old shaft holes and piles of tailings, Ted lost control of the bicycle and was hurled head-first towards a rusting windlass on which he struck his right eye, injuring it severely.[15]

At first it seemed to heal, but in the course of treatment it was discovered that his eyesight had been faulty all along. He was short-sighted and should have been wearing spectacles for long-range vision. With the aid of spectacles he might have seen that windlass in time to avoid it. Meanwhile, he could read perfectly without them, except that the injured eye became inflamed, thus leading to the start of chronic blurring and watering, especially when he was under stress. And even though he was aware of an increasing loss of power in the injured eye, he continued to read everything and anything he could lay hands on, so that his mother was constantly admonishing him: "Don't strain your eyes, so!"

As for his father, Jabez still practised what he had long preached to his family — "love one another" — and so, while his affection for Ted was no less, he could not help at times but treat him not only as a son second in seniority but also as something of a lame duck.

Chapter 4
Quiet Desperation

When Ted Banfield turned twenty-one on 4 September 1873, his father's present to him was a set of three volumes of the works of William Shakespeare, a sort of literary triptych around which his personal library was to be built.

The year 1873 was an eventful one for the Banfields of Ararat. The wooden building next door to the newspaper offices was demolished; and while the family occupied temporary premises nearby, a handsome six-room brick house was erected on the site, at a cost of £475 ($950).[1]

This was the year in which Jabez was licensed as a Church of England lay preacher by the Bishop's registry in Melbourne. There was a strong ecumenical streak in him. Originally a Baptist, he had become a Wesleyan under his first employer, John Rose of Liverpool; and then in Ararat, a member of the Church of England congregation at Holy Trinity. Old issues of his newspaper report him as having presided at anniversaries and other functions of the Methodist and Presbyterian churches at a time when he was taking up the Sunday collections at Holy Trinity and serving as treasurer and churchwarden.[2]

It was also about this time that he was gazetted as a Justice of the Peace and Honorary Magistrate, and for the next quarter of a century he took his place on the bench at the Ararat Court of Petty Sessions.[3]

The shanty town of canvas had given way to a well-ordered municipality with some fine civic and commercial buildings and private residences. The railway, which the newspaper (affectionately known as "The Tiser") had vigorously advocated, was now a reality. Thanks to the campaign and lobbying in the state parliament by the Railway League, of which Jabez was a prominent member, Ararat had become a junction town on the line connecting Melbourne and Ballarat with the pasture and wheat lands of the Western District, and later it was to be connected with the city of Adelaide in South Australia. Old mines were still worked in and around Ararat, but the gold scene had by now moved far northward to Queensland.

The newspaper took on a more august role and appearance, championing many causes. Starting from 1865, it sponsored the annual Ararat Easter Festival which was to become Jabez's pet promotion, an event famous throughout the colony, raising many thousands of pounds for local charities.

In the weeks preceding these festivals, Jabez inserted free advertisements in his paper, embellishing them not only with ornate and eye-catching combinations of type, but also lavishing high-flown blandishments which might well have been inspired by the passing reprobate, Henry Jerrold. The highlight would be the Grand Easter Monday Procession, an astonishing pageant, the whole spectacle "one bewildering scene of dazzling beauty", a mile-long cavalcade of young and old in fancy dress costume, including Chinese Mandarins and warriors in gorgeous robes and masks, parading a huge silken dragon.[4]

Some two years before the Easter festivals began, the newspaper suggested the building of an asylum for the care of the unfortunate minority in the locality suffering from mental instability. Once it came into existence it depended greatly on the annual festival for its upkeep, and the prime mover in its creation became a counsellor and friend to many in this institution; they knew him as someone to whom they could talk freely, knowing that they would receive understanding and sympathy.

Even in all the euphoria of his new, fulfilled and prosperous life in this new land, Jabez was still able to recall something of the dark despair he had suffered in Livepool, working long hours to support his wife and growing family while seeing the future becoming more and more clouded for them. His recurrent respiratory problems, which had briefly troubled him again when summoning the courage to give up the hunt for gold and to return to his trade, had all but completely vanished, even though inland Victoria could have spells of frigid weather, with sleet and icy winds. Certain enlightened doctors at the asylum believed that mental and physical illnesses were somehow linked with each other, and Jabez believed he had grounds to agree with this theory.

This cause remained something of a pet charity, one of the main recipients of the monies raised by the annual event sponsored by his newspaper.

As Harry took on greater responsibilities in the management and editorial sides of the newspaper, Ted outwardly appeared willing to coast along, handling general reporting and grasping any opportunity that arose to spread himself with a paragraph or two of fine descriptive writing where a few words would have sufficed. For his mother and sisters he had a special charm and a sunny, open nature, but he was adept at keeping certain feelings to himself. Despite consultations with Melbourne specialists, his injured eye continued to inflame and grow weaker, and so he began to resign himself to the belief that nothing could be done. The saying that there was printer's ink in his veins could not have applied more to anyone than Ted Banfield. At the same time, even with his injured eye, he would have been content, had such a way of life been possible, to spend it with his nose in a book. Harry had developed other interests, and so Ted found himself making solitary excursions into the bush, always taking a book to read when he rested. Some books helped him identify trees, shrubs, wild flowers, even grasses and weeds, while the works of the naturalist John Gould enabled him to recognize and name a wide variety of birds.

The year 1873 marked another family milestone. Ted's younger brother Walter secured a junior position with the London Chartered Bank. Jabez would have liked to have had all three of his boys on the paper, but he approved of Walter's step nevertheless. Such positions in well-established banks were highly prized — the sons of real gentlemen competed for vacancies — and Jabez was human enough to feel that he himself had achieved a certain standing for a son of his to be chosen.

After all the successes and achievements of 1873, the following year brought sadness. Sarah Wake Banfield, the third child and second daughter, had become Mrs A. McQueen, but after a short marriage she died at the age of twenty-four. Ted felt her death acutely as there had been a bond between them. They had been bracketed together all their lives, right back to Jabez's references to them in his letters from the gold fields; and even though to an extent his younger sister Eva took her place, Sarah's passing somehow made him even more solitary.

Nature and natural history engaged him more and more. He joined a wild life society and shared the concern of members at the threats to native birds and the dangers of introducing species from abroad. He began to delve into the philosophical writings of the leading naturalists of the day — Ralph Waldo Emerson, Walt Whitman and Henry David Thoreau — with whom he found himself instantly in accord.

Out in the bush with food in a rucksack, sometimes accompanied by one of his father's collie dogs, he would find a com-

E.J. Banfield with his father's dogs during a visit to Ararat in 1892. (Courtesy of Irene L. and Zoe Banfield, Ararat.)

fortable spot where he could lie back at an angle to read. Perhaps a mound of mine rubble now overgrown with cushioning grass. Here, where others had dug for gold, perhaps finding it, perhaps not, Ted struck it rich in the pages of Thoreau's best-known work, *Walden or, Life in the Woods*, during that afternoon hush, when "the sun has absorbed the energies of the most volatile of birds and insects".[5]

Phrases and passages stunned and astonished him the further he read. Ted's own life and feelings parallelled so much of what Thoreau wrote about: "Almost every New England boy among my contemporaries shouldered a fowling-piece between the ages of ten and fourteen"; fishing and hunting "early introduce us to and detain us in scenery with which otherwise, at that age, we should have little acquaintance"; "He goes thither at first as a hunter and fisher, until at last, if he has the seeds of a better life in him, he distinguishes his proper objects, as a poet or naturalist it may be, and leaves the gun and the fish-pole behind."[6]

How very true it rang when he read: "The mass of men lead lives of quiet desperation." And now, for the first time, he encountered those lines which were to stay with him throughout the rest of his life and still be with him in death: "Why should we be so desperate to succeed and in such desperate enterprises? If a man does not keep pace with his companions, perhaps it is because he hears a different drummer. Let him step to the music which he hears, however measured or far away."[7]

A sort of desperation had indeed crept into Ted's life. It seemed that his father and the rest of the family expected him to remain satisfied while there was only a limited future with Harry ahead of him.

His thoughts had been straying to other parts of the country where there were other challenges to be taken up. And so he came back from the bush, hearkening to a drumming from some distance away.

Chapter 5
A Drummer from Afar

Thoreau wrote: "How many a man has dated a new era in his life from the reading of a book."[1] The book in Ted Banfield's case was, of course, Thoreau's *Walden or, Life in the Woods*, and he carried a copy of it with him when he set out from Ararat in the late 1870s with a vast amount of small-town newspaper experience behind him.

After a short working period in Melbourne, he moved to Sydney where he joined *The Daily Telegraph* as a reader. His assistant was an aspiring young journalist, T.P. (Thomas Philip) Adlam, who was almost ten years Ted's junior.[2]

At the time, this metropolitan newspaper was said to be the only morning daily in the Australian colonies selling for a price of one penny. Its survival depended upon a large circulation, which in turn depended upon a wide range of news and topics. With his keen and lively interest in all and everything, Ted fitted in well.

He was aware of the advantages of Sydney with "the great natural beauty of the 'finest harbour in the world' ", a place where there were so many free attractions that "One does not need the purse of a millionaire to supply the needful for a stay of a couple of weeks".[3]

Despite all this, Sydney was not Ted's venue. Too crowded, too busy, an ant-heap of desperate people in desperate haste to succeed in desperate enterprises.

When setting out from Ararat, he had been determined to prove himself a success, if only in his father's eyes, and so when a combination of advancement in journalism and a position away from the bustling city came his way, he took the train west to the town of Penrith at the foot of the Blue Mountains to edit the local *Argus*.[4]

Here he remained for only three months. While his work on *The Daily Telegraph* in Sydney had given him the sort of experience which was needed by those who were launching a new penny morning newspaper in Townsville, Queensland, his qualifications included more than this. There were similarities between the Townsville area and Ararat in that settled communities were being established in the wake of gold rushes, and Ted had worked for many years on a newspaper under such circumstances. And there was another key contributing factor in the offer of the sub-editorship to Ted. His young colleague Adlam, smitten by Ted's talk about Robinson Crusoe islands strung along that far northern coast by the thousand, had already headed in that direction; as a member of the staff of the organization planning the new daily, he had suggested Ted as a likely man to the founder Dodd S. Clarke.

As Ted steamed north from Sydney in the middle of August 1882, dim and far-off memories of an earlier sea voyage, the long journey from Liverpool in the *Indian Queen*, were brought back to him as he watched the seagulls soaring in the wake of the ship. He did not recall whether he had suffered from something that was to cause him discomfort now — a proneness to seasickness. But after Brisbane, when the sea track north lay inside the greal coral bulwark that took the surge out of the incoming Pacific rollers, it was like sailing on an inland sea.

They travelled, as all did in these waters, along a passage pioneered by James Cook, who had methodically sounded and named his way northward, labelling natural features that had helped many a ship's officer to verify his position. Cape Upstart, for instance, so named because of its abrupt rise from the surrounding land; and Cape Bowling Green because of its smooth green sward.

On this trip, as the steamer threaded its way through strings and archipelagos of islands, Ted saw "some of the natural wonders of a portion of the earth's surface that is one vast wonder", especially between Mackay and Bowen, where Cook had written: "the whole passage is one Continued Safe Harbour . . . This passage I have named Whitsunday Passage, as it was discovered on the day the Church commemorates that Festival". Ted Banfield wrote:

> Islands and inlets of varied form and character are passed. Some of the islands are mere grassy mounds with flounces of creamy sand; others have wild rough cliffs shooting out from the deep with just the narrowest fringe of fleecy white, edging the intense blue that slowly heaves at their base. Some are passed within a stone's throw; others so far away on the edge of the ocean that they are but the very dreams of islands, so

etherealised by the magic hand of Nature that they seem scarce to belong to this terrestrial sphere.[5]

These were the Robinson Crusoe islands of boyhood magic lantern shows.

Of the approach to Townsville, Ted wrote:

The coastal country seen from the deck of the steamer is for the most part dry and forbidding, backed by blue ranges. No clue is given of the existence of the Burdekin Delta and its wealth of sugar lands, or of the great goldfield of Charters Towers, less than 100 miles inland. It was the fate of Captain Cook to miss the best natural harbour in Australia, if not the world — Sydney — and the second best on the east coast of Australia — Bowen — and to skirt upon what is considered by some, and quite unjustifiably, of course, one of the worst — that of Cleveland Bay.[6]

The town was reached by a channel dredged out into the shallow bay. Red-grey and brown seemed to be the predominating tints of the neighbourhood, and its most remarkable feature

the barren, treeless Castle Hill, the seaward aspect of which is a great cliff absolutely perpendicular. Old inhabitants tell of the time Castle Hill was covered with luxuriant vegetation, when the cliff itself was sparsely decorated with creeping plants and orchids. The visitor will be inclined to discredit these statements in view of the desolate aspect the hill now presents. It is a perpetual and dreary monument to the absorption of the citizens in business. So hard at work have all been in developing the resources of the port and district that none seems to have noticed the melancholy degeneration of the surroundings of the town. Even the base of the great rock which dominates the scene is used for advertising purposes.[7]

Despite this depressing appraisal of his new home, during the early stage of his residence in Townsville, Ted saw his surroundings from an altogether different aspect. He and another man shared a shack and the housekeeping on the beach facing Cleveland Bay and Magnetic Island, seeing other islands lying to the north.[8] At daybreak and sunset, and at times when the light had a special luminous quality, these islands, too, became "etherealised by the magic hand of Nature". And so they began to an exert an allure, an allure which did not diminish even though Ted's injured eye was fast becoming virtually useless.

This lively outpost took its name from Captain Robert Towns, an Englishman of many parts — ship owner, merchant, island trader, banker, to name some of the roles of this dynamic adventurer. Towns became a sailor at an early age on a collier plying between Shields and London. He had received only a little education at a village school, but his desire to succeed was such that when his ship was in port he attended a night school run by a retired mariner who taught him navigation. At sixteen

Towns became mate of the collier and a year later took command. A few years after this he became master of a brig trading in the Mediterranean, and amassed enough capital to build a ship of his own called *The Brothers*, which by 1827, when Towns was thirty-three, was one of the crack passenger and immigrant vessels to the colonies.[9]

Ted's new employer Dodd S. (Smith) Clarke, although from a different English background, was cast in something of the same adventurous mould — as were many of the larger-than-life pioneers who helped conquer this vast and forbidding part of the Australian continent. After receiving a public school education, Clarke came to Queensland as a youth to stay with relatives in the Wide Bay district. He joined the "Queensland and North-East Coast Expedition" led by G. Elphinstone Dalrymple, FRGS, as a boatman. Like others before him who were to become newspaper proprietors, Clarke had a fling at trying to find gold, in his case on the Palmer River field in the far north. From there he moved down to Cardwell where he obtained a detailed knowledge of one of the most beautiful stretches of coastline in Australia by nosing along its channels and into its inlets with a friend in an old iron punt fitted with an engine, with dugongs and turtles for company. Such sorties took them to that inlet where the settlement called Cairns was to be established.[10]

When the township took root here, Clarke formed a partnership with two compositors, J.K. Mehan and a Dane called Rhode, and started a newspaper. Clarke was able to give free rein to a talented pen; unfortunately, when a rival newspaper started up, his sarcastic references to it led to a court action in which he came off decidedly second best. So badly, in fact, that it sent him bankrupt. Putting Cairns and his failure there behind him, Clarke retreated down the coast to Townsville, where he and Mehan and Rhodes teamed up again to start *The Townsville Bulletin*, and in a short time, largely due to Clarke's outstanding all-round journalistic skills, it became a respected and powerful voice in the north.

Ted Banfield and Dodd Clarke were quick to recognize the talent in each other, and were alike in some ways — prone to highs and lows of mood, brimming with exuberance when all went well but depressed in the face of setbacks; although they dealt with the latter differently, Ted withdrawing into his shell while Clarke resorted to drink, a weakness that was to become a growing problem for him personally and for the paper. The two hit if off marvellously and Clarke was delighted with the young man he had recruited from the south, especially following the first issue of *The Bulletin* as a penny morning daily on 1 January 1883. According to T.P. Adlam, who was on hand to see it all happening, the new paper was "an immediate (and lasting) success, and its prosperity was in a great degree attributable to the energy, ability and devotion of the enthusiastic sub-editor."[11]

Ted's approach arose from the sense of duty instilled in him by his father. If you lived in a community, wherever it might be, it was incumbent upon you to take part in its affairs, which he had done from the outset — finding it no problem to do so, since he had an immediate rapport with the local people and somehow felt that he belonged among them. He was accepted at all levels and welcomed into the town's most influential circles. Thus, soon after his arrival he became friendly with one of Townsville's pioneer merchants, Thomas Hollis Hopkins, and a prominent alderman, Robert Philp, who was to describe Ted in his memoirs as "a bright young reporter".[12]

Opposite the site where Thomas Hollis Hopkins was to build a home, Ted sampled his first "strip of the tropics" as he took a stroll along the beach in the morning after working late into the night, collecting his first sea shells. At Robert Philp's home four miles out of town, he saw something of the potential of the north; a garden that boasted tropical fruits such as oranges, pineapples, pomelos and coconuts, all of which Philp claimed could be cultivated for profit. The garden also contained fruit which might not have been expected here — strawberries, thriving and luscious.

Philp had a kinship with other men of drive and vision, such as Robert Towns and Dodd Clarke. After arriving as a young man from Glasgow, he began work with a firm of merchants and shipping agents in Brisbane and was sent to Townsville where he became associated with James Burns, who had established a business as a storekeeper. When eventually they became partners in Burns, Philp and Co., they dealt in wool, wood, gold, and built up a fleet of steamers for the trade on the east coast and to the Pacific Islands and the East Indies.

In his letters home to Ararat, Ted had much to write about, although his mind moved too swiftly for his pen, and so his handwriting had become a streaming, rolling scrawl which recipients of his letters had difficulty in deciphering — to say nothing of compositors faced with his copy.

His father, Jabez, no doubt deplored this elementary failing, and saw no excuse for it. He himself had proudly preserved his fine copperplate hand, whether writing a leader for his paper, preparing an address for a public function or taking minutes at a meeting where he held office. Because of his father's attitude, Ted made an effort to write as legibly as possible, difficult as this was when he was overflowing with so much to relate about the people he had met, local affairs and issues, the delights of some of the scenery, and the prolific plant, insect and bird life. Some of the first shells he picked up on the Townsville beach were sent to Ararat to start the family collection there.

Although it was not in his nature to brag, he did have occasional lapses — but these were more in the nature of pleas for recognition. To impress his father in particular, he told how he was meeting some of the most imporant people in the far north: his employer, of course; Robert Philp, Thomas Hollis Hopkins, and Thankful Willmett, the Quaker settler, chairman of the harbour board and a prime moving force in the Townsville branch of the separation movement, which aimed to have the northern part of Queensland declared a colony in its own right under the crown.

This was an issue Dodd Clarke had championed in his paper, just as Jabez Banfield had campaigned for a railway and other causes considered vital for the best interests of local people. Ted was a ready convert, as much as if he had been born and reared in the far north.

To him the issue was so straightforward that it seemed incredible that it could not be adopted forthwith. There were two Queenslands (and there still are): the south, almost entirely within the temperate zone; the north within the tropics. On a climatic basis alone there was already a clear-cut division. With the centre of government at the bottom of that southern half, the north was too far away to be either properly or fairly administered, and it appeared that the capital saw to its own interests first. The movement had wide support; the idea had advanced so far that there were suggestions as to where the capital of the new colony should be sited — and, indeed, arguments about this secondary issue. Yet on the main issue, there were some against, so it was no foregone conclusion, and the fight had to be carried to the heart of the Empire, since it was only there, due to the existing form of colonial government, that any change could be made.

Ted became passionately involved in the issue, and willingly undertook extra work in the cause, but the intensive first year had left him exhausted, a condition partly brought about by worry over his injured eye. Stress finds out a man's weak point, and in Ted's case the target was all too vulnerable. Townsville had a number of well-qualified doctors, and Ted turned to one of the best of them. His verdict was not good. The eye could distinguish between light and dark, and discern vague shapes, but it was chronically infected and could cause serious trouble if it was not attended to, even affecting the brain. The advice was to go south to a Sydney or Melbourne eye specialist, in which case there just might be something that could be done.

This, then, was the cloud hanging over Ted's head at the end of 1883, in spite of the success of *The Townsville Daily Bulletin* in its first year.

During this year there had been little time to relax, although Ted had managed to take tentative steps into the islands, first by going across to Magnetic Island, the "magnetical island" named by Cook, and then away out to the main reefs of the Great Barrier to cover a report when a ketch from the Solomon Islands loaded with copra ran aground.

He had acquired a full copy of *A Voyage to Terra Australis* by Captain Matthew Flinders, and out here he experienced something of what the navigator had described:

> In the afternoon, I went upon the reef with a party of gentlemen; and the water being very clear around the edges, a new creation, as it was to us, but imitative of the old, was there presented to our view. We had wheat sheaves, mushrooms, stags horns, cabbage leaves, and a variety of other forms, glowing under water with vivid tints of every shade betwixt green, purple, brown, and white; ... but whilst contemplating the richness of the scene, we could not long forget with what destruction it was pregnant.[13]

Shortly before Christmas 1883, Ted first met the English journalist, James Troubridge Critchell, the London correspondent for a number of newspapers and periodicals, at different times include *The Pastoralists Review, The Sydney Morning Herald* and *The North Queensland Register*. He was also the author of books on such topics as the frozen meat trade, European markets and a guide to Queensland.[14]

Critchell was thirty-three on this trip to Australia, two years older than Ted; a rather grave, neat man, with a dark military moustache. At Christmas he was joining a boat party on a short cruise; Adlam was also going along. Critchell, knowing of Ted's eye trouble and seeing him looking so wan, suggested that he should risk a touch of seasickness (which had not worried him on the visit to the outer reefs) and join the party. Ted agreed, if only to savour Critchell's company.

Ted himself was to write a guide for tourists to this part of Australia. In it he described those islands stretching north from Townsville as "Summer Islets" and "stepping-stones" to Great Palm Island. Some of these stepping-stones had taken their names from ships: Rattlesnake Island, for instance, from the survey vessel commanded by Captain Owen Stanley and responsible for a major part of the charting in the area.[15]

If Ted suffered any seasickness, he did not recall it when writing of the experience: "A more delightful cruise than from Townsville to Challenger Bay, the port of Great Palm, and thence among the lesser islands of the Group, is scarcely to be imagined. Sport is plentiful, and the scenes of the seaward aspect among the coral reefs, which are miles in extent, reveal some of the wonders of the world."[16]

These wonders were first comprehensively catalogued by the English naturalist regarded as the "first biographer" of the Great Barrier Reef, Dr William Saville Kent, Director of Fisheries of the Queensland government. He carried out much of his research on and around the Palms, consolidating it in a magnificent tome partly illustrated with many of the scientist's own photographs taken on plates, using a heavy wood and brass camera which was supported by four extending legs. These photographs were (and remain) masterpieces of their kind, as are Saville Kent's own watercolour illustrations of the reef life — living corals, fish, anemones, molluscs — all painstakingly-executed scientific facsimiles magically converted into stunningly beautiful works of art. Saville Kent prefaced his book, *The Great Barrier Reef of Australia*, by stating that when he had been working on corals in the Natural History Department of the British Museum, it had been a daydream of its author to be "afforded an opportunity of seeing those organisms growing in their native seas and in their wonderful living tints".[17]

Such scenes were discovered by members of the Christmas holiday party when they went reefing, watched by some of the few white and coloured inhabitants who managed to live from fishing and gathering big clam shells and coral. Ted revelled in the spectacle, despite the nagging discomfort of his defective eye. He had his first close view of an eagle sitting upright as it guarded its nest of matted sticks of driftwood on the top of an isolated rock shaped like a giant grey egg. The party came upon a tiny inlet which was a treasure trove for the shell-hunters, a great heap of coral and shell debris containing isolated specimens, such as lustrous cowries, in perfect condition. To Ted it was like finding nuggets in a pile of tailings from an abandoned digging.

As the day on Great Palm reached into the afternoon, Ted's bad eye began to ache, so he detached himself from the party to go to a stream flowing out of the forest and down the beach. He knelt and bathed his eye with scoops of cool, pure water.

Critchell observed this. He knew that Ted had been advised to go to Sydney or Melbourne for a specialist verdict. He decided to take it upon himself to offer alternative advice, but waited until he and Ted went off together to hunt for butterflies, while the remaining members of the party fished, fossicked for shells, or just explored the shallows of the reefs.

Armed for the hunt with his net, Critchell enlisted the help of a local Aborigine who took him and Ted to glades where butterflies were plentiful. The Aboriginal name for them sounded something like "brammo". Ulysses and Cassandra butterflies were found rioting heedlessly "in curves and swoops of giddy flight"[18] and tumbled into Critchell's net.

As he and Ted rested, Critchell said, "I believe Adlam's going to Europe."

Ted knew all about it. "Yes," he said. "He's had enough of newspapers — wants to pick up some agencies and start up as an importer."

"Thought about going yourself at all?"

"To Europe?" said Ted in a startled tone, as if it was being suggested he might desert his post.

"Well, to be more specific — London. I'll be back there, so I'd be able to introduce you around. A pleasure, never fear." And then he took the plunge. "Besides, it would be an opportunity for you to consult the very best specialists in the world."

It was so genuinely put by a man who was so innately kind that Ted, even though feeling more of a lame duck than ever, suffered only a twinge of resentment before calming down and considering the hard realities of such a proposal.

"Of course I've thought about going to the old country," Ted admitted. "But not at this stage."

"Why not? The daily is well established now and ought to be able to spare you for a while. Especially if you're going to come back with wider experience — and fitter for the job. I have no doubt in my own mind that Clarke would see it in that way."

"It would cost money — and I'm hoping to buy a small place of my own. I just couldn't afford such a trip."

"There are ways and means. A certain influential gentleman, who speaks very highly of you, recently sought my advice on a confidential matter. He wants to attract attention to the Torres Straits route to England, in contrast to the better-known route south and across the Indian Ocean. His firm acts as agent for the British-India Steam Navigation Company."

"Robert Philp?"

Critchell nodded. "He wants to boost the Torres Straits route — get more passengers, more cargo. I had it in mind to suggest that I might do a series of articles for him. Now, if you were to undertake them, I feel sure he would be only too happy to arrange a complimentary return passage. And Clarke would surely welcome such articles — especially from your pen — extolling the advantages, both scenic and otherwise, of the northern route rather than its southern rival."

To Ted such a rivalry was related to the separation issue and he was immediately sympathetic to the idea, quite apart from the chance it would give him to obtain the world's best advice about his eye. So he gratefully accepted Critchell's offer to put the proposal to both Philp and Clarke. And when Critchell did so, each man wasted no time in agreeing: a complimentary passage in return for a series of articles for *The Townsville Daily Bulletin* by its "own Travelling Correspondent".

The party stayed on Great Palm for the night, setting up camp under "the very gates of heaven", a stupendous sunset of awesome splendour, partly caused by the volume of fine volcanic dust high in the atmosphere after the eruption of Krakatoa in Java a few months earlier.[19]

Chapter 6
Homeward Bound

The wet season was over and the threat of cyclones well past when Ted Banfield and his younger colleague Adlam boarded the British-India Steam Navigation Company's Royal Mail steamer *Chyebassa* as she lay at anchor off Bay Rock — some ten kilometres from Townsville — early in the evening of 26 April 1884.[1]

Ted was in a mood of high expectation, despite the disturbing reason for setting out on this voyage. Ships were floating islands, places of escape, and for him the whole journey was to be one long exhilarating escape, so much so that he avoided seasickness (so perhaps he was prone to it only when his mood was down near the lower end of his scale of emotions).

The British-India Steam Navigation Company had one of the largest fleets under any one house flag in the world — one or two paddle-wheelers and nearly eighty screw steamers ranging from a few hundred tonnes gross up to nearly five thousand.[2] The *Chyebassa* could not claim to be one of the line's finest ships, as were the *Manora* and the *Quetta*, but at 2,644 gross tonnage she was a comfortable ocean-going steamer, aided in the right conditions by sails, a feature of marine design at this time when the transition from sail to steam was still taking place. The *Chyebassa* was a roomy, well-ventilated vessel with inviting lounges and spacious decks under double canvas awnings to ward off the sun.

Throughout the night, the native crew of "Hindoo" seamen took the last consignments of cargo on board from lighters; it was still dark when the anchor was raised. The ship slipped past those "stepping-stones" Ted had already seen, and by daylight they were passing the Brook Islands, then another group, the Family Islands, named as such by Cook, leading to a much larger island — Dunk — which Ted now saw for the first time, from the outer side, with rocks and precipices shouldering off the sea, thus leaving its charms concealed and unsuspected.

Under the overall title "Homeward Bound", the "Travelling Correspondent" of *The Townsville Daily Bulletin* composed seven articles covering the voyage, all of which also appeared in his hometown newspaper in Ararat. Later when they were edited and published under the title *The Torres Straits Route*, Ted wrote: "I propose simply to unroll a panorama of a voyage from Queensland to England, with, perhaps, some faint sketches of the East as a kind of a side show." He proceeded to do just this, although he was being less than frank since he was engaged in what today would be described as a public relations exercise, and not a particularly subtle one at that.

> At the outset, I would with deference due and without prejudice, ask my readers to compare the routes to Aden (whence all roads lead directly to London) of the Peninsula and Oriental and Orient Companies with that of the British-India Steam Navigation Company. The former track, by Adelaide and Cape Leuwin . . . is so dreary and monotonous, so entirely innocent of that element so much desired and so keenly relished by your traveller — change . . . Compare, then, that uninteresting route with that which I shall endeavour to faithfully describe.[3]

Once he got down to unrolling the promised panorama, he betrayed something of a certain desire that had been implanted in him during the Christmas expedition to the Palm Islands. As the *Chyebassa* reached the Albany Passage at the top of Cape York, he found it to be "a place of even greater beauty than any we have yet passed". In among a group of islands, they came upon a quiet bay where several small vessels lay at anchor. Up above the bay was the lonely residence of Jardine, the wealthy squatter. Children played on the green in front of the house, and then in reply to a whistle blast from the *Chyebassa* they hoisted a flag to the top of their staff. The scene was soon shut out by a promontory of land, but the glimpse aroused something in Ted who wrote that "To the lover of all that is grand yet reposeful in scenery, to one who desires to absolve himself from the pleasures and conventionalities of city life", no finer place could be found.[4]

The panorama now began in earnest. They steamed through Torres Straits and dropped anchor off Thursday Island, where the *Chyebassa* loaded all the pearl-shell that had accumulated since the passing of the last boat. Heading into a raging sunset, that evening they had their last view of Australia.

In the Arafura Sea, with the Gulf of Carpentaria to the south, the ship ran into something closely connected with the reason for the current spate of spectacular sunsets. Spread out over the sea were fields of tinkling debris from the Krakatoa eruption, lightweight pumice stone floating amid scum of a dingy yellow colour.

There was a brief call at Timor, and more and more of those enticing fragments of sea-girt land which were always capable of somehow infusing Ted's pen with magic: "we sighted a few small islands, blue dots, which in the dazzling light of the early morning, appeared poised midway between sky and water — half celestial, half terrestrial — but altogether lovely."[5]

After steaming south of the crescent-shaped land mass, but almost always within sight of it, the *Chyebassa* headed up through the narrow Straits of Bali and along the coast of Java to Batavia. The Travelling Correspondent, whose writings parallelled the day to day progress of the ship, revealed himself to be a capable travel writer:

> The Chyebassa dropped anchor in Batavia Roads, in the midst of a considerable fleet of steamers and sailing vessels, about two miles from the shore. Scarcely had the anchor chains ceased rattling before several of the light "prows", which here fulfil the duties of lighters, were alongside, pitching and tumbling on the uneasy swell as if determined to rid themselves of their masts. Then commenced the clang and clamour consequent upon the receipt of cargo and coal.[6]

Leaving the *Chyebassa*, which "looked like a motherly old duck surrounded by a brood of uncouth but affectionate ducklings", in "a cloud of coal dust", the passengers were taken ashore in a powerful steam launch, passing the breakwater which had been damaged by the tidal wave following the Krakatoa eruption, and then along the canal which ran through the heart of Batavia. Ted was enthusiastic about many aspects of this "tropical Rotterdam", which he found to be a city set in a vast and shady garden.[7]

He was much impressed by the orderliness of the Dutch administration and the native inhabitants, particularly by their cleanliness and clothing:

> there was not a soil or a stain to mar the wholesomeness and picturesque appearance of their attire. Although, like a wise man, the Javanese does not encumber himself with much clothing, he invariably looks well dressed, for all that he wears is scrupulously clean. It would be well for the inhabitants of tropical Australia if some bold reformer were to introduce among the laboring classes, some such light, comfortable, consistent and cheap costume.[8]

What he saw here had brought to mind some of Thoreau's views of mankind's raiments: "perhaps we are led oftener by the love of novelty and a regard for the opinions of men, in procuring it, than by a true utility".[9] He had been delving into *Walden or, Life in the Woods* again, revelling in the freedom to read.

He also wrote that "long hours were devoted to lonely contemplation". Thoreau had written: "A man thinking or working is always alone, let him be where he will. Solitude is not measured by the miles of space that intervene between a man and his fellows. The really diligent student in one of the crowded hives of Cambridge College is as solitary as a dervis in a desert."[10]

However, it must not be thought that he devoted most of his free time during the voyage to such solitary pursuits. On his own admission he took part in another well-established shipboard diversion — flirting. Although "there was only one flirtable girl among an intolerable deal of mankind".[11]

Ted and Adlam decided to take turns every other evening in promenading her on the deck and discussing with her a subject which they had earlier agreed between them — the Southern Cross, before it began to go out of sight; cooped fowls; the noise of the engines; and other inconsequential subjects — so it was no wonder she appeared "a gloomy girl"; the unfortunate young lady must have been bewildered by their whimsies and exuberances.[12]

Before leaving Batavia, certain members there of the opposite sex attracted Ted's attention. In the course of the sightseeing he and others passed a ladies' school where

> we saw troops of happy school girls wending home. And here give me pause, while I endeavour, without shocking your modesty, to describe in simple homely terms, the simple, homely out-door costume of a Dutch school girl of Batavia — costume in which we saw girls of all ages, up to eighteen and nineteen, by the scores. Chemise loose and elongated, drawers abbreviated, stockings high, shoes low, hair in fat pigtails, or *a la Lucia* in the mad scene, parasol expensive — only this and nothing more — and all white, snowy white, save the shoes. Dress seems to be going out of fashion among the fair Batavians, and I expect that should it ever be my fortune to visit that lovely place again I shall find the rising generation clad in the simple style of our first parents before the fall.[13]

After leaving Java the ship had to work its way among "unseen sand-banks through a channel marked here and there with nothing but long bamboos stuck in the sand". Fortunately, they had a pilot on board at this stage. They passed the islet standing some twenty-four metres above sea level where thousands had perished when the wave from the volcano swept over it, and then

> Krackatoa hove in sight early in the afternoon, and we were abreast of it just as the sun went down. Previous to its last and most disastrous attack of internal disorder, the B.I.S.N. Co.'s steamer used to pass to the north, but the eruption so disorganised that channel, that another between mountain and the mainland had to be availed of. We did not, therefore, see the injured part of the mountain — the remains of the peak that was

blown away being to the north; but we saw a peak rising abruptly out of the sea, and tapering regularly from the base to the pinnacle, round which floated tiny clouds of thin vapour, which were ever waxing and waning; we saw that the peak was wild and horribly desolate, for in place of the dense vegetation which clothed from base to summit neighbouring island peaks, there was nothing but dull grey lava, seamed and scored by thousands of conflicting wrinkles. The mountain was dead. We saw the dry and withered exterior of what had once been an emblem of luxurious life, and we could not but be affected with its stern, gloomy, and forbidding aspect. It was soon lost in the brief twilight; but some of the passengers, after its form had been swallowed in the gloom of night, thought that they could perceive a faint pink — the sign of flickering life — where we had lost its summit.[14]

Island of Krakatoa in the Straits of Sunda before the volcanic eruption, August 1883.
(*The Illustrated London News*, 8 September 1883.)

They did not call at Colombo after all as they had taken on so much cargo at Batavia. When the equator approached "The line was crossed, without doing any damage to the ship", but there had been alarms. A cry of "fire!" when there was a minor outbreak, and "man overboard!" when the dark head of one of the seamen was seen bobbing astern before the ship stopped and a boat went to fetch him.[15]

The fairer sex continued to engage Ted and Adlam — not only the "one flirtable girl" but those who had joined the ship at Batavia. The reactions of the two men were obviously quite different to those of the ladies already aboard who grew to be exceedingly shocked in that the Dutch ladies chose to promenade the deck all morning and in the gloaming as well in very scanty clothing. They wore a fan, a loose white blouse open at the neck, and a short colored gown displaying robust calves, emphatic feet, and toes forced into tiny slippers, the high heels of which supported the middle of the foot, leaving something less than a yard of heel sticking out into space in unrelieved loveliness. The girls affected the lovely costume which is fashionable among the Batavian school girls, and both young and old allowed the wayward wind to revel in the loose abundance of their hair.[16]

As the panorama continued to unroll, there were stretches of open sea with no land in sight, but these were no longer deserted watery wastes to Ted as he found constant bird life — gulls and petrels, and sometimes at night, against the stars, flocks and detachments of migratory species.

Other mountains were seen — before Suez and Port Said, the "inhospitable bulk of Mount Sinai — rising out of a wilderness of brown sand". They sighted it on a Sunday evening: "Among those dreary ravines had not Moses communed with the God of Israel for forty days and forty nights? ... No sermon preached aboard that day had half the influence for good." After Ferdinand de Lesseps' canal and Port Said, a small white cloud "like a pearl on the blue rim of the ocean" — the vapour hovering above the summit of Mount Etna. After a glimpse of Malta and its capital Valetta, the "vine-clad hills of Spain". They passed from the Mediterranean into the Atlantic "Under the shadow of the grim old rock of Gibraltar". And then: "Solemn, gloomy, pall-like clouds hung over Trafalgar's Bay, and a danger light cast a blood-red gleam through the misty air from a point which overlooks the scene of Nelson's glorious victory."[17]

Early in the morning of 16 June 1884, the Eddystone lighthouse hove into sight, and "on the port side was the misty outline of the shore of Old England. Soon the *Chyebassa* passed into smoother water inside of the Plymouth Breakwater, and the passengers had leisure to admire the greenness of the irregular fields and the freshness of the woods, and to inspire deep draughts of the soft air that came off the land."[18]

From Plymouth they proceeded up the Channel: "That morning the coast was scarcely ever out of sight. It was now rocky, barren, dreary; now checkered with woods, green fields, and quiet cosy villages; now faint and unreal in the green haze; but it was there and that was enough."[19]

Another night on board and "morning brought the white cliffs of Dover, which glistened in the fitful sunlight, and a far-off view of the coast of France, and afternoon — the mighty city of London".[20]

The following year when Ted collated the seven instalments of "Homeward Bound" into a promotional pamphlet, he added an introduction in which he stated that the journey from almost

Foundering of SS *Quetta* in Torres Straits, 28 February 1890. She sank in three minutes after having her bottom ripped open by an uncharted rock.
(Courtesy of John Oxley Library, Brisbane.)

any part of Australia was simple and easy: "The odds of being shipwrecked and tossed about for a week or two upon a raft made of ancient hen-coops, and being cast up on a deserted island, where highly-flavoured birds' eggs, seal's blood, and sea weeds are perennial luxuries, are so remote that they do not come within calculation."[21]

The odds, alas, were not so remote. Early in 1890, when the Torres Straits route could have been expected to be even better charted, better known, and thus safer, one of the British-India Steam Navigation Company's finest screw steamers, the *Quetta*, was heading north through the Adolphus Passage when disaster struck. One moment the ship was forging smoothly on across a calm moonlit sea, the next its bottom was ripped open by an unknown rock. She sank in three minutes with the loss of 133 lives and great hardship for those who survived.

As Matthew Flinders had observed when confronted with the beauty, the mystery and the might of the Great Barrier Reef: "with what destruction it was pregnant".

Chapter 7
Erratic Rovings

After the seventh of the "Homeward Bound" articles there was an interval of some two months before the publication of any further dispatch from Ted in either Townsville or Ararat.

"Erratic Rovings" began to appear early in November 1884; four articles in all. In the first, Ted wrote: "My last was dated from London, but ere I had the opportunity of acquiring beyond a very casual knowledge of the more prominent and striking features of the great city — while yet I knew it in only one or two of its multitudinous aspects — circumstances drove me to the country."[1]

He made contact with J.T. Critchell, who was eager to assist with information, introductions and friendly advice, to both Ted and Adlam, who both spent a few adulatory days taking in some of the traditional sights. Trafalgar Square was invested with added interest for them since they had passed through the waters where the historic sea battle had been fought, and had seen it in a brooding mood that might well have been caused by the presence of spirits from the past. They stood before the soaring, fluted column with the figure of Nelson high above; just high enough, should he have been able to "see" with his one good eye, to allow him to follow the loops and reaches of the River Thames to its mouth and to glimpse the sea.

With one eye already useless, Ted felt he had a sort of kinship with Nelson. He shared the same slight build and ascetic appearance. A man who was to become one of Ted's closest friends — E.G. (George) Barrymore — was to observe this and make a detailed comparison: "His head was small, well-shaped and poised gallantly. His wavy hair, thinning off the temples, ran back, displaying a fine brow. A high-bridged nose, but not a predatory one . . . The chin was long, determined and finely cut. It was essentially a sensitive face, the face of a poet. It always reminded me of Nelson's. He was of that lean and sensitive type."[2]

Critchell had made tentative arrangements ahead of Ted's arrival for him to see a leading eye specialist. The appointment was confirmed and shortly after stepping ashore from the *Chyebassa*, Ted was to hear the expert verdict. Deep down he had continued to harbour the hope that a man of such distinction might divine a cure or know of an operation that could restore the eye. The decision was categorical. Unless the eye was removed, it was only a matter of time before it infected the brain.

Leaving Adlam to see wholesalers and manufacturers whose goods he hoped to import to North Queensland, Ted surrendered to the arrangements made on his behalf, and was admitted to one of the London teaching hospitals where the operation was carried out. Before he could be fitted with an artificial glass eye, the socket had to be given time to heal and harden — and to assist and hasten this process, it was recommended that the socket should be exposed to the air. Not to air laden with smoke, fumes and grit, as was London's air, but good clean country air.

Critchell invited Ted to stay at his cottage in the small Essex town of Billericay which was connected by railway to the Liverpool Street station, which in turn was within walking distance of the hospital where Ted was to report for check-ups and for the fitting of the artificial eye. Ted was only too happy to accept the kind invitation, and so was introduced to the charming, thatched "Queensland Cottage", with a garden in which imported Australian shrubs shared the soft summer sunshine with hollyhocks and English roses. Inside the cottage, he found himself even more at home in the presence of Critchell's array of souvenirs from the Australian colonies — sea shells, native artefacts and a collection of butterflies mounted in glass cases, including several captured on Great Palm Island the previous Christmas.

In the cottage, and outside when he might meet or be seen by villagers, he wore a small black patch under his spectacles; but on his own in the lanes and fields, he removed the patch and let the air get at the empty socket. He made excellent progress, and within the expected six weeks the socket was declared well healed and sufficiently hardened for the fitting of the artificial glass eye, two of which were "made to measure" for him, resembling as closely as possible the colour of the iris of his healthy eye, the size of its pupil and the shade of its white. At the hospital he was instructed in the handling and care of an artificial eye, how to insert and remove it, how to wash it, how to look after the socket, thus starting a daily ritual which he would have to observe for the rest of his life.

He had to accustom himself to this ritual, and at the same time become used to the actual wearing of the glass eye, so he was faced with a second convalescent period. He decided to combine this with a visit to a part of England that had long fascinated him, a part not far from Essex as the birds flew — the county of Kent, where, as a small boy, his father Jabez remembered working holidays spent harvesting hops. It also had another association for him, as the place where one of his idols had spent some of his early life and much of his later life — that friend of the brother of the impecunious Henry Jerrold — Charles Dickens.

To reach Chatham meant returning to London and taking another train from another station. Here, where his father Jabez had been born and where his grandfather had worked as a pierhead master, Ted saw the early home of the Dickens family and the stylish mansion on Gad's Hill which became the master writer's main residence. He found something familiar in many of the people, which was understandable, for were they not descendants of some of those individuals who had become characters in Dickens' stories? Now that his good eye had finally parted company with its ailing companion, he had somehow been set free to see the world about him and its inhabitants with greater clarity. With this heightened perception came a sharpening of all his other senses.

Chance took him inland to the Kentish village of Lenham, where he felt that the true character of Merrie England had been preserved "as yet unsoiled and unadulterated by contact with the turbid overflowings of the cities", despite the fact that he reached it by the newly-opened railway line which had apparently terrorized some of the older and staider citizens.[3] His description of the fearful intruder's effect on these villagers is one that stands comparison with those of Dickens who excelled in writing on such subjects:

> To them this dreadful, awe-inspiring railway, which tears along and screeches as it goes, quaking the solid earth as though it would rouse their ancestors who have slept so long and, up to the present, so peacefully beneath the yew trees yonder, is as a sign — it is the beginning of the end. They will not approach the station where the strange monster stops for a moment and then rushes off again, panting in its eagerness to be away.[4]

In one of the public houses in the village square, where ancient cottages with latticed windows and projecting upper stories were some three and four hundred years old, he found comfortable accommodation. While ceasing to be an object of wonder, and establishing friendly relations with the locals, he explored his surroundings. To the sound of the fitful tinkle of a blacksmith's hammer upon an anvil, and the musical chimings of the clock in a massive square church tower, he took a path up a hillside vocal with bird song to its highest point:

> All the country below is one unbounded garden; save for the old grey church and a few isolated houses, the village is blotted out with dense foliage; there are great dark patches of wood, and thousands of small fields all unalike as to size, shape and color; some are of golden yellow, others of the darkest green, and others tinged with grey; there are others of pale green, others pink and warm with clover, others ruddy and aflame with poppies. There are pastures dotted with sheep, and others enlivened with groups of cattle. In the midst of a fair domain, surrounded by noble trees, and beside a miniature lake, stands the lofty many-gabled manor-house. Beyond are the low fertile hop-clad hills, which overlook the spacious low land called the Weald of Kent; and in the far far distance — just where earth and sky seem to meet — there is a gleam and flashing of the sea. A softness and a harmony — a passive glory — peculiarly wholesome and satisfactory to one used to the excessive brightness and monotonous glare of the Australian landscape — pervades the scene.[5]

At The Dog and Bear, The Chequers and The Red Lion where mild and bitter ales were always on draught, Ted was accepted by the locals. He was appalled to learn of the low wages paid here in comparison with those in the Australian colonies. Why didn't these men migrate? His enquiring mind sought an answer for it, and in reporting his conclusions he revealed his flair for being able to mimic accents and dialects and to render them visually into words.

"If I am to speak according to my convictions," he wrote, "I must say beer, nothing but beer." He theorized that if the emigration authorities could supply free beer "they would have no difficulty in thickening the population of bush townships". When he revealed himself as being an Australian, one of the questions put to him was: "An' waat mighten 'e pay for a point o' be-or out'en thee ar?" When Ted supplied the information, the comment would be: "Thaat wouldn't do for the loikes o' me. I must ha' be-or regular."[6]

His underlying awareness of the attractions of the fairer sex, which had been a feature running through the "Homeward Bound" articles, appeared at the very end of the second of his "Erratic Rovings"; although it was enigmatic, to say the least: "I assert that the Lenham girls have expressive feet".[7]

Intrigued Ararat readers had to wait from 18 November to 23 December 1884 for an answer: "Anyone who stands upon the leads at the top of the belfry tower, as I have done, will see enough to convince him of this." For generations it had been the practice for young men to escort young ladies up to the top of the dark and dusty staircase and for the men to mark the outlines of one of the young ladies' bare feet on the soft lead.

> Now, one cannot walk upon the belfry-tower without treading upon dozens of these romantic mementoes. In some cases it is quite apparent that the young lady has insisted upon her pedal autograph being accompanied by that of her companion . . . The smaller footprint will be inscribed, perhaps, "Anne", and the larger "George" . . . The old, old story told in yet another form! . . . It signifies to all whom it may concern that "Anne" and "George" have hobbled themselves to one another, and that they intend to walk through life together. One strange perplexing thought this leggy mode of declaration does suggest! It is on which limb does the young lady wear the engagement ring?[8]

He felt that he owed it to the kindly villagers to provide some sort of explanation for his leisurely stay in Lenham with the village as headquarters as he made trips to other parts of Kent. So he confided that he was adjusting himself to the wearing of a glass eye. While this brought veiled but penetrating scrutiny from the villagers, he was able to quietly gloat when he gathered that he had grown to wear the artificial substitute with such assurance that there was growing conjecture as to which of the two eyes behind his spectacles was real and which was false. With this discovery came the realization that his stay here must now come to an end. After one of his last visits to the belfry tower, he wrote:

> In my memory may be kept green the glorious view so expressive of peace and content. An hour ago the sun set, and yet every feature of the landscape is warmed with a tender glow from a bank of "daffodil sky" in the west. In one of the vicarage fields below there is a troop of noisy cricketers, and in the orchard adjoining are "young-men and maidens, old men and children", robbing tall cherry trees of their ruddy fruit. Above the shouts of the cricketers, the murmurs of the fruit-gatherers, and the lowing of the cattle, floats the thrush's song, and close on hand, on the mossy parapet of the old church, there are twittering sparrows. A sweet perfume is wafted from the fields of beans and clover, and from each cottage ascends a thin column of smoke. It is at a time such as this that one realizes how potent must be the influence which will attract a home-keeping Englishman from the scenes of his youth, and that after all beer is not quite the only tie which attaches the poorest labourer to his native soil.[9]

His sojourn in Kent had roused within him "an earnest love for old England and old English institutions, a pride in her history and a personal interest in her well-being that distance shall never qualify nor time distort".[10] But Australia, in particular North Queensland, had become *his* native soil, and he had no desire to live here in Kent, despite its peaceful way of life and his inclination to escape from the hurly-burly.

Lenham still observed an ancient annual curfew which took place in ceremony only. Starting at a quarter to eight on each 28 September, the church bell was rung for fifteen minutes every evening until 25 May the following year. By the time this ritual had started in 1884, Ted was working his way north to visit the city where he was born and to call on some of his parents' old friends.

Chapter 8
Pedal Autographs

Ted had promised his mother that he would make contact with her friend, Eleanor Golding, with whom she had been corresponding for thirty years. When he wrote to Mrs Golding to tell her that he planned to visit Liverpool, back came an immediate reply insisting that he must stay at the Golding home. Much as he would have liked to remain independent — still being highly conscious of his glass eye — the invitation was so warm and welcoming that he could not refuse it.

What Ted's mother apparently did not know — nor his father, nor Harry and his other brother and his sisters — was the real reason behind his journey abroad as Travelling Correspondent. It would seem that he had revealed nothing to any of them about the operation to remove his diseased eye, and so he was confident that neither Eleanor Golding nor any member of her family would have any prior knowledge of his glass eye. But he was exposing himself to a test and a certain ordeal nevertheless.

He arrived in Liverpool, expecting to stay a day or two at the most. He had in mind a visit to the Lake District, which, now that autumn had taken over, would have its splendours on display. According to Critchell, this was one of the best times to visit the area. And according to the German writer-philosopher Goethe: "To understand a poet, one must go to his home country." By coming to England, Ted felt that he had somehow come closer to Shakespeare and Dickens — and to Keats and Goldsmith — and he hoped to gain a deeper appreciation of the works of Coleridge, Southey, Wordsworth and other poets of the Lake District school by visiting the scenes that had inspired them. His overseas trip had, in a sense, turned into a literary pilgrimage.

After a preliminary look at Liverpool, which included the River Mersey down which the *Indian Queen* had sailed as he had set out for Australia, he made his way to the Golding home. As he approached the front door of the house, a substantial dwelling built by George Golding[1] to his own design, he was greeted by sounds that took him back to Ararat when his mother and his sisters practised singing. A piano played ascending scales, and a young but unsure female voice accompanied them: "Do, re, mi, fa, so, la, ti, do!" A moment later the piano repeated the scales, this time accompanied by an older female voice, one that was sure, languid and sweet. Another ascent, then a descent of the scales in reverse order by this same voice, as Ted stood confronting the knocker on the door, somehow feeling that if he were to rap it he might be guilty of some ungentlemanly intrusion.

As it happened, he did not need to knock. Eleanor Golding had been keeping a lookout for him from a front window, and as he reached to grasp the brass knocker, the door swung inward — and there stood his mother's old friend, beaming a welcome.

The piano and the two voices were louder now, and Mrs Golding hastened to explain that her daughter Bertha was a music teacher[2] and was giving a private lesson to a new recruit to her church choir. The voice of the recruit did not impress Ted as having much to offer the choir, but as a man who had a keen ear for a songster he found the voice of the teacher unusually light and lovely, and so he remained fascinated by it, becoming increasingly interested in meeting its owner.

Eleanor Golding said that Bertha should be free soon; meanwhile, she introduced him to George Golding and a son, both of whom also accorded him a very warm welcome. They spoke with Lancashire accents, and Ted realized that his father Jabez had retained a strong trace of this same accent in his speech.

"You 'ave certainly growed up more'n a little since last I saw ye," George Golding told Ted.

George had been on the dock, farewelling the *Indian Queen*; but Ted had to confess that he had no recollection whatsoever of those first two years and two months of his life which he had spent in Liverpool. Eleanor told him that he had been a happy child; and that his mother Sarah Ann had left with him in her arms, while Eliza, Harry and little Sarah tightly held one another by the hand to make sure they stayed together and were not left behind. Mrs Golding recalled the presence of Mary Gearing and her children, too — and of how it seemed that the two young mothers and their little ones were setting out on a journey so far that they would never be seen again.

Yet here was young Edmund back in their midst! And hadn't his father done well in the land of his adoption! Eleanor Golding had a number of copies of *The Ararat and Pleasant Creek Advertiser* which Ted's mother sent her from time to time, the most recent being the one covering the 1884 Easter Festival. Mrs Golding knew all about the major part played by Jabez Banfield in organizing this annual event. In every issue, on the front page, was a report on the Ararat Court of Petty Sessions held before Justices of the Peace, including Mr J.W. Banfield.

As Eleanor and George Golding went on to outline what they had arranged for Ted to do during his stay, he found himself surrendering to being here for longer than the day or two he had anticipated. The piano and the singing advanced from scales to an air and then came several hymns, while Mrs Golding prepared to serve afternoon tea. Presently the singing lessons stopped. Ted heard the pupil being ushered out, and moments later the owner of the tantalizingly sweet voice entered the sitting room, a petite young woman in a white lace dress, her light-brown hair worn short,[3] her eyes clear and sparkling, and a beautiful warm smile blooming on her lips. And so Ted Banfield was introduced to Bertha Golding, who had been born three and a half years after her parents had been on the Liverpool dock to see him on his way to Australia.

Afternoon tea was served, the floor being Ted's by right as the visitor from afar; and, as always when in the presence of someone with whom he felt an affinity or a rapport — and in this case he had a whole family — he was taken over by his own enthusiasms. Firstly, his impressions of the great city of London and its wonders; the beauty of the countrysides of Essex and Kent, their neatness and softness after the wide sweeps, the stronger light and deeper distances of the Australian landscapes. Much as his audience enjoyed hearing all this, he found himself being encouraged to describe the countryside around Ararat and the scene in North Queensland — and inevitably something about the Great Barrier Reef.

In comparison with the knowledge he was to amass of this vast structure, what he knew at this stage was limited, but he had gathered some arresting facts about it. James Cook had described it as a wall rising perpendicular out of the unfathomable ocean, and other early navigators such as Philip Parker King and Francis Blackwood had confirmed this by taking soundings. Inside the reef those soundings could be only sixteen or twenty fathoms, while outside the sheer wall there were depths of nearly three hundred fathoms *without touching bottom*. All built by tiny animals, the coral polyps. To the builder, George Golding, this was indeed a wonder — a sort of underwater Great Wall of China. Above water it was a Milky Way of islands, with exquisite coral gardens, untrodden beaches strewn and heaped with peerless sea shells: "half-terrestrial, half-celestial" fragments of Paradise providing uninhabited domains for a thousand Robinson Crusoes.

Ted had been under Bertha's spell since he had heard her voice as he waited on the doorstep; now it was her turn to be under his spell. Because Bertha had to hold music classes at a ladies' school, Eleanor escorted him on his visit down a narrow street to see his parents' first home.[4] And then to the house by Queen's Pier where his grandfather had lived. The printers Robert Dickinson and John Rose had long since passed on, but Ted saw the printing shop where his father had been apprenticed and the office where he had later worked as foreman. It seemed to him that crannies and crevasses harboured the grime and moss of centuries, and he was thankful that his father had had the courage and enterprise to try his luck in Australia.

On his first Sunday with the Goldings, he accompanied Eleanor and George to the church where Bertha had gone earlier to take her place in the choir.[5] By dint of intense listening, he believed he could isolate that voice of special sweetness which had greeted him a few days earlier.

When it came Bertha's turn to show Ted something of Liverpool, she put an end to a certain formality that had so far prevailed. From the outset her parents had addressed him by his full christian name, but to Bertha he had been Mr Banfield, while to him she had been Miss Golding. No more of that.

"I'm Bertha, if you don't mind."

Only too happy to comply, Ted laughed and began to say, "In that case I'm . . ."

"Edmund."

"No," he said. "Ted — if *you* don't mind."

Bertha laughingly agreed. Alone together for the first time, they became at ease in each other's company. They discovered common interests; Bertha confirmed what Ted had suspected from the number of books about the Golding home — a love of reading and literature. She had a special fondness for Charles Lamb[6] and an appreciation of his delightful sense of humour and richness of fancy, traits which she had already detected in Ted. She was also keen on the countryside and belonged to a Ramblers' Club which had adopted a guest house in the Lake District as its headquarters.

When Ted revealed how keen he was to at least glimpse the scenes which had captivated the pick of the English poets, Bertha suggested a one-day train excursion to Kendal. It meant a very early start and a late return, but it enabled Ted to view the vistas which had inspired not only Coleridge, Southey and Wordsworth but also Keats, Shelley, Gray, De Quincey, Scott, Carlyle and, most recently, Tennyson.

The hills were canopied with russet and gold. After looking down onto a lake surface that mirrored these rich autumn hues, they turned to descend a muddy path and found themselves confronted with the footprints made on their ascent. Ted started to shake his head and chuckle.

Bertha did not understand, and so, in a teasing yet forthright way, she sought an explanation.

"I don't know how people behave in the colonies; here it's considered bad manners to laugh at private jokes."

After hastening to apologize, Ted revealed how the two pairs of footprints on the path had reminded him of those "pedal autographs" on the soft lead on the belfry tower of the Lenham Church. Bertha was intrigued and encouraged him to tell her more about it. And so he told her what he had written in the third of his "Erratic Rovings" about the expressive feet of the Lenham girls, and of the novel way they and the young men of the village plighted their troth.[7]

As he did so, he became aware that Bertha was very still and looking deeply into his eyes; in a panic that she might discover that one of his eyes was false, he laughingly dismissed the custom as being another of those endearingly eccentric aspects of the English way of life.

Without the spectacle glass over his artificial eye, Ted felt it would have been impossible for it to have gone so long unsuspected. He had endured some awkward and anxious moments, such as when Eleanor Golding had produced a copy of the Banfield family photograph taken in Ararat outside the new brick house. It was the work of a travelling photographer from Melbourne, and Ted was asked to name his brothers and sisters. Being near-sighted, he had to remove his spectacles so that he could see clearly enough to be able to identify everyone. Much the same problem arose when he was given an open book to read after Bertha had located one of her favourite Lamb essays.

Despite the look which Bertha had given him on their excursion to the Lake District, he was still unsure of himself, and of her feelings. The expected stay of a day or two had become almost a fortnight. He felt he could not leave without somehow ensuring that his friendship with her would continue, so he suggested that they write to each other. Bertha at once declared this a splendid idea.

It would have been easier to leave matters at this, but he felt he had to be honest with her, and so on the day before he was due to return to London, he told her what in fact had brought him to England, something he had yet to break to his own family in Ararat.

"Well!" she said with an unexpected gasp of astonishment.

"For someone with just one eye you seem to see more than a dozen people do with two."

She was thinking of all he had spotted and enthused about on their excursion to Kendal — birds, trees, flowers, waterfalls, panoramas, skies. After shaking her head in amazement, she went on to make a very curious remark.

"You must have noticed that I keep on placing myself to your left."

Now that he thought about it Ted realized that this had in fact been happening. When they walked together, when they sat down, Bertha had moved around so that she would be on his left side. He gave a slow nod, but the remark still bewildered him.

Treating her left ear to a weary little tap with her fingers, she said, "I'm afraid the hearing's almost gone in my left ear since I went down with what the doctors said was rheumatic fever. Makes us quite a pair, doesn't it."

Ted laughed, but it was a nervous reaction. Bertha again looked at him as she had done when he told her how the young couples in Lenham expressed their affection for each other. But he continued to remain unsure of himself, and so at this stage he still hesitated to try to take matters any further.

Chapter 9
Rob Krusoe

On his return to North Queensland, the Travelling Correspondent of *The Townsville Daily Bulletin* prepared the seven "Homeward Bound" articles as a pamphlet to be distributed by the British-India Steam Navigation Company. In the introduction he wrote:

> Released from all responsibility of providing for his everyday needs, and having banished for the time being the petty duties as well as the great concerns of life, the traveller during the voyage will live in luxurious ease, and at the termination discover that he has, like the eagle, renewed his youth. He will plunge into the business of the world again with refreshed energy.[1]

Ted felt a new man. After having rid himself of a canker that had been dragging him down physically and mentally, he had become fully accustomed to wearing an artificial eye; he had seen something of the old world and he'd had enriching and wonderful experiences, most exhilarating of all being his meeting with Bertha Golding to whom he had written en route back to North Queensland by the Torres Straits.

Dodd Clarke, Robert Philp and the staff of the shipping department of Burns, Philp and Co. were pleased with the articles and with the pamphlet, which made out a strong case for the continuation of the £55,000 ($110,000) government mail subsidy to British-India rather than to rival shipping interests pushed by an opposition group in the south of the colony. The pamphlet also helped strengthen the case of those in the "forgotten" north who wanted a colony of their own, and those members of the Separation Council led by Thankful

Willmett, who were already busy collecting signatures to back up their petition to Queen Victoria. It had certainly unfolded an exciting panorama to entice the prospective traveller to the Old Country, making the southern route by Adelaide and Cape Leuwin colourless in comparison — and it had presented the firm of Burns, Philp and Co. as enlightened champions of the causes, concerns and development of the north.

The "Homeward Bound" and "Erratic Rovings" articles had also been well received when reprinted in Ararat, by both the readers of the newspaper and members of the Banfield family. Jabez, who had not been obliged to decipher the riotous scrawl which had faced the compositors in Townsville, had been proud to publish all pieces in full and had been delighted with their literary excellence to the point of including excerpts from them in a number of his readings and recitals in Ararat and neighbouring townships. Such acknowledgment from his father was a source of deep satisfaction to Ted. As for his mother, it was somehow as if through her second son her dream of a trip back "Home" had at least in part been fulfilled — even if she did not altogether approve of what in her opinion was cavalier conduct by Ted and his colleague Adlam towards the only eligible young woman on board the *Chyebassa*. She hoped he had not carried on in the same way at the Goldings, and was relieved to receive a letter from Liverpool giving an enthusiastic account of Ted's visit and a hint that their daughter Bertha had been — and remained — much attracted to her handsome and charming son.

Shortly after telling Bertha about the operation to remove his eye, Ted had written home to Ararat, thus revealing the real purpose of his visit to England, and at the same time leaving no one in any doubt that something which could have caused grave trouble had been successfully dealt with.

During his absence, Harry had continued to send Ted's complimentary copies of the newspaper to Townsville. Going through them and catching up on hometown news, he discovered that there had been sweeping changes. It was now simply *The Ararat Advertiser*, as from 1 January 1885. Also from this date, the proprietor, J.W. Banfield, had announced that the paper would be on sale at the reduced price of £1 ($2) per annum or threepence (2½ cents) per single copy. By the use of a new type of smaller grade and by the lengthening of the columns, it would be permanently enlarged. Jabez had been turning his hand to the odd leader, and Ted thought he could recognize his father's in one which began: "The mission of the journalist is to catch the humor and phases of every passing hour; to mirror life as it presents itself to him; to make history by recording that which he observes."[2]

Ted felt he was doing precisely this as he plunged back into his role as second in command of *The Townsville Daily Bulletin* while Dodd Clarke, although showing no signs of curbing alcoholic excesses, remained in charge.

Few could claim to know the north, its potentials and its problems, better than Dodd Clarke. After all, he had been a member of a major exploration party and had set up camp at places where no white men had been before, but where now there were thriving towns and settlements. As one of the boatmen attached to the 1873 Elphinstone Dalrymple expedition, he had taken part in the probing of all inlets between Cardwell and Endeavour River to ascertain how far the rivers were navigable and to assess the suitability of the soil on or near the banks for agricultural purposes. He and the newspaper were very strongly behind the separation movement, and so was its sub-editor, E.J. Banfield.

In the course of 1885, Ted became increasingly involved in this crusade, and in local parliamentary politics, especially after Robert Philp agreed to stand for the newly-created electorate of Musgrave as a candidate supporting the incumbent Queensland Premier, Sir Thomas M'Ilwraith, a Scottish immigrant.

Clarke put it to Philp that the north had done a great deal for him and that it was up to him to do something for the north in return. What did Clarke want him to do? It was quite simple: stand for the new parliamentary seat.[3] This was followed by a direct personal request from Sir Thomas M'Ilwraith.

Philp claimed in his memoirs that he did not seek public office, and that he had no special interest in politics; but he was wholeheartedly behind the cause championed by Dodd Clarke and so he agreed. At the end of the year, he found himself conducting an electioneering campaign throughout a huge area, including country which, though settled, was still as harsh and unpredictable as it had been when the Dalrymple party had explored it.

He began this campaign just before Christmas 1885 when he left Townsville by steamer. His intention was to cover the Herbert River and go upstream as far as Ingham, but the wet season had started and conditions were so bad that they had to berth much nearer the river mouth, at Halifax. Philp reached Ingham by buggy and it was here that he made his opening speech. Returning to Halifax by the locomotive on the sugar tramline, he found the engineer of the steamer so drunk after celebrating the festive season that he and his party had to get the vessel under way down the river by themselves. The engineer sobered up enough to help the campaigners to proceed north to Cardwell, where Ted Banfield had been waiting to report on their progress.

At the time, Robert Philp was the North Queensland agent for the insurance underwriters Lloyd's of London. The captain of a small steamer the *Glaucus* had come in by lifeboat from King's Reef where his vessel was aground. He believed that it was hopelessly trapped in a coral fissure and that he had no alternative but to abandon it. Philp decided to assess the situation for himself, and set out from Cardwell with the captain of the abandoned vessel on another small steamer the *Ada Dent*. Philp invited Ted Banfield to accompany them.

The weather had eased, so that the threat of seasickness to Ted was not as bad as it could have been. The going was in fact comparatively smooth. After heading out of the Hinchinbrook Channel, the *Ada Dent* took the inner steamer route between the coastline and the islands of the Family Group, and so crossed the gap of five kilometres that separated Dunk Island from the Australian mainland, making this the nearest Ted had so far been to that "delicious Isle" which was to become his home.[4] Not that much could be seen of it, even though they were so close. The light was still poor after their early start, and the island itself under wraps; cloud hung over its peaks and mist blanketed its valleys, its bays and inlets.

King's Reef, first charted in 1819 by Captain (afterwards Admiral) Philip Parker King, lay north of Dunk and was not one but in fact many reefs. Coral-rock and sandy shallows extended from the mainland to the South Barnard Islands, these being part of the overall formation which King had named after a friend, Edward Barnard. Although at high tides smaller coastal steamers could pass in almost any direction with impunity, the actual passage through the reefs was intricate and highly dangerous without precise local knowledge. It was not an area noted for the beauty of its coral growths but rather for bold and prominent formations like giant black-headed busts — "huge blocks standing on sturdy pedestals, tipsy toadstools, and irregular mushrooms".[5]

Brought face to face with his stricken ship as it lay awry in the grip of the exposed coral, the captain of the *Glaucus* bemoaned its situation as being impossible and claimed that its fate was sealed.

Not so Robert Philp. He told the captain how he should go about getting his ship off the reef; then, leaving him to carry out the exercise, proceeded to the next stage of his electioneering campaign, a meeting at Geraldton (now Innisfail).[6]

The captain of the *Glaucus*, meanwhile, was unsuccessful, and it was left to Philp to organize another attempt after he got back to Townsville. Acting to his instructions, those making the second attempt managed to get the little steamer water-borne again, after which it was fitted with a new bottom and continued to trade for many years.[7]

Rounding the South Barnard Islands, which consist of a number of isolated, jungle-covered knolls with fig and umbrella trees, pandanus palms and hibiscus bushes overhanging cliffs, they passed what had been rookeries for thousands of years for the migratory white nutmeg pigeons — now back again in vast numbers, to mate and rear families. When the *Ada Dent's* whistle blew as it steamed past, a tumult of startled birds took to the wing in great snowy patches. Known also as Torres Straits pigeons, they were in the habit of frequenting the tops of wild nutmeg trees. Ted had never seen such a spectacular congregation of birds, one that had a certain biblical quality, for these were of the dove family, symbols of gentleness and innocence, and their presence here made it a very special sort of retreat.

As the birds circled and wheeled, Ted was appalled at their vulnerability. He had heard how boats hove to while those on board blasted away at such unprotected flocks. It was more than just wanton killing; it was sacrilege.

The meeting at Geraldton on Boxing Day night was a spirited one, conducted in the wake of the local regatta held during the day on the Johnstone River. Then the weather worsened again. Ted retained such vivid recollections of it that some twenty years later in an article for *The Northern Miner* he was able to recall many of its sidelights:

> A fierce wind, a great grey sea, and torrents of warm rain made travelling by the little steam launch between the Johnstone River and Cairns anything but pleasurable. It was wet on deck, ever dismal wet. The atmosphere of the little cabin below was a combination of stale eggs, rancid oil, steam, moist blankets, and agitated bilge water. It was hot and stifling and jolted on the sensations — the stomach particularly. We lunched on deck, and of all things in the world the chief dish was pork and cabbage; pork, which slipped and slid over the plate, and sloppy cabbage that was greased to perfection, that is if perfection was to create conflict in the stomach afterwards.[8]

Needless to say, when dry biscuits were offered as alternative fare, Ted was among those quite satisfied to settle for them, hard and stale as they might be.

Cairns was awash, so trying to reach the town of Herberton, where Philp planned to speak, was a matter of riding, walking or wading, since it was before the building of a railway. The party pressed on by hired horses, carrying light equipment on their saddles. Ted had covered election campaigns from Ararat, but never against such a backdrop as this vast, rugged terrain, nor under such primitive conditions. However, he was physically up to the challenge and when the weather relented he found the going delightful.

> Once free from the swamps of Cairns, the country became pleasant. The odour of the wet soil, the warmth of the jungle, and the greeting of the birds inspired the thought that the uncomfor-

table part of the journey was over and that up among the mountains all would be joyous and dry, that the rivers would grant safe and easy passage, and that victory at the poll would crown a pleasant undertaking.[9]

Alas, a mist crept down, the horses and mules turned the track into a slime box, the rain fell in lumps, the creeks and the rivers rose. The animals had to be left behind as the journey was undertaken on foot with the help of expert bushmen, until the electioneering party, after abandoning everything except the clothes in which they stood, managed to fight their way across the range to Herberton where they received an uproarious welcome — as did the intrepid parliamentary candidate from township to township after this, and from camp to camp.

The upshot of the campaign was a great victory at the polls for Robert Philp, who was in time to become the premier of Queensland.

Ted Banfield wrote this article after he had started to practise the gentle art of beachcombing on his strip of the tropics, and did so under one of his early pen-names, "Rob Krusoe".

When Robert Philp left the far north to take up residence in Brisbane, among the 250 citizens of Townsville who presented him with an illuminated Morocco-bound testimonial address were Ted Banfield, Dodd Clarke and Thomas Hollis Hopkins. And when Philp made his maiden speech in the Legislative Assembly, he began:

> Mr Speaker: I must commence by saying I am a strong believer in separation. I am one of the members recently elected to this House, and my principal grounds for standing was that I am a strong believer in separation. Until we get it, the north will not obtain justice from this end of the colony.[10]

This speech was delivered in Brisbane on 27 August 1886. Exactly two weeks earlier, in Townsville, at a marriage ceremony in St James' Anglican Church, followed by a wedding reception at the home of Thomas Hollis Hopkins, Bertha Golding had become Mrs E.J. Banfield.[11]

Chapter 10
First Whispers

Following his return from England, Ted Banfield had thrown himself into his newspaper work with characteristic energy, as always conscientious to the point of obsession. However, at least mentally, he had taken time off for another matter: his relationship with Bertha Golding.

He began his first letter to her in the Bay of Biscay, and when the ship stood off Valetta to discharge cargo and to pick up passengers, he arranged for the letter to be taken ashore and posted. By managing to get a letter to Bertha so soon, it was not all that long after his return to Townsville that he heard from her.

She wrote in a firm, precise, no-nonsense hand that somehow matched her endearing forthrightness; yet in its graceful curves Ted undoubtedly saw something of her petite femininity, and in its loops those soft-lipped smiles of hers. She invited him to picture her trudging through the snow with other ramblers, making an atrocious hotchpotch with all their footprints, something that would never do on the belfry tower in the village of Lenham. She mentioned that she had seen a wedge of high-flying geese leaving the lakes for warmer climes in the south; and she went on to picture Ted back in Townsville, free to gaze out on all those entrancing islands he had described in Liverpool. He reread this letter many times, now without any doubt in his mind as he recalled that tense look Bertha had given him.

The islands were in fact even more entrancing than ever, Ted wrote in his reply; perhaps because he was obliged to work so hard that he could only observe them from a distance. He referred to the local weather, to the high winds, the torrential rains, and the damage they caused; but he looked forward to that part of the year that made tropical Australia one of the most desirable "winter" climates in the world.[1] Would she, he wondered, care to think about the possibility of sharing the local scenes and climate with him? If so, as convention seemed to prescribe, he would write to her father seeking her hand in marriage.

While he took care to restrain himself from lapsing into the scrawl which was either a joke or a nightmare to the compositors, depending on their temperaments or moods, it could cause him actual physical pain to have to make sure that his handwriting remained legible. One of the steamers of the shipping line he had so highly praised was due to sail in a few days, so he caught an early outgoing mail to England. Delivery was now being guaranteed in eight weeks. Allow at least a week for Bertha to make up her mind, and add another eight weeks for delivery back to Australia. Seventeen weeks — four months — an eternity.

However, in just over two months he received a cryptic reply by cablegram. In such matters Bertha made up her own mind, knowing that her father would agree to whatever she decided. She would be delighted to accept. It took another six months of letters and visits to the telegraph office for Bertha's passage on an immigrant ship to be confirmed. She would embark from London late in May the next year so as to be able to arrive in North Queensland when the weather would be perfection. And so she travelled by the Torres Straits route on one of the British-India steamers, which in those days rarely made an outward voyage without a quota of brides and glory-boxes.

Bertha had read all the "Homeward Bound" articles in copies of the Ararat newspaper sent to her mother, so she knew what to look for on the voyage.[2] After the Mediterranean, Port Said, Suez, Aden, the information from articles was most helpful when it came to the rather intricate course followed by the ship once they reached the East Indies. She was able to glimpse for herself that gaunt volcano which had been responsible for the glorious sunsets over the Irish Sea and the Lake District; and then the irregular chain of islands all the way to Townsville. She became friendly with others heading to North Queensland to make it their home, including several who were to remain close to her for the rest of her life.

In preparation for her arrival, Ted had become the owner of a small house on Stanton Hill, one of the high points under the domination of Castle Hill — a neat, white-painted bungalow on wooden stumps, with a deep verandah the full width of the building, and three sets of French windows. The views in all

directions were stunning: Cleveland Bay with Magnetic Island, and the Palms and other islands looming away to the north. And far to the east, beyond the coral reefs and sandbanks that just emerged at low tides, was the Great Barrier Reef.

On their wedding day, 3 August 1886, Ted was a month off thirty-four and Bertha was twenty-eight. They took a steamer north and spent part of their honeymoon at Geraldton, thus twice by-passing Dunk and the Family Islands. Although they had a good view of Dunk and a glimpse of the sweep of its main strand, islands such as Timana and Bedarra, which were compact and more in keeping with the romantic appearance of south sea islands, impressed them more. Dunk, in contrast, had a shy bear-like quality about it; but then it was still quietly keeping its many charms and wonders to itself.

Back at the bungalow under Castle Hill, Bertha had plenty to occupy her while those distracting views continued to beckon. For Ted, except when he undertook reporting assignments, going north as far as Cairns and west to Charters Towers, it was again long hours well into the night at the *Bulletin* office as sub-editor, the second in command.

The family in Ararat, after having first been deeply concerned to learn that Ted's boyhood accident should have resulted in the loss of an eye, were delighted with the romantic

Bertha and Ted Banfield at their home, Stanton Hill, under Castle Hill, Townsville.
(Courtesy of Irene L. and Zoe Banfield, Ararat.)

developments which had followed his trip to the Old Country. They had hoped that the newlyweds would come south for their honeymoon.

Ted explained that he could afford neither the time nor expense as he had invested in a house. He had also taken steps to obtain a little security for himself and Bertha by buying a small parcel of shares in the newspaper company. This was mainly at the instigation — if not insistence — of Dodd Clarke, who, besides being manager and editor, was also a substantial shareholder. He believed that it was in the parent company's interest for senior employees to have an investment in it. Quite apart from the matter of finance, which faced most newlyweds, something else could have been standing in the way of a trip to the south — Bertha and Ted could have been starting a family. In Ararat, this would certainly have been considered an explanation.

Three years had passed without any sign of a child when Ted at last took Bertha south by steamer and train to meet the family. She had already met Ted's youngest sister, Eva, who had come north to stay at Castle Hill with her favourite brother and with Bertha, who was to become a much-loved sister-in-law.

. In May 1889, before the southern trip, a quaint little Irish woman, Essie McDonough, had joined the couple as housekeeper and general help. In the care of this plain-looking but dry-witted pixie, the bungalow and Rowdy, one of the first in a long succession of canine members of the family (which are often substitutes for children), were in good hands. Essie was nearly forty when she was first employed, and was to be devoted to the E.J. Banfields for many years and to share the major part of their great adventure as scouts "on the van of civilization".[3]

Bertha was very much aware that while this was a long over-due visit to Ararat, it was also a most necessary break for Ted. She had been dismayed at the way he pushed himself to keep working and by his constant striving for perfection. While much of his life was lived at a level of bubbling enthusiasm, that mercurial quality which had first captivated her in Liverpool, his spirits could plummet. If he worked too hard and too long, issues — more often other peoples' problems and those of the world at large — could be magnified out of proportion to their importance.

The separation issue still simmered, but with no resolution in sight. And he had been prepared to wage war single-handed against the owners of a lugger that had come into Townsville laden with the skins of slaughtered birds for sale to buyers in America.

Such aggravations were left behind, and in Ararat Bertha

found herself very warmly welcomed by the family and accepted as a member of it. Jabez was so open in his delight with his new daughter-in-law that Ted felt that through his wife he had gained much esteem in his father's eyes. Jabez wanted to hear about his old haunts and favourite places in Liverpool, and Bertha was most happy to refresh his recollections. As for Ararat, Bertha had heard enough about it from Ted to feel she had already been introduced to it. Jabez insisted on making her better acquainted with it and escorted her on a sightseeing tour. With Harry taking on more and more of the managing and editing of the newspaper, Jabez had more time for outside interests.

After inviting Bertha to sit in the Court of Petty Sessions where he took his place on the bench, Jabez invited her to the Asylum for the Insane, where he frequently had afternoon tea

Essie McDonough, housekeeper, on Dunk Island.
(A.H. Chisholm Papers, courtesy of Mitchell Library.)

with inmates he had taken under his wing. He did not impose this on Bertha, he just wondered whether she might be interested; and since she knew that it was one of her father-in-law's special charities, she readily agreed. In the court, Bertha had been impressed by Jabez's kind but firm handling of those who came before him and his fellow Justices of the Peace;[4] now she was to observe his gentle and sympathetic handling of the asylum patients.

What she also saw was that while Jabez gave these inmates much comfort, he himself obtained a certain solace. Here were men and women whose temperamental weaknesses were so much beyond their control that they found themselves unable to cope with life in the outside world. To Bertha, it was as if Jabez were aware of something of this same weakness in himself, and that through contact with those in whom it was in a greater degree, he obtained a certain insight into his own vulnerability and gained the strength to master it. She realized that what she had fathomed in Jabez was also part of Ted's make-up; and that Ted's elations and enthusiasms on the one hand, and predisposition to depression on the other, were traits inherited from his father. It was a valuable revelation to her, something which heredity had ordained and with which she must contend as best she could.

Ted returned to the north greatly restored by the trip which, to judge from the letter he wrote to his father on 5 November 1890, had sustained him for the next twelve months:

> My Dear Dad, It is exactly a year today since we landed in Townsville from our ever memorable visit to Ararat, and I am thinking it would be pleasant to commemorate the occasion by having a chat with you. We never cease recalling the many delightful episodes of our sojourn in old Ararat and are ever anticipating the time when we shall have another edition of it.[5]

In Eva's letters to them, Ted and Bertha had learnt that Jabez had been troubled with pains at the back of the head. Ted expressed the view that his father still spent too much time in the office, although he was pleased at the hint Eva had dropped that his parents were thinking of a holiday.

> Is there any chance of your bringing Mother up here for a month next winter? Bertha and I often talk of the delight such a visit would give us, and I really think you would be pleased to see our little estate at the foot of Castle Hill. There are such splendid boats on this coast now that you would be as comfortable while on the water as in one of your favourite Melbourne hotels.[6]

Neither Jabez nor Sarah was much inclined to hazard a sea trip that would take them into tropical waters, certainly not so soon after the *Quetta* disaster. Still seeking to improve his image in his father's eyes, Ted revealed that for the first time since leaving home he had indulged in a little mining speculation. For the investment of £7.10s.0d. he expected to make a cool £100. He went on to say: "If I see a chance I propose putting in £10 for you and Harry, for I am certain there is going to be a big boom." Alas, the boom failed to eventuate, and later Ted was to write to Harry: ". . . it has been my hard fate to lose every penny I have put into a spec."[7]

In the letter to his father, with the same object of ingratiating himself, he wrote in some detail about the recent Separation Carnival in Townsville, one which had been organized along the lines of the annual Easter Festival in Ararat:

> The people were very enthusiastic and we had visitors from hundreds of miles away, all being surprised at the unique character of the carnival and the throng of spectators. It is something to be able to reflect upon the fact that one has been the means of getting together by far the greatest concourse of people ever seen in tropical Australia and of entertaining them in an entirely novel manner . . . You, who started the Ararat Fairs, will be pleased to think that worthy institutions and worthy folk in this far off town will reap benefits and advantages from your originality and charitable designs.[8]

While Jabez Banfield's ideas added to the funds of the Separation Council, his son's efforts did not seem to make much headway in advancing the cause. Ted believed as strongly as ever that there should be a division of the colony to allow the inhabitants of the north to control their own destinies. But there were procrastinations in England, while at home opponents to the movement continued to emerge. To Ted this was blind stupidity and wilful perversity; the issue was a matter of simple justice, and he could not conceive any right-minded person not being in favour of the change. Yet even those in favour of it were split among themselves as they argued over the site for the capital of the new colony. Townsville, Mackay and other centres pushed their own interests; someone even suggested that the site should be inland behind Cardwell at the Valley of Lagoons. Shortly before Bertha's arrival, the Separation Council had sent the eight-metre-long petition to England; but even though it contained just over ten thousand signatures, the authorities remained unmoved.

To go on supporting a cause in the face of all this left Ted dispirited. And to get him down even more, it was about this time that he suffered a most upsetting turnabout of fortune at *The Bulletin*.

Dodd Clarke's alcoholic problems had grown so bad that he vacated the editor's chair, leaving Ted to take over. Ted saw this as an opportunity to bring in a very talented newspaperman to occupy his former post as sub-editor — Humphrey David Green, who was born on one of the Victorian gold fields near Ararat, and had entered journalism on a small paper in Herberton.[9] It was here that he had been so angered at the way some whites were treating the Aborigines that he wrote a letter about it to *The Townsville Standard*. On the strength of this, the editor offered him a job; and it was by coming to Townsville that he met Ted Banfield, who was thereafter one of his best friends.

David Green was a big man in build and in outlook, a great footballer and cricketer, a man of culture and taste, with a love and appreciation of the gracious things of life, even though when the occasion arose his language could be colourful. He and Ted delighted in each other's company. David Green was the younger by some four years, but Ted came to have a certain hero-worship of him; so much so that he became a sort of father figure as the years were to go by.

With Ted as editor and Green as his assistant, all seemed set for a congenial and highly stimulating working relationship. But then, as is often the erratic way with alcoholics, however charming or inherently kind they may be, Dodd Clarke took it into his head that he wanted the chair back, so Ted stepped down. This meant a drop in rank for Green, who became a senior reporter; not that it appeared to worry him as he revelled in his work. It was not long before he moved on to *The Northern Miner* in Charters Towers to make a great success managing it, while Ted remained with *The Townsville Daily Bulletin*, no doubt in the expectation that Clarke would vacate the editor's chair again, and this time permanently.

The uncertainty was unsettling, even though Ted remained on cordial terms with Dodd Clarke. The stress of this and the daily grind, which continued into the early hours of the morning, began to take their toll. Ted loved his newspaper work; but when it consumed so much of his time and energy, he began to resent not being able to get on with his one mastering pastime, reading. He had set himself a programme to absorb as much as possible of the great body of literature. Almost the only time he had for this was in the mornings after working late at the newspaper office. Before having to return to the office to go through the routine of getting out another paper, he would sit in a deck chair on the verandah of the bungalow and try to immerse himself in one of the many books on his list. After the strain of having used his one eye well past midnight, Bertha would tactfully try to urge him to rest — although sometimes this was not necessary as he dozed off with the book in his lap. At other times, if he did put down his book, it would be to gaze out over those islands, where when his fancy roamed, he could imagine runaway drummers finding refuge.

Bertha was conscious that he had begun to lose weight; and when others remarked upon it, she insisted that he must take some of the vacation due to him, and so they set out up the coast a little by horse and buggy on a camping-out expedition.

If any one time could have been pinpointed as Ted Banfield's first attempt to "absolve himself from the pleasures and conventionalities of city life" and to escape to somewhere "as yet unsoiled and unadulterated by contact with the turbid overflowings of the cities", this was it.[10]

Anyone who has been fortunate enough to come upon a small volume of Kenneth Grahame's letters to his young son entitled *First Whisper of Wind in the Willows* will have seen the beginnings of a major work. If anything by Ted Banfield could be entitled "First Whispers of The Confessions of a Beachcomber", a strong contender would be the article he wrote in 1891 for *The Ararat Advertiser* under the pen-name "Rambler".[11]

Not far north of Townsville near Cape Pallarenda, the two, "with whom everything is common",[12] pitched a tent among pandanus palms under a spur not far from a mangrove creek — just a short stroll to the sea. It was across hot white sand; but a covering of long green tendrils and frail puce-coloured flowers of a plant of the convolvulus tribe offered some protection to the soles of their feet until they reached the wet sand and the water.

What he wrote as "Rambler" he was to repeat, but this was the first time it appeared:

> The stalled ox is not here, nor the fatted calf, nor any of the ordinary luxuries of the table; but there are fish in the sea, wallabies on the hill, game on the plains, and oysters on the rocks; and, else, contentment and merriment and a universal atmosphere of freshness, light and satisfaction. The heat, the clatter, the stuffy odours, the toilsomeness, the fatigue of town life, are abandoned; the quiet, the calm, the refreshment of the whole air, the whole sea are ours. From the moment when the sun touches the hills with the faintest pink, until it drops so suddenly out of sight . . . the whole realm of nature seems to be at our command.

Thoreau had written: "I go and come with a strange liberty in Nature, a part of herself."[13]

They breakfasted on fresh fish fried in the sweetest, softest oil — whiting, bream, rock cod, flathead. Wearing broad hats they rested in the shade of big rocks "after the fashion of born idlers, such as we are, and watch the slowly receding tide until a mile or so of sand and mud separates us from the sea". Here they saw oyster-peckers and curlews feeding; and elsewhere, butcher-birds and magpies whistling and warbling, and cooing little bluish grey doves. "Sometimes we wander up the hills and lie in wait for the wallaby in the shade of rocks covered with orchids, whose bronze flowers catch every ray of the sun.

Sometimes we devote ourselves to the delights of botanising on this rich field; and then are discovered many entertaining specimens."[14] The cotton tree spangled with bright golden flowers; rocks festooned with wax plants; a bottle tree stretching out gaunt bare arms from its bulb-shaped trunk; the creamy white flowers of wild gardenia, filling the gullies with whiffs and gusts of sweetness; umbrella trees with strings of crimson beads; and wild liquorice or paternoster pea, so called because in some countries the seeds are made into rosaries.

There were actually three members of the party because they were accompanied by Rowdy their dog, who hunted down wild pigs which had been gobbling up plovers' eggs foolishly laid on bare ground.

On the water's edge, with the island-studded Halifax Bay in one direction, and in the other, big ocean steamers lying safely at anchor in the deep channel between Cape Cleveland and Magnetic Island, they fossicked in the debris, finding shells, pieces of coral from reefs far out at sea, and an abundance of pumice stone ejected from tropical volcanoes — such as Krakatoa, which they had both seen. On this strip of the tropics, with bare feet, Ted and Bertha both imprinted their "pedal autographs" as he began to enjoy the sport of beach-combing.

The mangrove swamp was the home of the walking fish. The "whole realm of nature" was to be Ted's to describe, its wonders, misfits and fugitives, which he always saw and depicted in an individual way: "Perched on the bare roots, staring at you with pedestal eyes — like those of a crayfish — it waits your approach and then leaps airily into the water and skips along the surface like the flat stones we used to throw."[15]

A fortnight passed: "There is no conventionality nor domestic restraint — we are free in this aromatic air (for the drupes of the pandanus give a special flavour to the smoke of the fire on which the billy boils) from the petty fetters of propriety". Then they folded up their tent and turned their faces to where "the bare sunburnt crags of Castle Hill show bustling Townsville to be".[16]

Chapter 11
Runaway Redcoat

As Bertha and Ted had been married for over five years now, the same question must have been asked in both Ararat and Liverpool: are they ever going to have any children?

No actual declaration of their wish to have children has been encountered; but they were fitted in so many ways to being parents, and showed such affection for young people, that it must be assumed they wanted their own. That very best of friends, Edward George Barrymore, was to write that Ted was at his best with children and that his letters to them were "simply delightful, so full of fun, whimsicality and fancy".[1]

Was it, then, that the couple could not have children because of some impediment on the part of one or even both of them? This could well have been the case, as Bertha suffered from internal problems over a period and finally had to undergo surgery to relieve the pain.[2] Underlying all these years there could have been the sorrow of having to face up to the fact that, much as they wanted children, it was never going to happen.

They both took great interest in the children of Ted's brothers, and an opportunity to see something of them came in August 1892 by making another visit to Ararat, to be present at the Golden Wedding Anniversary of Sarah and Jabez.

Eliza would be there with her second husband, James Maclean; Harry with his wife Belle and their two-year-old daughter Lorna; Walter and his wife Ada with their daughter Dorothy; and Eva with her fiance.

Ted had at first been daunted at the suggestion of another journey south; there was not all that much money in the bank, and he doubted whether he could be spared from the newspaper for the length of time necessary. Bertha quietly worked on him; she believed it would be something he would always regret if he was not present at such a celebration. Besides, even though the short break at Cape Pallarenda had been a tonic to him, he was again showing symptoms of over-work — and she was supported by Dodd Clarke who believed that Ted should take more time off from his job.

For Sarah and Jabez, Bertha's presence was not the only link with Liverpool and lifelong friendships started there. James Gearing and his wife Mary came over from neighbouring Maryborough. The two mates were together again — not that they had ever been far from each other, either geographically or in terms of their ways of life. Gearing had remained with *The Maryborough Advertiser* until it had been sold; but that was many years earlier. He had started *The Maryborough Standard* with which he was still associated. Like Jabez, he had played a promi-nent part in community affairs and was in fact the reigning Mayor of Maryborough. Each had helped establish a bowling club in their respective towns, and they met from time to time on their home greens. Having been married at St Bride's Church, Liverpool, just a year after the Banfields — with Jabez best man — the Gearings' Golden Wedding Anniversary was not far off. Although, as was recalled at the Banfields' celebra-tion, Jabez had very nearly put an end to all the Gearings' wedding anniversaries beyond their ninth when his pistol had gone off accidently and a rolled-up pair of gloves had "palmed" the bullet and saved James's life.[3]

After the warmth of North Queensland, inland Victoria in August was bleak with bitter winds, even if the days were sunny. Ted could not imagine himself ever being able to retreat south to live in such a climate again. Although she had not com-plained, Bertha had found the torrid Townsville summers exhausting; but now she confessed that the tropics seemed to have got into her blood, too. They had become Queenslanders — North Queenslanders — both of them.

Harry realized this, and when out on a stroll to the river with Ted, he revealed a certain envy. "I think I'd like the life up there," he said, and went on to tell Ted that his article under the pen-name "Rambler" had reminded him of the old magic lantern shows and the life led by Robinson Crusoe on his tropical island.

Ted had to laugh. "That's the sort of life I'd like to lead myself," he said. "I'll be forty in a couple of weeks. By fifty I'd like to be able to retire from journalism and start a new life. In my opinion, there's a great future for tropical produce — bananas, pineapples, mangoes, coffee, cocoa — and there's land going begging. But how on journalism can one amass the capital to start out?"

Having taken Harry into his confidence, Ted was to continue to do so in his letters after he returned to Townsville, but only to a degree. Harry and his wife Belle had something that Ted on his part had to envy — one child already and every expectation of others to follow.

The hoped-for visit to Townsville by Ted's parents never eventuated; nor did Sarah's trip back to the Old Country. She and Jabez became beset by similar arthritic problems and went no further than Melbourne, and at greater intervals.

Bertha had hoped to contribute to their savings by giving singing and music lessons, and did so for some time, but the deafness in one ear and the first sign of impaired hearing in the other had made it increasingly difficult for her to judge a note, and so she had given up this outlet for her talents. But it was not her own affliction that really concerned her. She became constantly worried that Ted was imposing too great a strain on his one sound eye, not only through office work with its long hours in gaslight, but also by trying to keep abreast of his private reading. He devoured books and journals which had little or nothing to do with his newspaper work, although at the same time he continued to give to that work his utmost application and dedication, despite growing problems and irritations.

Separation, for all its support, seemed doomed to perennial frustration. There were a number of reasons for this, among

Family group at the time of the Golden Wedding of E.J. Banfield's parents, Ararat, 1892. Standing (left to right): Walter and Harry's wife, Belle; Harry holding daughter Lorna; Eliza and her husband James Maclean; Bertha and Ted. Seated: Walter's wife Ada and their daughter Dorothy; Sarah Ann and Jabez Walter Banfield. In front: Eva and her fiance, F.E. Strangward.
(Courtesy of Irene L. and Zoe Banfield, Ararat.)

them the attitude of the authorities in London, which was that as a self-governing colony Queensland had to formally request London to take action; but no such request was forthcoming from the Queensland parliament because the southern members, who wanted to keep on administering the whole colony, repeatedly out-voted the northern separationists. On the other hand, it suited London to take no action as many people in Britain had invested in Queensland bonds and the authorities there were afraid that the breaking up of the colony could affect the security of these investments. To an extent, Ted managed to see both sides of these aspects to the issue, but it was with utter disbelief that he found himself having to report and publish the views of some of the anti-separationists who claimed that the advocates of a new colony were sugar producers who wished to protect their supplies of cheap coloured labour.

In some of his articles and leaders, such as those about the imported coloured labour and preservation of wild life, Ted became far too worked up; and "at least on one occasion his righteous indignation caused him and his paper a lot of trouble".[4] While Dodd Clarke and his colleagues amusedly treated Ted as a somewhat wayward innocent meaning no real harm, at the same time they kept a close watch and curb on his pen. On several occasions Clarke sent back articles on the grounds they were too long, so Ted got around this by completely rewriting them in a smaller hand without making any changes.

He began to labour under a growing feeling that it was all very well to take the attitude that a newspaper must be the voice of freedom in the community and a guiding hand, the policy his father had advocated and pursued, but when it came down to hard reality, in certain circles and on many issues, the paper had little positive influence. Such a feeling could not help but leave him defeated and depressed.

Dodd Clarke's alcoholic problem was still with him, but his business judgment was not impaired. He concentrated on the managerial side of the newspaper, leaving Ted to take on more of the duties of editor. This led Ted to believe that, despite misgivings on the part of others about his fitness for the senior post, it was still only a matter of time before he was officially installed, and on permanent basis.

While this hope kept him going, he and Bertha embarked on several more camping-out expeditions, heading further up the coast by launch and steamer — to the Palm Islands and Hinchinbrook. He always came back restored, although each time to a lesser degree, all too aware of leading another life of "quiet desperation". He was not keeping pace with his companions; he was starting to listen for, if not yet clearly hear, a different drummer.

Although Ted had not confided the full extent of his feelings to Bertha, she knew that each camping-out expedition had become part of a search for a retreat, a place of their own where they might take short breaks and holidays in seclusion away from the hustle and bustle of Townsville, a place where they could be close to nature, to its creatures, its growths, its wonders, its mysteries. She herself felt an increasing need for such an occasional refuge after the strain of trying to converse with people who either did not know about her hearing impediment or were aware of it and so shouted at her.

As they sat on deck chairs on the bungalow verandah, Magnetic Island lazed out in front of them; it was still only sparsely settled, both by permanent residents and those using it as a holiday retreat, but it was not remote enough. Ted gazed in another direction and farther afield, to that region where shining leaves and sparkling waters on and around distant islands heliographed their welcomes.

The year 1896 did not start well for anyone in Townsville. In the last week of January, Cyclone Sigma struck. Not since the first small pioneer settlements had been established on this part of the coast had anything of such ferocity and magnitude been experienced.[5]

One of the French windows of the bungalow was blown in and the sitting room drenched. Papaw trees in the front were flattened and the gate torn off its hinges. Below them, roofs had vanished and bedrooms lay revealed. Ships and boats had been swept up into the streets. Scarcely any property had escaped; but Ted was more concerned at what damage might have been done in terms of Bertha's feelings about staying on after having experienced nature's "irresponsibleness and mischievousness".[6]

He need not have worried. There was no question of even remotely considering a move. Bertha could recall some storms that had brewed up in the Irish Sea and lashed Liverpool up and down every narrow alleyway until there was hardly a household that escaped some part of the battering. Her father had been busy for weeks attending to damaged rooftops.

Their wedding anniversary this year was a special one — the tenth — and when the day to celebrate it came in early August, the so-called "winter" weather was sublime, and all the terror of the January cyclone had been forgotten and most of its scars had gone. Ted took the day off so that he and Bertha could spend all of it together. His marriage was something for which Ted remained constantly and overwhelmingly grateful. Bertha might well have a man of a difficult temperament on her hands, but she had his total love and affection, as he had hers. As he began to tell her, he could not endure the trials and aggravations of these years without her.

Six weeks after this anniversary, they set out on a more far-ranging camping-out expedition with friends. Thomas Hollis Hopkins had acquired property at Tam O'Shanter Point and had suggested that Ted might do well to look over the land and sites offering in this area. This was where the barque *Tam O'Shanter* had landed members of the Kennedy exploring expedition from Sydney in 1848. Such parts of the coast could only be reached by boat and remained as isolated as if they were surrounded by sea, so in a sense they were islands.

Knowing of Ted's plans, Dodd Clarke ventured the suggestion that since a visit to Tam O'Shanter Point would take them so close to the Family Group, a visit to some of these islands might help them discover what they were searching for. He had landed on a number of them with the 1873 Elphinstone Dalrymple expedition. With the exception of Dunk, the islands of the Family Group were known only by their native names, until 1886-88, when Lieutenant G.E. Richards, RN, called them after the staff of the surveying party he commanded.[7]

"Timana is a gem of an island," Clarke told Ted. "But it's probably too small. Besides which it has no permanent water. Bedarra is another gem, larger, and has a *little* water. I'd take a serious look at Dunk. It has plenty of permanent water. We weren't the first to fill our barrels and tanks there — ships have been dropping in since Philip Parker King anchored in the *Mermaid*."

After deciding that Tam O'Shanter Point, being still part of the mainland, just did not have the atmosphere of isolation he was seeking, Ted headed out to Timana, where he found running water; but as Dodd Clarke had said it was not permanent. Then to Bedarra. Both were Robinson Crusoe islands, each with a sand-spit shooting out to the north-west and a well-sheltered bay or cove. At the same time they were the tops of hills in a sunken chain continuing up from those stepping-stones to the south.

Ted had accepted the theory that the outline of the Australian continent, and in turn the shapes of the offshore islands, had come about as a result of the melting of the polar ice-caps. But he had heard this theory disputed: the land had contributed to the outline and shapes by subsiding. Perhaps so, but there was no question that the level of the sea had risen — and risen to a magical degree — to isolate hill tops and turn them into such exquisite isles.

After experiencing the feeling that the hand of the Creator had been at work here, Ted turned towards Dunk. Once again it looked a shy bear of an island. It was a lump of mainland cut off from the continent. But then, as the boat approached the north-west tip of its sand-spit, its tiny satellite became visible, an islet of such delicate proportions that again the Creator must have played a part in controlling the rise of the sea and the subsidence of the land to bring about such perfection.

This was Mound Islet, named by Owen Stanley when it became a fixed point in his surveys. These surveys were for the first charts to be produced after those made by the then Lieutenant James Cook, who had attached the name Dunk to the island in whose shelter it lay, doing so after the family name of his noble patron the Earl of Sandwich, and making a mistake which even Ted Banfield was not to discover for some time to come.[8]

Now Ted was not long in realizing he had been badly mistaken in his early impressions of the island. The islet stood out from a sheltering bay which greeted the incoming campers with the long sweep of its white strand, as if all the time it had been hiding a dazzling smile.

To the natives, the island was Coonanglebah, and the islet Purtaboi. Ted learnt this soon after he and Bertha and their friends had set up camp on the beach. Their presence here had been detected from the mainland, and while they were cooking fish caught off the rocks, a frail bark canoe appeared with a sturdy Aborigine propelling it with a hand paddle of bark, "crouching forward like a jockey on the withers of his mount, and sending it along by alternate strokes".[9]

The native beached his featherweight craft and introduced himself as Tom, one of the four remaining descendants of about four hundred who had lived on the island before clashes with the white newcomers had scattered them and reduced their numbers. Here, where his ancestors had once had a whole fleet of bark canoes, he returned from time to time to sit down and eat oysters with a few members of his family.

Tom was eager to be of service, and Ted was only too pleased to be taken on a guided tour and shown which creeks could be depended upon for an all-year flow of water; the whereabouts of springs; where tasty pigeons could be snared and wild bananas gathered; the best places to fish and which species could be caught there; and where to gather the best oysters — rocks were corniced, shelved and bridged with masses of them. As revealed by Tom the island was a sort of living larder.

After his encounter with the natives on the Palm Islands, and elsewhere in the course of his search for a retreat, Ted knew that they named places mainly because of some association — an incident which had taken place there, in memory of someone, because a spirit was believed to dwell there. In other cases names were attached simply to distinguish one place or part from another. He knew that basic names — those for the sun, the sea, water, fish, birds — differed between groups or

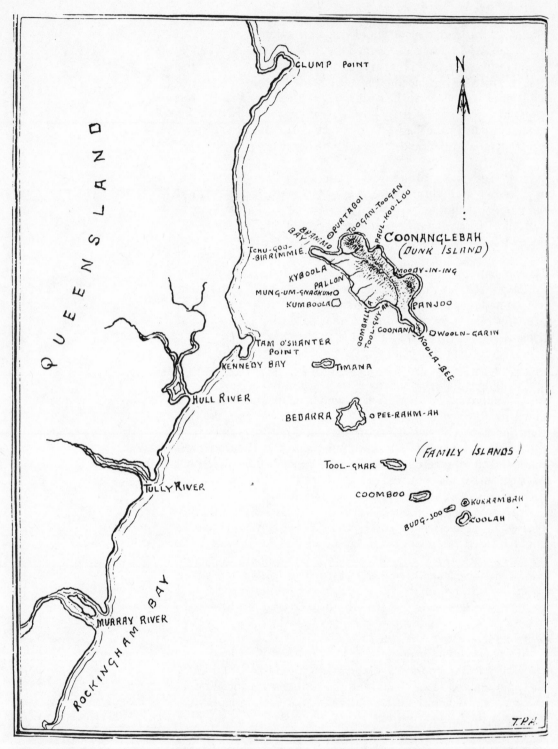

Revised chart of Dunk and Family Islands as in the first edition of *The Confessions of a Beachcomber*, 1908.

tribes. He also knew the word for butterflies, and here on Dunk, where a stream emptied into the bay after emerging through a leafy tunnel of forest and jungle, gorgeous specimens tumbled and frolicked in and out of the sunlight.

In Tom's tongue, the word for this lovely insect was "Cookee-Cookee". To Ted this seemed "an anti-climax as well as a trivial though endearing play on the name of the discoverer of the Island". That was why he borrowed a term from the vocabulary of the Palm Island natives "with a slight amendment of pronunciation as a concession to brevity. 'Brammo' Bay accordingly stands for butterfly; butterflies, it may well be hoped, will for ever by their illuminating presence render lettering superfluous".[10] Having, so to speak, turned the butter-flies into living signposts, it was the only time Ted Banfield in-terfered with existing names or terms.

Purtaboi was a name and nothing more, although when Ted first heard it the emphasis was on the second syllable — Pur-*tab*-oi — so he was ever to insist, to the point of being finicky about it, on this pronunciation. As for Coonanglebah, as Ted understood it from Tom, it meant it was a place of evil repute since it was here that there had been a deadly fight between native factions. Later he was to learn that some natives con-sidered it a sacred island and would never fight one another here, but go elsewhere to such places as Clump Point and Murdering Bay. It was an island "bearing the old English name of Dunk", and Ted liked simple direct Anglo-Saxon words (except when carried away with the sonorous and high-flown), so of the two existing names, the Aborigines' and Cook's, he stuck to the latter. When asked why Ted had left Dunk un-changed and rarely used the native name, Bertha's view was that Coonanglebah was "a terrible mouthful".[11]

With their willing guide, the Banfields and their friends were also introduced to Dunk's lovely garden of coral, to groves of bloodwoods and other fine trees, to places where colonies of the recently-arrived white nutmeg pigeons and metallic starlings were repairing old nests and building new ones in readiness for the breeding season here. Both were handsome birds. The white nutmeg or Torres Straits pigeon was "white with part of each flight feather black, and with down of pale buff". The hen birds stayed at home during the day while the males went foraging. The metallic starling, or the Shining Caloris, which had rich red eyes "like polished gems", was "gleaming black, with purple and green sheen". Ted likened its wonderful radiance to "A soap bubble, black yet retaining all its changing lights and flashing reflections".[12]

Bertha remained at the camp site. The other couple chipped oysters off the rocks while Tom groped under mushroom coral for crayfish. Ted explored the forest and jungle on his own,

Dunk Island, view from
heights looking south.
(A.H. Chisholm Papers,
courtesy of Mitchell
Library.)

carrying a rifle just in case he spotted a likely table bird. He
glimpsed metallic starlings "wheeling into the wilderness of
leaves with the rapidity of thought, and with such graceful
precision that the sunlight flashes from their shoulders as an arc
of light".[13]

As he wandered to "the accompaniment of that subdued
aerial buzz by which Nature manifests the more secret of her
functions and art — that ineffable minstrelsy to which her
battalions keep step",[14] he began to hear other sounds — drips
of water, scrapings of leaves, chirps of insects, chirrups of birds,
a host of noises mainly unidentifiable yet concerted as if

somehow being orchestrated. And then woven into all this he began to hear a distinct measured beat. He stopped to listen. It could be a drum. It continued — from behind a wall of greenery — and then he glimpsed a flash of red.

Ever since first reading about that "different drummer" in Thoreau, he had pictured a runaway Redcoat, a deserter from the barbaric ranks of the human race. It was not with the expectation of finding any such person that he crashed through the wall of greenery, but because he was in the grip of his own runaway imagination. A startled scrub hen scurried away and he found himself staring at a red hibiscus bloom. The beat kept on — and, whirling in another direction, he glimpsed red again and plunged towards it, doing so just in time to see a forest parrot, a red-winged lory, soaring up to the tree-tops and into the sunlight. Still the beat kept on, and once again he spotted the gleam of red, and headed towards it, to find a coral tree in bloom. Now the beat was even louder — and in the direction from which it came was a steady blaze of red.

Becoming short of breath, Ted struggled down through the undergrowth until he was out of the forest, and staring at a flame tree bedecked and bedazzling with clusters of red flowers — and not far from it, where they had set up their tents, Bertha was tapping the head of a pickle jar on one of the tent pegs to try to loosen it so that she could open it.

Ted was still in a daze when he joined her, and muttered something that sounded like "It was only you", before declaring that up on a low plateau he had found the very spot for "a modest castle".[15] He went back up on it and there fired his rifle as if laying claim to it (as Cook to the far north had claimed the eastern coastline in the name of King George the Third).

That different drummer was no longer distant nor far away; if only in spirit it was here that he dwelt, somewhere on this desirable island, and so in the lives of Ted and Bertha "the result of the first day's exploration decided a revolutionary change".[16]

Chapter 12

Escape to Live

Ted got back to Townsville in the grip of panic — the fear that someone might step in ahead of him and secure some hold on Dunk. It surprised him that no one had yet laid claim to any substantial part of the island, one that was "wholly uninhabited, entirely free from traces of the mauling paws of humanity"; a place where "an empty jam tin or broken bottle, spoors of the rude hoofs of civilization, you might search for in vain".[1]

He wasted no time in making an application for a lease on an area embracing the hitherto unnamed bay which he had called Brammo and the land behind it, including the plateau which he had decided was the site for his modest castle. There was no prior claim or application, so he was granted a special lease by the Queensland Government for a term of thirty years at a rental of 2s. 6d. (25 cents) per acre per annum.

It was rare for Ted to be less than lyrical when describing Dunk, which is well within the tropical zone, its bearing being 146 deg. 11 min. 20 sec. E. long, and 17 deg. 55 min. 25 sec. S. lat. However, he managed to confine himself to the bare facts in "Dunk Island. Its General Characteristics", a paper read before the Royal Geographical Society of Australasia, Queensland, on 28 May 1908, by E.J.T. Barton in the absence of E.J. Banfield:

> Dunk Island is situated 110 miles up the coast from Townsville and about 60 miles south from Cairns. It is merely a range of hills running parallel to the main coast range — high and bluff at the northern extremity, broad and bulging at the waist, and falling away, to a somewhat shabby and common-place ending — low, narrow, and comparatively barren — to the south, while a

central spur points towards the S.W. The superficial area is about 3 ½ sq. miles; greatest length three miles; greatest breadth about two miles; and the coast line measures between ten and twelve miles.[2]

Like an artist who keeps coming back again and again to a subject or scene which obsesses him (as the French painter Paul Gauguin was currently doing on much the same latitude in the Pacific Ocean at Tahiti), Ted was to create a succession of pen portraits of the island, one of his earliest being in a letter to his brother Harry following the visit to Dunk of September 1896. At the same time Bertha wrote to Eva, who was to be married in the New Year and become Mrs F.E. Strangward. Both extolled its perfection as a holiday retreat. Fortunately Ted also mentioned to Harry that he expected it to prove to be a profitable investment, so his father Jabez was prepared to consider it a worthwhile enterprise, certainly with infinitely more to recommend it than some of Ted's dubious mining tips (and with gold booming over the range in the Charters Towers district, such tips were winging their way to Townsville like flocks of gilded bats).

Now that he had a piece of paper confirming his hold on a corner of Eden, Ted became absorbed in planning their next break on the island. He made lists of equipment, tools, stores to be ordered and shipped to Cardwell; also seeds and seedlings to be planted. He envisaged something more substantial than a tent which they would have to pitch and then dismantle at the beginning and end of each holiday visit. A hut. And he rather fancied one of the prefabricated type he had seen advertised, made of scented cedar and imported from Canada, and said to be so simple to put together that a child could do the job blindfold.

While Bertha was delighted to see the perennial boy in Ted coming out again — and she was to marvel constantly at his effervescences, and sigh that it seemed he was destined never really to grow up — with the arrival of another wet season and its winds and rain, other clouds descended.

The causes for which he had striven seemed to have been forgotten or abandoned. The separation issue was now secondary to the move to federate the colonies into the one commonwealth. While Dodd Clarke continued to maintain a firm control of the managerial side of the newspapers, Ted was the editor of *The Townsville Daily Bulletin* in all but name. Yet the actual post continued to be denied him, so in a sense he was still back in Ararat, doomed to remain second in line of succession.

Try as he might to accept the situation, the injustice of it kept eating into him. He began to sleep badly, although he rallied after a visit to Dunk once the wet season was over. Back in Townsville, he made further arrangements for materials and

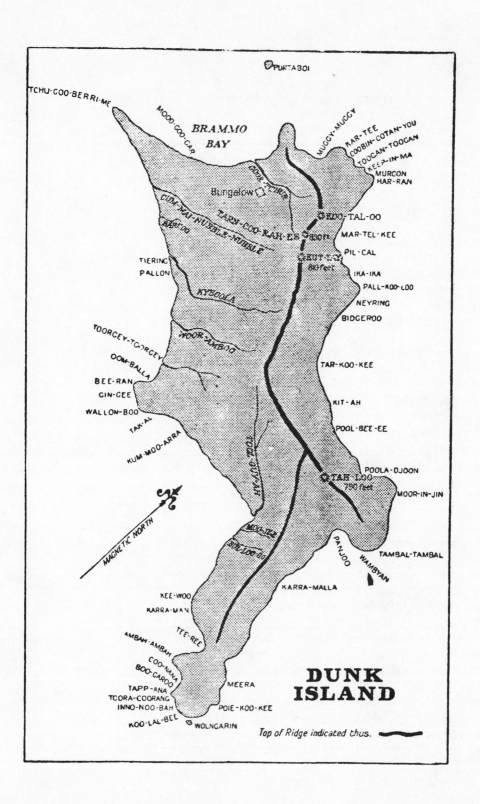

PURTABOI

TCHU-GOO-BERRI-ME

MOO-GOO-GAR

BRAMMO
BAY

MUGGY-MUGGY

KAR-TEE
COOBIN-COTAN-YOU
TOOGAN-TOOGAN
KEEP-IN-MA
MURCON
HAR-RAN

COO-TOO-RA

Bungalow

CUM-MAI-NUBBLE-NUBBLE

TARS-COO-RAH-EE

KOO-TAL-OO
780 ft

BARSOO

MAR-TEL-KEE

PIL-CAL

KUT-LY
80 feet

IKA-IKA

PALL-KOO-LOO

TIERING
PALLON

NEYRING

KYBOOLA

BIDGEROO

TOORGEY-TOORGEY

MOOR-AMBOO

TAR-KOO-KEE

OOM-BALLA

BEE-RAN

GIN-GEE

KIT-AH

WALLON-BOO

POOL-BEE-EE

TAK-AL

KUM-MOO-ARRA

KULL-OO-GOOL

POOLA-DJOON

TAH-LOO
750 feet

MOOR-IN-JIN

MAGNETIC NORTH

MOO-TEE

BOO-LOO-BOO

PANJOO

TAMBAL-TAMBAL

WAMBYAN

KARRA-MALLA

KEE-WOO

KARRA-MAN

TEE-REE

AMBAH-AMBAH

COO-NANA

BOO-CAROO

MEERA

TAPP-ANA

TCORA-COORANG

INNO-NOO-BAH

POIE-KOO-KEE

KOO-LAL-BEE

WOLNGARIN

DUNK
ISLAND

Top of Ridge indicated thus. ━━━

DUNK ISLAND — PLACE NAMES

Goor-tchur	Trumpet shell
Mood-goo-gar	Fish resembling trevalley
Tchu-goo-berri-me	Swarm of bees
Cum-mai-nubble-nubble	Creek in which a sucker fish was tethered
Barcoo	Blue pike
Kyboola	The looking-glass tree (*Heritiera litoralis*)
Tiering	Round, smooth, hard nut, spur on one end
Pallon	Name of a gin
Woor-amboo	Favourite camp of an old man so named
Toorgey-toorgey	Pinna shell
Oom-balla	Fish (yellow tail)
Bee-ran	Tree (*Barringtonia speciosa*)
Gin-gee	Sunflower tree (*Diplanthera tetraphylla*)
Tak-al	Block of dead coral
Wallon-boo	Half-tide rocks
Kum-moo-arra	The Alexandrian laurel (*Calophyllum inaphyllum*)
Tool-guy-ah	Eel
Moo-jee	*Terminalia melanocrapa*
Bul-loo-go	Stone fish
Kee-woo	Yellow plum (*Ximenia americana*); also known as Bedyewrie
Karra-man	Red snapper
Tee-ree	White stone (quartz)
Ambah-ambah	Big wind
Coo-nana	A bulky rock, isolated
Boo-garoo	Native banana
Tapp-ana	Resort of turtle
Toora-coorang	Small fish frequenting rock crevices
Inno-noo-bah	Black palm
Koo-lal-bee	Black cockatoo
Wolngarin	Palm with coconut-like fronds
Poie-koo-kee	Booby (brown gannet)
Meera	Stone knife quarry
Karra-malla	Sea urchin
Panjoo	Nice place
Wambyan	Burial place of a boy so named
Tambal-tambal	Mainsail fish
Moor-in-jin	Spangled drongo
Pool-bee-ee	Thunderstone
Kit-ah	Fish spear tree
Tar-koo-kee	Name of a man who died on the spot a long time ago, and who is believed to haunt it
Bidgeroo	"Debil debil" who kills fish with a stone-pointed spear
Neyring	Native taro (*Colocasia antiquorum*)
Pall-koo-loo	Group of isolated rocks perpetuating a legend of men who came across from the mainland to fight
Ika-ika	Round-headed, half-tide rock, supposed to have been rolled down the mountain by a "debil debil"
Pil-cal	Favourite camp of an old man so named
Mar-tel-kee	Fish like catfish seen in fine weather in clear water
Har-ran	Coral patch awash at low water
Murgon	Quandong (*Elaeocarpus grandis*)
Toogan-toogan	*Macaranga tanara.* Shrub providing fish spears, twine for lines, and a cement
Coobin-cotan-you	Falling-star cave
Kar-tee	Coral rock
Muggy-muggy	Coral mushroom where crayfish lurk

Dunk Island. The Beachcomber's map and list of place names, found among his papers and published in *Last Leaves from Dunk Island*, 1925.
(Courtesy of Helen and David Green.)

stores to be shipped to Cardwell, where they were picked up and taken by launch to the island. The climate in Townsville was at its best, but it did not help. He started to go into a depressive decline. He became too tired, through worsening loss of sleep, to progress with his private reading. War threats were coming from the other side of the world and from South Africa, and from Kissing Point came the thunder of guns as the artillery practised.

Life that had not been properly lived was slipping away. Ted's appetite for food deserted him and he began to lose weight visibly and at an increasing rate. He resisted Bertha's attempts to persuade him to see their doctor, until he lacked the energy to protest. His condition has been said to have been a form of phthisis, a progressive wasting disease, possibly pulmonary consumption — and Ted had certainly pushed and exposed himself to a degree that had left him highly vulnerable to such an illness. Bertha refused to accept this diagnosis, but what she had to accept was the doctor's prognosis. Unless Ted gave up his work at the newspaper office and had an immediate change of scene and occupation, he had at the most only six months to live — possibly as little as three months.

His situation had become desperate. According to Bertha, in a letter to Alec Chisholm: "He was absolutely worn out with day *and* night work and want of sleep, and I believe it was slowly but surely killing him". According to George (E.G.) Barrymore, in whom Ted later confided, so terrifying was his craving for sleep that "he resorted to chloroform. This could not go on, and in his great distress the longing came for the peace and seclusion of Dunk Island". T.P. Adlam was a witness to it all, and according to him: "Utterly disillusioned with daily journalism, jaded, tired, almost worn out, Mr Banfield shook the dust of the streets of Townsville from his shoes, and set sail for Dunk Island."[3]

According to Thoreau: "To the sick the doctors wisely recommend a change of air and scenery."[4] Bearing this in mind, Ted agreed to a lengthy change, although at this stage no more than a trial period of six months. The prefabricated hut was waiting at Cardwell, and it was essential that if they were to establish themselves on the island, they should do so while the weather was good.

The question of Essie accompanying them arose, but their means were slender and they could not guarantee her present wages. Besides, they did not want to involve her in having to rough it with them — and since other people, friends and neighbours, had been interested in securing Essie's services as housekeeper to the point of trying to poach her, she had no problem in obtaining another agreeable position.

As for the house under Castle Hill, it was put up for rent —

they could do with the money it might fetch — but no one came forward immediately.

By the time they took the steamer north with goods and stores to supplement what was already on the island, and with such possessions as Ted's books, including his treasured three volumes of Shakespeare, his weight was down to just over eight stone. He was wretchedly seasick when the steamer was exposed to a beam sea in the "paddock", that open stretch between Magnetic Island and the Palms. This did not augur well for a man with a camp to build. At Cardwell they engaged a workman to help them with the initial setting up of their camp, and he assisted in the loading of the launch for the island.

It was 28 September 1897 when, with a strong buffeting wind from the north-east, they began the final crossing. Although it took only a few hours, Ted suffered even worse seasickness. By the time they landed he was so exhausted that Bertha and the workman had to help him ashore on to the beach where he flopped down and literally crawled up to the soft sand.

They did not land unwelcomed. In the year since they had first met him, Tom had gleaned something of their plans and movements, even though they had kept such matters much to themselves. He had gathered that they were due on Dunk about this time, so was on hand to offer his services again and, if required, those of his gin, his mother-in-law and other relatives.

Rugs were spread near the tree line, and Ted lay there as the workman and Tom, under Bertha's watchful eyes, handled the unloading of the launch. Out in the open they prepared food and drink, but Ted did little more than peck and sip before turning away — and he had scarcely strength even to do that. Above them the trees rustled noisily and the casuarinas, which were never totally silent, sighed and moaned. It seemed at first that even here, sleep was to be denied; but without any potion of a medicinal type, Ted eventually fell into a deep, dreamless sleep, thanks to draughts of unadulterated air — as when he had camped many, many years before, first in Melbourne and then in Ararat.

During the night the casuarinas ceased their harping and by daybreak were whispering contentedly. On this, "the first morning of the new life", what Ted saw when he woke mid the camp equipment was a scene of utter tranquillity: the sea shining, the sky cloudless, the sand immaculate, the air pure and scented with the fragrances of the forest and jungle. Accepting the invitation of the sea, he entered the water on unsure legs, as Tom set about cooking fish already speared out on the reef. As Ted was to put it: "Feebleness and dismay vanished with the first plunge into the still sleepy sea, and alertness and vigour returned, as the incense of the first morning's sacrifice went straight as a column to the sky."[5] To Bertha, who watched fearfully, what happened was just miraculous.

After declaring his fish breakfast delicious, Ted now somehow found the strength to take part in the clearing of a small patch of bush, and by sunset that first day they had pitched tents on the spot. More space had to be cleared for the cedar hut, and this meant cutting down bloodwood trees. Although he had the hired labourer and had engaged Tom and one of his native cousins each on a small wage, Ted tried to undertake his share of the work. These trees were big and tough, and Ted was unaccustomed to such work, but he managed. The erection of the hut proceeded smoothly, all the numbered sections and parts fitting and bolting together. A roof and a ceiling of corrugated iron and boards an inch thick intervened "between us and the noisy tramplings of the rain and heat of the sun"; the main item of the rudimentary furniture, their bed, was set up inside — and they were at home.[6]

In the succeeding weeks, more land was cleared. In fact, just over a month after landing, when Ted made time to reply to a letter received the previous week from his brother Harry, he was able to report that they had cleared in all about three acres. However, he remained deeply conscious of what they were doing:

> What justification existed for the defacement of the virginal scene by an unlovely dwelling — the imposition of a scar on the unspotted landscape? None, save that the arrogant intruder needed shelter . . . It was resolved that the shelter should by way of compensation be unobtrusive, hidden in a wilderness of leaves. The sacrifice of those trees unhaply in prior occupation of the site selected would be atoned for by the creation of a modest garden of pleasant-hued shrubs and fruit-trees and lines and groves of coconut-palms.[7]

Following printed instructions, Ted set about building a kitchen and a slab hut to act as a storeroom. Although he'd had no formal training as a carpenter, early in life he had displayed an ability to improvise, as when he and Harry, with the guidance of the Ararat undertaker, constructed their "bone-shaker" bicycle. He found the splitting of timber into thin slabs an art which took much trial and error before any degree of success could be achieved; but in the end he managed. Inspection of the adjoining domain, which was a vast aviary and tropical hothouse combined, had to be reserved as a sort of reward for toil. And even then, as he threaded "the sunless mazes of the jungle — that region of shadow where all the leaves are dumb", he was still conscious of work in hand.[8]

Part of an overhanging tree branch might have just the shape

One of the chairs made
by the Beachcomber.
(Courtesy of Helen Dyer,
Townsville.)

or curve he needed for the household furniture he was constructing, a chair for instance — and while he seemed to get on famously with tables, cupboards and bookshelves, chairs were to be the most fiendish, obstinate, perverse and contrary things, animate or inanimate, with which he had ever become involved. Each time he tackled one, he revelled in the challenge of trying to tame it.

> Tender-footed, it stands awry, heaving one leg aloft — as crooked and as perverse as Caliban. In good time, botching here, violent constraint there, the chair finds itself or is forced to do so, for he is a weak man who is not stronger than his own chair. So, after many days' intense toil — toil which even troubled the night watches, for have I not lain awake with thoughts automatically concentrated on a seemingly impossible problem, plotting by what illicit and awful torture it might be possible for the tough and stubborn parts to be brought into juxtaposition — there is a chair — a solid, sitable chair, which neither squeaks, nor shuffles, nor shivers.[9]

Ted was in good company. Thoreau had made some of his furniture, as had Robinson Crusoe. Thoreau stated: "None is so poor that he need sit on a pumpkin", while in his journal the castaway recorded that he had spent nearly five days making a chair, and that he had with much ado "brought it to a tolerable shape, but never to please me; and even in the making I pulled it in pieces several times".[10]

As Bertha and Ted occupied and used the hut, the kitchen, the shed, others moved in with them. Grey, bead-eyed geckoes, house lizards that stalked the incoming moths and beetles. In the walls, wasps built terra-cotta warehouses to store spiders and grubs. A bee constructed a comb among the books. Sharp-toothed bats with pin-point eyes swooped in one door, quartered in the roof and departed by the other door. Even a snake paid a visit, but that proved to be — for the reptile — a fatal call.

Before the rains came they had "comfortable if circumscribed shelter". They had brought two months' provisions with them — plenty of tinned meat and jam. Thanks to a friend in one of the shipping companies, arrangements had been made for a steamer to call once a week. They imported fowls and ducks, and so had fresh eggs. A goat arrived to provide them with fresh milk. Meanwhile, they had Tom and the sea to furnish them with fish, oysters, crabs and crayfish. And they had plenty on which to feast their eyes, birds for instance, such as the tiny sunbird "garbed in rich olive green, royal blue, and bright yellow . . . The best part of his life is passed among blossoms, and he seems to partake of their beauty and frailness."[11]

In his *Confessions*, Ted's description of this period echoed what he had written under the pen-name "Rambler" for his hometown newspaper:

> The heat, the clatter, the stuffy odours, the toilsomeness, the fatigue of the town life are abandoned; the careless quiet, the calm, the refreshment of the whole air, the tonic of the wide sea are gained. From the moment the sun illumines our hills and isles with glowing yellow until it drops in fiery splendour suddenly out of sight leaving a band of gleaming red above the purple western range, and a rippling red path across to Australia, the whole realm of nature seems ours to command.[12]

This still remained a trial period. In Ted's first letter to Harry from Dunk, in which he gave his address as "Brammo Bay", he wrote: "We have still no very definite aims regarding the future for I want to see how Bertha likes the life before we put any of our little capital into cultivation". If at the end of six months the secluded island life proved too difficult for them, then their main dwelling, the hut, could be dismantled, packed and taken away, so all would not be lost. "We shall probably not make up our minds until after the wet season, but, of course, will in the meantime persevere with the clearing and burning off."[13]

In this same letter, Ted also wrote: "To me the life is charming after the restraints and annoyances of journalism and I am glad to know you seriously think of adopting some other means of earning daily bread."

Harry, of course, was not seriously thinking of making any such change. With a wife and children to support, with ageing parents to stand by, and with a secure future as heir to the proprietorship of a thriving newspaper business, he had little choice but to continue where he was. And, by becoming a councillor, he was following his father's footsteps in another way.

However, he had shared explorations of the bush and adventures on the river with Ted, and had been present at the magic lantern shows when ravishing images from vivid hand-painted slides were thrown on to a sheet hanging on the wall. Ted was free to sail his little boat through such scenes, across waters teeming with fish, dugong and turtle, so it was not surprising that Harry should be unsettled when he compared his own routine life to the one in which Ted now revelled. All the same, Harry had what Ted — and Bertha — still lacked. Something of Ted's attitude towards children, and his regret at not having any of his own, showed in a postscript he added to the foregoing letter: "We both read with special interest what you said about your kiddies. I would dearly love to see them and hope to do so one of these days. Lorna and the Boy must be a great joy to you both."

Perhaps in the place of children, Ted was to have an island to love and cherish. The real decision to try the life there was

Bertha's — and for her it meant a certain final surrender, since it is inconceivable that she or Ted would have considered isolating themselves had there been the slightest possibility that even at this very late stage they might have had an addition to the family. Ted was obviously all too conscious of their situation when, in *The Confessions*, he wrote that they were "not youthful enthusiasts, but beings who had arrived at an age when many of the minor romances are of the past".[14]

Sarah and Jabez had been greatly concerned to learn of Ted's failing health. After news came through that he and Bertha were moving to their island retreat for an indefinite stay, Sarah was relieved. It would give Ted a chance to recover. But Jabez had strong reservations. He could not see how in the long run his second son could solve his problems by isolating himself on a remote island. It seemed to him to be an abandonment of one's dutiful place in the community, to be avoiding life.

To Bertha, who closely watched Ted's reactions to this new life (as he, on his part, did hers), Ted was a man transformed. Daily she marvelled at what she saw him undertaking. His decline had not been constitutional, but rather a severe manifestation of the depression to which he was prone by heredity and temperament. By coming here he may, in some eyes, have appeared to escape, but as she saw the situation he was really starting to live.

Chapter 13
Man of Many Parts

The weekly steamer was a boon, a link with the outside world,
bringing mail, newspapers, journals, and sometimes fresh meat.

"Listen to this!" Ted loudly cried to Bertha, after opening and
scanning a letter in the most recent delivery, one made shortly
after their arrival on the island. "Someone really knows why
we've come here — gold!"[1]

"Gold?" said Bertha. Her functioning ear must be playing
tricks on her!

"That's the rumour. During our camping-out last year, we
made a rich find — and we've crept off to mine the yellow
stuff."

"What utter nonsense!"

"Nevertheless," Ted went on, quietly laughing at Bertha's
forthright dismissal of the suggestion, "here's a letter from a
man — a complete stranger to us, too — offering to go fifty-
fifty on the basis that he'll finance the shaft if we tell him where
to sink it."

"How on earth could anyone come by such a ridiculous
notion?"

"Apparently traces of gold have been found on Hinchinbrook, so other islands could have some. In fact it's rumoured
that here on Dunk the natives have used a great lump of it for
generations to pound nuts."

Bertha wagged a finger at him. "I've always been afraid that
those mining tips of yours might get you into real trouble."

Laughing all the more, Ted rose from his chair. "I'll have a
word with Tom about this."

Tom, who was digging out tree stumps with Willie the other

hired native, thought the suggestion of the gold lump highly amusing but offered to take Ted to see one. Ted, naturally, hastened to accept — and was escorted to a spot where piles of old shells indicated that Tom's ancestors had sat down here to feast. Tom cleared away some undergrowth to expose a "gold" lump so weighty that no man could lift it — an ingot of crude copper, "probably portion of the ballast from some ancient wreck".[2]

According to Tom, the rumours did not stop at this lump; it was also claimed that one of his ancestors had gone fishing from the edge of the reef with a line made from lawyer vine — and that he had used a golden sinker.

While Tom laughed, Ted was deeply concerned: "The very worst that could happen would be the discovery on this spot of anything more precious than an orchid."[3]

He hurried back to the hut to write a reply to the man who had offered cooperation. There was no gold here, there never had been gold, and there would be no shafts sunk. It was a groundless rumour. All the same, before that rumour had been abandoned, prospectors came to the island, some going about their search quite brazenly in the face of Ted's furious denials, others behind his back. But no colours were found, and so the prospectors withdrew and the rumour died. All the same, it had been a highly upsetting development and could well have hastened Ted in taking steps to obtain a greater hold on the island.

It seems evident that, well before the completion of the six months' trial period, Ted Banfield had already committed himself deep down to a prolonged stay. In the way he was clearing land, planting seeds and trees, erecting buildings, all his plans were long-range. If, at the end of the six months, he and Bertha decided it was all too much for them, they could still take the cedar hut with them, but a great deal would have to be abandoned.

If the diaries Ted started to keep are to be taken as an indication, then it would appear that his decision to try permanent residence was made soon after having been on the island for three months, because he started a day-to-day record of his life on Dunk on 7 January 1898. In one of the standard-sized Lett's diaries he began with an entry stating that he had finished painting his boat.[4]

As wet seasons go, their first on the island was a routine one, with no repetition of cyclones in the area as had been the case two years before when Sigma struck. This is not to say that it was an easy period for them; the heat and humidity wore down their resistance and both suffered attacks of dengue fever and malaria and had to dose themselves with quinine. Every month or so, one or the other would go down again. Worse still, Bertha had severe bilious attacks. This could well have been a form of fish poisoning, for some of the fish caught in the area were noxious; Tom and his companions could not be entirely relied upon to caution them because the natives seemed to be immune from some of the poisons that affected the whites. But her internal pains were another matter.

Towards the end of August 1898, Bertha suffered such a distressing attack that Ted prepared the boat to row out into the inner passage to intercept a steamer due to pass on the way to Cairns, but Bertha started to recover and insisted that she would be all right.

Even so, it had been a crisis, and they were imposing a serious hazard on themselves by being so far from professional medical attention. Ted was now almost forty-six and Bertha forty, so their ages were against them in terms of living a remote secluded life. In addition, each was already saddled with a disturbing physical disability — Ted with but one eye and Bertha already deaf in one ear.

The island itself, while on the one hand an idyllic refuge, presented certain hazards if only because of its rugged terrain. The coastline in parts was far from hospitable, as Ted and Bertha were to learn. A sampan was to be smashed to pieces on its southern end and its two Chinese occupants just able to scramble ashore with their lives. Ted himself got lost when exploring the heights, so it was little wonder that a naval rating, in much the same area, should find himself in the same predicament, and perilously so with precipices and deep gullies concealed by forest and jungle. The rating was adrift for twenty-four hours before being guided to safety by a powerful searchlight trained on the heights from a warship anchored near Purtaboi.[5]

Ted was a romantic to the core. As fellow romantic George Barrymore was to record, "He had a mania for justice. Every wrong thing, be it personal, municipal or political, worked him to a frenzy. He felt things too keenly, and his sympathies were always for the underdog." But his "nature was sunny, and essentially happy". Despite illness and setbacks, basically he bore no grudges against individuals, groups, mankind, fate, destiny or fortune. Just as he had an inclination towards bouts of dark depression, he had that mercurial ability to rise above it all. He had a marvellous capability to forgive and forget, no matter how worked up he may have been about an issue or what manner of injustice had been done to him personally. In fact, of those early traumas on the island, he wrote: "Why recall the memory of those acheful days, when all the pleasant and restful features of the island are uncatalogued?"[6]

Shortly before it seemed that he would have to intercept the

Cairns-bound steamer to obtain medical help for Bertha, Ted confirmed that they had made the decision to settle on the island. Rather than lease part of Dunk, he applied to actually possess it.

Although this involved the writing of letters and the filling in of official forms and the furnishing of personal information — and the delays of governmental and municipal officers and offices — in principle it was a straightforward procedure in terms of a Land Act designed to promote settlement. In fact, in Ted's estimation it meant that in North Queensland: "Literally the meekest of men may inherit the choicest part of the earth."[7]

Following such an application, the first move by the authorities was to declare the area open to selection — that is, anyone could select it with a view to obtaining ownership. However, the original applicant had the prior right, and so the way was clear for Ted to apply for an agricultural homestead of 320 acres (130 hectares), for which he would be called upon to pay 2s. 6d. (25 cents) per acre at the rate of 3d. (2½ cents) per acre for ten years. Five years were allowed for developments such as clearing, fencing and construction of buildings, all of which would be assessed in relation to the valuation of the land. There were further conditions as time and tenure progressed, but once the first commitment was made it meant continuous occupation by the applicant, and so Ted made himself a permanent islander.

In addition to needing money for day to day living, he had to finance the improvements, and in this regard he wrote: "The affairs of the busy world were discarded, not upon the strength of large accumulated savings or the possession of means by inheritance or by the success of investments or by mere luck, but upon merely imperative, theoretic anticipations upon the cost of living the secluded life. We had little in reserve, how little it would be unbecoming to say."[8]

They had the rent from the Townsville house when it was occupied, and Ted planned to supplement their income by selling produce in excess of that needed for himself, Bertha and their native hands. Here where indigenous plants and trees, some with edible roots and fruits, thrived in fertile ground, he introduced a whole new order of seeds and seedlings, a profusion of vegetables, fruits, herbs and flowers: potatoes, sweet potatoes, onions, shallots, carrots, parsnips, turnips, tomatoes, beans, peas, corn, chillies, cabbage, leeks, celery, lettuce, beet, sprouts, cress, radishes, marrow, maize, watermelon, rock melon, papaw, mangoes, custard apples, cape gooseberries, pomelos, oranges, limes, lemons, bananas, mandarins, thyme, sage, parsley, marigolds, nasturtiums — to mention most of the many but by no means all.[9]

He hoped for outlets in Townsville, Cardwell, Geraldton and

Cairns for this produce — and for fowls, ducks, eggs; and oysters, crabs and crayfish. And especially for honey. He built hives and introduced bees of Italian stock, and anticipated a variety of types of golden nectar.

One of the most serious symptoms of his depressive illness had been his loss of energy, something highly conspicuous in a person noted as Ted was for his industry and capacity for work. Now that he had turned away from journalism to concentrate his efforts in different directions, his energy was prodigious, and he thrived on physical exercise and began to put on condition.

His roles were many. He was "his own magistrate, postman, architect, carpenter, painter, boatbuilder, boatman, tinker, goatherd, gardener, woodcutter, water-carrier and general labourer"; and he found himself "compelled to chip the super-fine edges of his sentiments with the repugnant craft of the butcher"; and, after setting the stove fire and kneading the dough, he was, with Bertha's help, his own baker.[10]

While the inspection of his domain remained to a large extent a reward for work well done, he was conscious as the favoured resident of "a duty to exhaustively comprehend it". And so he began to explore "its sunny places, its deepest shades". Although he became rich in knowledge of the ways of plants and trees, of streams and waterfalls, birds and insects, and other creatures of the land and the sea, Ted Banfield never saw himself as a methodical or skilled scientific investigator, but an observer "eager to know how Nature, not under the microscope, behaved; what were her maiden fancies, what the art with which she allures".[11]

He observed and explored, and early in his occupation, when he was about to build the kitchen to go with the prefabricated hut —

Good fortune presented, greatly to the easement of labour, two splendid pieces of driftwood for posts for one of the doors. To the sea also I was indebted for long pieces to serve as wall plates, one being the jibboom of what must have been a sturdily-built boat, while the broken mast of a cutter fitted in splendidly as a ridge-pole. For the walls I visited an old bean-tree log in the jungle, cut off blocks in suitable lengths, and split them with maul and wedges into rough slabs.[12]

In September 1898 came two anniversaries, that of their camping-out expedition two years earlier and that of their landing twelve months after that. Their abode was not yet the modest castle Ted had envisaged, although they now referred to the hut as a house since they had added a verandah — even though one with an earthen floor — and painted it white. In his diary he wrote: "1898 has been a good prosperous year. Good-bye to it. May 1899 be as happy and prosperous."[13]

Although Ted had claimed that the meekest of men were granted land here, it did not pay to be too meek. He found that the granting of an agricultural homestead was beset with interminable letter-writing, form-filling and visits from government officials.

Meanwhile, some crops did not flourish as he had hoped. A market was found for oysters in Geraldton and Cairns, only to dry up. Bertha's repeated bilious attacks and internal pains had to be investigated, so she went to Townsville where their doctor decided that a small operation was essential. She was away for two months from March to May, and although Ted was greatly agitated, Bertha assured him all would be well. He was overjoyed at her return — especially as she came back greatly improved in health and with her fortitude strengthened to stand by him in the frustrations and sadnesses ahead.[14]

Early in August a telegram arrived from Ararat informing Ted that his mother had died, and in subsequent letters from the family he realized that his father was bereft and in failing health — although still taking his place as a Justice of the Peace on the bench.

The negotiations for the land still dragged on, so Ted decided he could be meek no longer. He wrote to a friend who was shortly to become premier of the colony — Robert Philp — and received a reply indicating that his case would be looked into and some action taken. However, he very nearly did not live long enough to be formally granted tenure.

The water in the inner passage between Dunk and the mainland was at times so clear that the bottom could be seen nine fathoms down. Turtles idled along and browsed on marine grasses and weeds, and hovering fish "nibbled daintily the green and lazy slime on the batten of the bilge, their gently waving shadows being barely perceptible, for their delicate, semi-transparent bodies absorbed but the merest particle of the brightness of noonday".[15]

Yet winds could suddenly spring up, as when Ted was confidently sailing his boat for Clump Point with Bertha and two native boys, Charlie and Willie, on board. Also Paddy, the dog. They were bowling along happily when

> a vagrant and wanton puff skipped on the hill-top, snoodled between two steep ridges, whisked coyly out of a bottle-necked gorge, impudently slapped the big jib, and in a trice the skimming dish-boat had made an unbecoming exhibition. Half a mile from land — and not a soul within many miles to send us aid; clinging to the up-turned boat while contemplating the fact that the intense calm of the morning was giving way before a stiff north-easterly breeze.[16]

Bertha could not swim, and Ted supported her while grasping the ornamental tiller in the other hand; he used it to threaten Willie and Charlie — the former to swim for the shore, the latter to stay — for if both reached the beach and looked back, their courage might fail and neither might return with the punt.

As Willie swam away, there was no sign of Paddy. Charlie had an explanation — and in recording it, Ted displayed once again his flair for capturing dialect and putting it down on paper: "That fella drown — finish! Him tie up alonga rigging. No come up one time. My word, poor pfella Paddy; good-bye. Me plenty sorry."[17]

Ted believed that the dog must have swum to the shore with Willie, but there was no sign of the animal in that direction, so while Bertha was left to cling to the bottom of the boat, first Charlie, and then Ted, probed under it — and so Paddy was discovered, his paws working as if on a treadmill as he kept his nose up in the bubble of air trapped inside.

Willie paddled the punt to the capsized boat which was towed ashore to Brammo Bay. Coats and Bertha's shawl were lost, but the rudder was recovered later. So there was no damage — that is, apart from Bertha's loss of confidence in Ted's ability to handle craft of this type. From this time, she boarded small boats only when absolutely necessary, and she never sailed with Ted again, even though he circumnavigated his island and the neighbouring isles, and ventured alone as far as Townsville.

Ted was to have a turn at being trapped under his boat. It happened some fourteen months later, when they were spending Christmas, 1899, with their neighbours and friends the Cuttens on the mainland at Bicton. On Christmas night a rising wind, with thunder and lightning, brought up the sea. Ted considered it risky to leave his boat moored in open water, so he went out with two sons of their hostess to bring the craft into the shelter of the stone jetty. They got on board the boat, but the storm broke and "A huge white sea fondled her; she rolled over in its embrace, helpless. My companions sprang clear . . . while the boat, the mast snapping off short, came over and trapped me."[18]

In an article "The Sensation of Drowning", prefaced by a quotation from Keats, "I have been half in love with easeful death", Ted wrote of this experience, and at one stage it seemed he surrendered to his fate: "The world was slipping away. All resentment against fate was of the past. Storm and terror were gone. This, then, was the end — a new sense — aesthetic, delicate, a purified appreciation of physical comfort, surcease of mental striving, desire for delicious rest. So to die was not to die, but to sleep, dreaming softly."[19]

Bertha was deeply dismayed when she later read the longhand draft of the article, although Ted had not completely surrendered. "As the nerveless fingers relaxed, my feet touched Mother Earth, and Mother Earth, prompt and decisive, administered a galvanic shock." He fought back. A halyard had looped itself around his legs, but he broke free, and a breaker threw him on the sand. "The episode, which to me had stretched into infinitude, had trespassed but a few idle moments of the good time of Providence."[20]

It confirmed what Bertha had suspected, that in Ted's delicately-balanced mental make-up there was an inclination towards death. While it shocked her, she was grateful to have discovered this indirect admission of its existence, because this, too, would enable her to cope with his swings of mood. Such admissions were to surface from time to time in his writings, occasionally in reflective prose which verged on poetry, as when he described himself floating in "This peace-lulled, beguiling sea, teeming with myriad forms scintillating on the verge of nothingness":

Thus musing,
the sorcery of the sea became invincible.
My thoughts drifted, until I dozed,
and dozing dreamt —
a vague incomprehensible dream
of floating in some purer ether,
some diviner air
than ever belonged to wormy earth.[21]

A week after Robert Philp became Queensland's premier on 7 December 1899, Ted received word that his father had died in Ararat — a few days after preaching for the last time at Holy Trinity.

Although Ted was prepared for this news, knowing that Jabez had been lost without Sarah and in worsening health, he was still devastated. He had never really envisaged life without the challenge of having to acquit himself in his father's eyes. It somehow drew the curtain on the long twilight of boyhood in which he had been standing despite the passage of the years. He felt an overwhelming sense of having failed to justify himself, especially in his decision to try to make a go of the island life. He just had not had the time to do that; he did not even have a full legal right to the part of the island he had chosen.

He wrote to Harry, regretting not being with him and his eldest sister Eliza at their father's bedside, although knowing that even if he had been there, he could have done little to vindicate himself. He did not consider himself entitled to anything much in the way of an inheritance, although he wished to have a keepsake, so he wrote: "There is something I would like and feel great comfort in possessing. Dad's copy of Milton's works, that small old fashioned book from which he learned the beauties of Paradise Lost and which at his request and advice I read." He also asked if he might be permitted to have his father's fishing rod "as a remembrance of Dad's fondness in years gone by of fishing and of those walks we used to take to the Hopkins".[22]

It had been, as he wrote in his diary, a sad year with the passing of both of his parents. He hoped that 1900 would be happier. Well, it was to see the approval of his application for the Dunk Island land in June, and at least one of his money-making enterprises was succeeding.

There was gold on the island after all. Hives full of combs of it. Liquid gold. So much so that Ted was in danger of running out of receptacles into which to pour it before shipping it to Townsville.

Chapter 14
Sea-Girt Hermitage

In May 1900 Ted erected a flagstaff on the sand-spit facing the
inner steamer track and the mainland — and two days later had
occasion to hoist a red flag in honour of the relief of Mafeking,
the lifting of the siege of British forces by the Boers.[1]

The erection of the flagstaff was one of the first projects in an
on-going programme which was to include the building of a
boatshed in the tree-line at the back of the Brammo Bay beach;
the laying of a tramway of three-by-three hardwood for a
trolley to run Ted's boat down to the water; the construction of
a suspension bridge over the gully to allow shorter access to
one of the main areas cleared for cultivation; a pump at the
bottom of the gully and a storage tank up above it; the planting
of sprouting coconuts to form a long avenue of palms down to
the beach.

Within a month, the flagstaff was called upon to help mark
other occasions. Up went a flag on the June day in 1900 when
the telegram arrived informing them that the application for
Dunk Island had at long last been approved.[2] Up again on 3
August, which had been declared a holiday for the anniversary
of the wedding of Edmund James Banfield and Bertha Golding.
Up again on the first day of the first year of the twentieth century when the Australian colonies became federated into a
commonwealth. There were, unhappily, occasions when the
flag was to fly at half-mast, and the first of these was in late
January 1901 when news was received of the death of Queen
Victoria.

The masters of passing ships may not always have realized
why a flag had been raised; but if one did happen to be flying,

E.J. Banfield, 1901, aged forty-nine. (A.H. Chisholm Papers, courtesy of Mitchell Library.)

Bertha Banfield, 1901, aged forty-three, dressed for visit to Townsville. (A.H. Chisholm Papers, courtesy of Mitchell Library.)

they usually responded with a whistle blast — some, no doubt, doing so with relief after using glasses to make sure that the flag was not upside down, for that would have meant someone on the island was in need of assistance.

Little could be done to overcome the danger of isolation should crises arise, even though they were close to the mainland and to the inner steamer track where passing ships could be intercepted. Certain signals came into use based on smoke, mirror flashes and fires. In emergencies any two signals meant that help was needed; three that the worst had happened. One signal, perhaps between Ted and Bertha when she was spending a few days on the mainland with friends, meant that all was well. Some signals were in simple pre-arranged codes; for instance, in the case of natives returning after holiday breaks or walkabouts, asking for a boat to be sent to fetch them. And in the case of two who were sweethearts, one a visitor to the island and the other a mainland settler, lanterns were used to say goodnight across the five kilometres of water.

Emergency signals were no guarantee that help would come. When the young son of a visiting family took ill on the island, the signals to a passing steamer were ignored and the boy died. Ted was so upset about this, and made such a protest, that instructions were issued by the shipping companies that *any* signal from Dunk Island had to be investigated.

The perils remained, nevertheless, with reminders from time to time, such as when the raising of the flag for the coronation of King Edward the Seventh had to be postponed because he had been stricken with appendicitis. Despite such perils, now that the land application had been granted, Ted felt free to consolidate their position. Firstly, he marked off a 40 acre (16 hectare) strip of land at the southern extremity of his 320 acre (130 hectare) block and Bertha applied for it in her name, thus increasing their joint holding by one eighth.[3] At the same time he embarked on a major development. The existing house was still basically the prefabricated hut with attendant structures all of a temporary nature. In short, his modest castle had still to be built and he set about planning it, using the layout of the Townsville house as a guide, with central hallway and French windows opening on to a wide verandah. However, unlike the Townsville dwelling (which they still kept just in case they might have to go back there), his island bungalow was to have the same wide verandah on three sides.

Although he had received a legacy of £300 ($600) from his father, the new bungalow would involve a big financial outlay.[4] From his own plans he prepared estimates of the amounts and types of timber required, all of which the Cutten Brothers at Bicton assured him they could supply. Added to the timber were the costs of such items as nails, brackets and bolts, and iron roofing, and he could not undertake the erection of such a substantial building — and expect it to withstand the forces of cyclones — without at some stage the expertise of at least one skilled tradesman, whose wages would increase the drain on his capital.

The sight of a pen may have nauseated him for a time after his escape to Dunk, but he could not lay his aside for long — especially when through it he could make some money by writing leaders. The first he did were for the *Cairns Argus*, and then he wrote up to four a week for *The Townsville Evening Star* at the request of his old friend T.P. Adlam.[5]

Whatever the fate of his venture into importing and selling "London and Continental Novelties", Adlam had not been away from the newspaper business for long. After becoming sole proprietor of *The Star*, he was now a director and shareholder of the company owning it, as well as being editor.[6] In 1901 he planned another trip overseas. Would Ted take over in his absence? For Ted this was not only a vindication after having been denied the editorial chair of *The Townsville Daily Bulletin*, but also a most timely opportunity to earn some extra money.

Under the terms of his grant, he had to be in continuous occupation of the land; but provision had been made for periods of absence, so he applied for permission to be away for six months: "The grounds of my application are that by accepting a temporary appointment I may acquire additional capital to enable me to undertake further substantial improvements on the homestead". This was made on 18 May 1901, and on 13 June the land commissioner recommended that the condition of occupation be suspended for six months.[7]

Ted had apparently bent the rules, because in fact he and Bertha had shut up the house on the island on 21 February, leaving the natives to keep an eye on things, including the bee hives. While Ted worked in *The Star* office, Bertha took the opportunity to visit friends in Charters Towers and Brisbane. They returned to the island on 13 November, after nine months rather than the permitted six, so it would appear that like the man he was said to resemble in some ways, he was capable of turning a blind eye to edicts from on high.

The natives welcomed them back — Tom and his gin Little Jinny, and two boys Willie and Mickie. The buildings were in good order but the gardens were heavily overgrown and the boat leaked. All this could easily be put right, but what puzzled and dismayed Ted was that only four of the bee hives were occupied, and by a handful of alarmingly listless and undemonstrative members of the species in comparison with the busy battalions he had left in residence.

Having started with two hives, he had increased the number to a dozen. His hopes had run high of "the earning of a modest profit from one of the cleanest, nicest and most entertaining and innoxious of pursuits". Before leaving for Townsville, he had shipped up to seventy pounds (thirty-two kilograms) at a time of wholesome white, golden and tawny-brown honey, after whirling the dripping combs in the separator. If any hive was tapped, there would be "a furious and instant alarm and angry outpouring of excited and wrathful citizens"; but now there was "merely a buzzing remonstrance, indicative of decreased population, weakness and disconsolation". The cause was investigated and revealed

> in the presence of two species of birds, the Australian bee-eater (*Merops ornatus*) and the white-rumped wood-swallow (*Artamus leucogasta*). The former is one of the handsomest of the smaller birds of Australia, its chief colouring being varying shades of green with bronze-brown and black head and blue back; and to add to its appearance and pride two graceful feather-shafts of black protrude from the green and yellow of the tail.[8]

They caught their victims on the wing. As for the partner in crime, the wood-swallow, it

> wears a becoming suit of soft pearly grey and white, to contrast with its black head and throat. It has a graceful, soaring flight and a cheerful chirrup. At certain seasons scores congregate on a branch, perching in a row, so closely compact that their breasts show as a continuous band of white. When one leaves its place to catch an insect, the others close up the ranks and dress the line, and on returning, wrangle and scold as he may, he needs must take an outside place.

These were the "marauders who confounded anticipations of a comfortable livelihood in the decent calling of an apiarist. They devoured bees by the hundred every day."[9]

Ted was faced with a problem. If he declared war on these two species of birds, he would be going against his wish to establish the island as a place for the preservation of bird life, as a "sea-girt hermitage". Since his occupancy he could claim that it had become "a sanctuary, a city of refuge, a safe abiding place, a kingdom where all birds of the air — save tyrants and cannibals — were welcomed with gladness and enthusiasm", the tyrants and cannibals being birds of prey such as eagles, falcons, goshawks and kestrels.[10]

Yet the two vagrant species had the right of prior occupancy of the island — and other claims to dispensation. For instance: "they were eminently useful in the work of keeping within bounds the rampant host of insects to which mankind is in the habit of applying the term injurious." Had the Banfields taken steps to ensure that the production of honey was allowed to proceed "it would have been at the cost of the lives of hundreds of graceful birds". And not only these two species, but the "hundreds of others that now merrily make so free would have been scared away".[11]

Rather than do any violence to the marauders, Ted decided to abandon the enterprise. A mainland friend fortunately took the whole honey plant and the hives off his hands, and he rationalized that he would be able to use the money which would have been spent on cartridges to purchase honey from other sources.

This led to a sweeping decree by Ted and Bertha, and the discovery of a "grand objective".[12] Interference with all bird life in their domain would henceforth be forbidden. The island would be proclaimed a sanctuary for all manner of birds, except the murderous and cannibalistic, such as the falcon who had killed their pet butcher bird and had therefore been summarily shot.

And now, thanks to those nine months of wages in Townsville, Ted was ready to proceed with the construction of his modest castle, even without the hoped-for income from the sale of honey.

Chapter 15
The Modest Castle

"In designing the bungalow," Ted wrote, "two essentials were supreme, cost and comfort — minimum of cost, maximum of comfort."

> There was no alignment to obey, no rigid rules as to style and material . . . Low walls, unaspiring roof, and sheltering veranda, so contrived as to create, not tickling, fidgety draughts, but smooth currents . . . to flush each room so sweetly and softly that no perceptible difference between the air under the roof and of the forest is at any time perceptible.[1]

Bertha was handed the spade to turn the first sod when the first block of the bungalow was put in on 23 September 1902. Many years later she wrote:

> our home here has not been the usual rough bush building, but rather an absolutely comfortable one, with an English air about it, although in the midst of tropical surroundings. For the first five years, until we were assured that the life would be the right thing from a health point of view, we had only the cedar hut and a kitchen, but after that we considered that we would make for lasting comfort.[2]

The timber ordered from the Cutten Brothers was shipped across and unloaded in Brammo Bay. In the early stage, Ted engaged an itinerant Norwegian called Jack at £1 ($2) per week, but he proved most unsatisfactory and construction proceed without him. A few of the Aborigines lent a hand — even Bertha, and for her pains she suffered a nasty head wound from falling timber when assisting in the erection of verandah posts. This was not the only hazard — a death adder was found in one of the post-holes and had to be dispatched. An important of-

The bungalow as it was during A.H. Chisholm's visit.
(Courtesy of Mitchell Library.)

ficial, Dr Roth, the Protector of Aborigines, was also enlisted as a helper while he used Dunk as a base for visits to the outer reefs. After two months of ground work, and when all the basic components for the new abode had been assembled, a skilled tradesman was employed. Wm. Tait, a carpenter, arrived early in December 1902 and started work at 50s. ($5) per week and keep, and in six weeks the floor was laid, the walls were up, the overhead timbers and rafters in place and a shiny new iron roof heliographing its presence to distant parts.[3]

In *My Tropic Isle*, Ted stated that he and Bertha celebrated Christmas 1903 by moving into this modest castle. It must have been one of the displeasing blunders he discovered in the book because the occupation of the new bungalow began much sooner — on 8 January of that year — when furniture was shifted from the old cedar hut into the new abode, and he and Bertha were able to rejoice in "the roomy airy pleasant apartments".[4]

Carpenter Tait's task was finished with the roofing of the new guest chamber, and he returned to Townsville on board the *Lass O'Gowrie*. Heavy rains fell following his departure, thus testing his handiwork. The bungalow proved sound. Within a month it was put to a further and much more severe test. In the wake of mountainous seas and high winds a cyclone struck, leaving parts of the forest bare of leaves.[5] Part of the sand-spit was carried away and mounds of seaweed piled on the beach. The bungalow came through the test unscathed.

There was, however, a major catastrophe. In terms of the damage a cyclone could inflict, this one did relatively little harm to the island itself, but out in Brammo Bay it

destroyed most of the fantastic forms which made the coral garden enchanting. In its commotion, too, the sea lost its purity. The sediment and ooze of decades were churned up, and, as the agitation ceased, were precipitated — a brown, furry, slimy mud, all over the garden — smothering the industrious polyps to whom all its prettiness was due.[6]

The Banfield bungalow and coconut avenue, as painted by Noel Wood of Bedarra Island. (Courtesy of Lorna L. Banfield, Ararat.)

Much construction still remained for Ted to handle on his own — the fastening down of verandah boards, the finishing of the bathroom, painting doors and window frames, the building of a gangway between the back of the bungalow and the kitchen, then whitewashing the exterior.

Parallel to this he completed a wardrobe for Bertha, a china cupboard, bookshelves for his office, even a wheelbarrow. He had plans to install running water in every room, a project that would, when it could be tackled, require some help from a real plumber. The range of projects dazed Bertha — a stockyard, more fencing, more outhouses, thatching the boatshed; and within the bungalow more, too — a revolving square bookcase for the volumes of *Encyclopaedia Britannica*; a lectern for the big dictionary; and the hanging of framed prints including several of the languorous classical nudes popular at the time. The natives also made a contribution to the embellishment of the interior with thick-weave pandanus palm mats for the floor.[7]

After the cedar hut, which had become hopelessly crowded, there was room on the walls for the collections of Aboriginal weapons, implements and musical instruments. On shelves and in showcases, some of Ted's beachcombing loot could be displayed — sea shells, small black pearls, pearl-shell fish hooks in all stages of their creation from the actual untouched shell to the fragile-looking hook that was "a thousand times more durable in this climate than the hooks of steel" made by the European intruders. In large jars were fish and snakes caught by Ted and pickled by Bertha, among them a diamond-patterned yellow and green snake and a gruesome marine specimen:

> the death adder of the sea . . . the warty ghoul . . . Loathsome, secretive, inert, rough and jagged in outline, wearing tufts and sprays of sea-weed on its back, scarcely to be distinguished from the rocks among which it lurks, it is armed with spines steeped in the cruellest venom. Many fish are capable of inflicting painful and even dangerous wounds, but none is to be more dreaded than the ugly and repulsive "stone fish".[8]

In this display were a globe that had shone in a ship's saloon; part of the figure-head of a Fijian canoe; and a broken paddle from the New Hebrides. Also several empty bottles which were of little significance to visitors until Ted explained that they had contained printed forms from American researchers asking for them to be returned so that the pattern of world's currents would be better understood.

Each day Ted walked his "promenade" in Brammo Bay, sometimes with Bertha, both in bare feet and relishing the smooth feel of the sand as they left their "pedal autographs" imprinted side by side. Alone on other strips of the tropics, with the combinations of land, sea and air such that Ted was to be constantly finding new and fresh ways to describe the shining wonder of the magical light that clothed everything; the calms when the sea was a living mirror; the air resplendent, luminous and delicious with fragrance; days of stunning beauty as he inspected "what the winds and tides may have spread out" for "on these radiant shores, I boldly and with glee give way to my beachcombing instincts".[9]

The wreck of a German barque driven onto an uncharted part of the Great Barrier Reef about three hundred kilometres to the south was "the greatest favour bestowed" on Ted in his

profession of Beachcombing: "Long and heavy pieces of angle-iron came bolted to raft-like sections of the deck; various kinds of timber proved useful in a variety of ways", and the grating of the battered barque

> upon which many a wet and weary steersman had stood, now fulfils placid duty as a front gate. No more to be trampled and stamped upon with shifty, sloppy feet — no more to be scrubbed and scored with sand and holystone; painted white, it creaks gratefully every time it swings — the symbol of security, the first outward visible sign of home, the guardian of the sacred rights of private property.[10]

Paddy, one of the long line of faithful canine friends, had his own gate at the back — a tin flap with "PUSH" painted on either side.

As Ted was now to say: "We had won disregard of all the bother and contradictions, the vanities and absurdities of the toilful, wayward, human world, and had acquired a glorious sense of irresponsibleness and independence". But it was a sense at all times tempered by discipline. The mornings for work on the property. The afternoons for exploration, observation and

"The Gate of Hospitality", made from sailing ship grating, with the Beachcomber going out to meet visiting Queensland Governor. (Courtesy of Mrs L. Webb, Winchester, England.)

121

beachcombing. Marvellously brilliant cloudless days spent wallowing in such luxuries:

> Then at sundown to plunge into the tepid sea, to frolic and splash therein, while the red light in the west began to pale and the pink and silver surface of the ocean faded to grey; then to a vigorous soaping and scrubbing in the shady creek, where the orange-tinted drupes of pandanus-palms give the cool water a balsamic savour; then, clad in clean cotton, to the evening meal with a prodigious appetite; and to bed at nine o'clock to sleep murmurlessly for eight hours — tell me if thus you are not fitted for another day's toil in the sublimating sunshine?[11]

This was the man who in Townsville, after those long hours of newspaper work, had been nearly out of his mind with craving for sleep. He was now just over ten stone in weight with his skin deeply tanned. He believed he owed his salvation to "His Majesty the Sun", to the glorious planet Sol "whose medicinable eye" in the words of Shakespeare "corrects the ill aspects of planets evil".[12]

When he wrote of the "wholesome effects of the free and vitalising life", the "tonic" of the sea, and the "sublimating sunshine", he was doing so in terms of modern tranquillizing therapy.[13]

This was also the man who had scarcely been able to take any food, yet now he could consume on his own a large specimen of one of the commonest yet most delectable North Queensland fruits, the papaw: "That which makes women beautiful for ever; which renews the strength of man." He believed that the true eater of fruit belonged to the most etherealized branch of epicureanism, more so than even the most selective connoisseurs of wines, and that: "Only those . . . who can time their acceptance of it from the tree, so that it shall possess all its fleeting elements in the happy blending of full maturity, can know how good and great a papaw really is."[14]

Between dining and retiring for the night, there were to be further explorations and another sort of beachcombing in the main room of the bungalow, sometimes with silence seeping in from the dark, sometimes night insects and night-jars and the rustle of the sea on the beach. A strong kerosene lamp hung from a rafter and threw a sharp cone of light from under its metal shade.[15] Within this cone, and with his back to the lamp, Ted would sit and delight in exploring the strands of islands of another kind, for books provided that other form of beachcombing. One of the reasons why he had shaken the dust of civilization from his feet was so that he could pursue another programme — catching up on the reading for which on the mainland he'd never had enough time.

A book was an island, and the three volumes of Shakespeare,

which he visited constantly, were special islands with gemstones and pearls cast up along with sea shells and other spoils of the ocean. A word was such a prize and he would turn to the lectern, which was also placed within the radiance of the lamp, to consult his big dictionary. The English author and critic, C.E. Montague, had not yet published his book *A Writer's Notes on His Trade*, but what he was to write was something that Ted Banfield had been practising many years before:

> A sculptor alone in his studio will fondly stroke a lump of un-worked marble or bronze . . . A writer or a good reader will do much the same: his mind will finger single words and caress them, adoring the mellow fullness or granular hardness of their several sounds, the balance, undulation or trailing fall of their syllables, or the core of sunlike splendour in the broad, warm, central vowel of such a word as "auroral". Each word's evocative value or virtue, its individual power of touching springs of the mind and of initiating visions, becomes a treasure to revel in.[16]

Ted was now writing regular articles. With so much happening in the north — separatism, federalism, the meat trade, fruit-growing, natives' problems, climate, clothing, to mention a few — he had no shortage of subjects, and it was from his nightly beachcombing that he garnered much of his material. Time and again he would break off from his reading to quote something to Bertha — a word, a phrase — as she herself read a book, or patched his dungaree trousers, or confined her participation in his sea-going activities to making a new sail for his boat. He would frequently record such pickings when he came to the final task before calling it a day, the writing up of his diary.

One of his earliest pen-names, one through which he celebrated his fascination with Robinson Crusoe islands, was "Rob Krusoe" — used when recalling Robert Philp's first electioneering campaign. Although Bertha was to tell Alec Chisholm that she recalled nothing of his adoption of "Rob Krusoe" and that in her opinion it had no part in their life on the island, he wrote "A Beachcombing Exploit" for *The North Queensland Register* under the pseudonym "Rob Krusoe" while he and Bertha occupied the cedar hut. It related how Ted and Tom had allowed themselves to believe that what appeared to be a derelict mastless boat was from the French penal colony of New Caledonia, and that it contained a runaway French patriot whose frail craft had come in through the Great Barrier Reef. It was one of those days when "there is no far-off sea, no sky-line, but a silvery expanse in which blue islets float", the sort of day when fancy could be excused for running wild. As it happened, when the derelict craft was approached it turned out to be no more than a dead cow — much to Tom's undisguised hilarity.[17]

It was in this article that Ted's handwriting got the better of the compositor who made "Queen's Jubilee politics" out of what Ted had intended to be read as "Queer jumble politics".[18]

"Rob Krusoe" did not make many appearances and did not survive for long. When Ted began his "Rural Homilies", he adopted a pen-name more in keeping with the role he played on his island, although one of its first appearances again confounded the compositor and so an early Christmas special for *The North Queensland Register* was by someone who would appear to have incorporated a well-known species of tree into his pseudonym by calling himself "BEECH-COMBER".[19]

Thereafter he was either "The Beachcomber" or just plain "Beachcomber". His journalistic colleagues in Townsville and Charters Towers entered into the spirit of it and adopted this name; at the same time, as his articles grew in strength in terms of content, style, range and impact, the former "Travelling Correspondent" became to them a sort of "Our Man in Eden".

Chapter 16

A Lunatic on the Coast

Almost twenty years after the appearance of *The Torres Straits Route*, Ted began work on *Within the Barrier*, a tourist guide to the North Queensland Coast, also published by the firm founded in Townsville by Thankful Willmett. This was to be at least his third publication, since he and G.H. Pritchard had already brought out *Townsville Illustrated*, a short historical sketch with splendid views of the city, the harbour and panoramas from Castle Hill, together with a short historical sketch of the city and some latest statistics.[1]

Some of the photographs illustrating *Within the Barrier*, which had a cover titled "The Winter Paradise of Australia", were taken on Dunk. A review of the work in *The North Queensland Register* stated: "Mr. Banfield has found his field . . . we await his next work, or any work he does, with pleasure, as we have confident assurance that we will not be disappointed." When referring to the islands of Rockingham Bay, Ted wrote: "Counting the Brook Group — twenty miles out from Cardwell — Goold and Garden Islands, the Family Group and Dunk Island with its satellites, the steamer passes eighteen in as many miles, the largest and fairest being Dunk Island, whereon is a solitary but ideally located homestead."[2]

Despite this rather coy reference, the homestead was indeed ideally located, and in more ways than one. Although it might be the residence of an "Unprofessional Beachcomber",[3] Ted's credentials were above reproach: he was a man of standing in his chosen field, he had been appointed a Justice of the Peace in 1899, and he was a gentleman (even if he put this description of himself rather than journalist or settler on some of the documents which required him to state his occupation). He was an entertaining host with a charming and cultured wife, so what better stopping-off place to recommend to those important people from southern parts who were taking to cruising among the islands and wonders of the Great Barrier Reef. Some such recommendations came from his friend, the Honourable Robert Philp, MLA, premier of Queensland, and they were made to people ranging up to vice regal rank, so that governors and governor-generals were among those who were to be treated to conducted tours of his domain by the Beachcomber. Quite apart from its undoubted claims to being the fairest and best island, it was also a sort of safe house.

Another distinguished visitor came at the suggestion of Ted's good friend in England, J.T. Critchell; although before this man presented *his* credentials he took the precaution of first looking over both the island and the owner of the solitary homestead from the deck of the *Lass O'Gowrie* when Ted rowed out to pick up the mail and stores.

Ted was unaware that he was under close examination, but when the time came he was able to recall this man in vivid detail and write about him in one of his "Rural Homilies":

> Some years ago a queerly arrayed, red-faced, fair-haired man glanced over the side of the faithful steamer which keeps this isle in weekly touch with the busy world. He might have been mistaken for a tramp, and an eccentric tramp, for the remnants of his hat were stayed with linen bands and linked with bold brass safety pins; his coat was soiled and frayed and he wore no necktie. But in spite of his odd attire there was something about the passer-by which riveted attention. A week or so later [8 September 1903] a letter came from Walter Strickland, asking, in most courtly terms, for permission to visit the isle, and commending to perusal a bundle of credentials, which amply proved the possessor to be a remarkable man — scholar, world-wide traveller, philosopher, author, natural history enthusiast.[4]

Ted had heard of a "lunatic on the coast"[5] who spent his nights wading in the shallows and mud flats with a lantern and collecting night fish. This was the man, and his interests embraced marine shells, certain forms of insect life, snakes and botany. Despite Bertha's reservations, Ted extended an invitation, and he arrived on 10 October with luggage that was at one and the same time both scanty and weighty:

> It comprised little in the way of raiment, but several things contributory to the successful pursuit of hobbying, specimen bottles, a gallon of formalin, and some simple appliances. Being excessively susceptible to the alteration of the sun, he was wont, as a preliminary to a collecting expedition, to anoint his radiant countenance with a brown unguent, and, careless, or indifferent to appearances, a blob would be applied to the tip of a nose positively cerise, and erratic streaks to rosy chin and cheeks. He would also unhook a couple of safety pins to let down a rear cur-

tain from his hapless hat for the protection of his neck. Then, with old boots and trousers shortened to his knees and ludicrously frayed, discovering very ruddy legs, he would joyously venture forth, on the coral reef, and return with marine wonders, upon which he would talk with rare eloquence.[6]

At times Ted could endure fools and bores, although never knaves, but ever since his boyhood encounters with Henry Jerrold in Ararat he had been indulgent to genuine eccentrics — and here was an eccentric of the highest order, a master of many tongues, overflowing with knowledge, a man who had lived in remote parts of Europe and the East, and had turned his back on England where he was in line to inherit a famous Yorkshire Castle and an illustrious baronetcy.[7] Walter William Strickland was fifty-two when he came to Dunk Island with his paraphernalia, one year older than Ted who was visibly mesmerized by him, and gave over all his time so that they could wander about the island and out on the reef together.

Strickland was of that small tribe of fearless Englishmen, robust or frail, charming or charmless, honest or unscrupulous, usually rich, who were to be found on the slopes of hitherto unconquered mountain peaks in distant parts of the world, at the head waters of hitherto unnavigated rivers, in blazing deserts and in freezing arctic wastes, eagerly and industriously revealing new aspects of the planet earth to their fellow men. Some were pure delight, others pains in the neck, most were motivated by seemingly crazy ideas — but all were unabashedly and without apology stepping to the music they heard. In Ted's view Henry David Thoreau would have delighted in the presence of such a person as Walter William Strickland, a man "who saw life from a different angle than most of us".[8]

Bertha was markedly less enthused. While being impressed by a graduate of Trinity College, Cambridge, and by the author of many published literary works — dramatic pieces, verses, translations in many languages, pamphlets, leaflets and essays on a great variety of topics — and a high-born man of wealth to boot, she did not respond when he began to extol the virtues of the squalid ways of life of lowly dwellers in almost inaccessible parts of Europe and Asia. She had no problem at all hearing him without her cardboard "tube"; he addressed her as if she might be up the back feeding the fowls. This she could endure, but when Strickland came to express disgust with his own people, and to decry England's achievements and greatness, this was disloyal, profane and disgusting. When he attacked the notion of monarchy and the sham of religion, she would hear no more of it.

"Really, Mr Strickland — is nothing sacred?"

"To be sure, my dear Mrs Banfield — truth. Truth is sacred — and truth is what I seek."

127

Ted dismissed Bertha's disapproval of their guest; his knowledge, achievements and dedication were of such magnitude that they cancelled out those shortcomings which concerned and shocked Bertha. (After all, had not Thoreau written "Rather than love, than money, than fame, give me truth.")[9]

Strickland's visit came at a time when Ted, after personally declaring Dunk a sanctuary for bird life, was becoming involved in the moves to have his island and others in Rockingham Bay proclaimed officially as perpetual reserves, so Strickland's opinions of those who killed wild life, whether for food, for fashion or for profit, were eagerly heeded. Strickland's powers of invective and castigation were demonstrated in a passage from his work *The Extinction of Mankind*, quoted by Ted in one of his later "Rural Homilies" in which he attacked the irresponsible attitudes of sportsmen, men of science and collectors of natural history specimens to the birds of the world. Referring to those Anglo-Christian missions which were said to be realizing large sums of money from the industry, Stickland wrote:

> The whole order of Birds of Paradise is threatened with extinction in the near future to tar and feather these Christian female ruffians, and render them more hideous by contrast than nature has created them. The same fate awaits the divinist and most gorgeous forms of life evolved in nature's prism house — those unrivalled living gems — the humming-birds.[10]

Ted and Bertha gathered that in England he had a wife, but no children, and that she took little part in his life. Bertha could well understand this. How could any woman share the sort of life he apparently led, lowering himself to the level of primitive villagers in order to learn their languages and folklore?

Strickland on his part had something to learn from Ted. The garden of coral was still ruined after the March cyclone earlier that year, but Ted was able to describe those vanished few acres in such a way that he brought the scene alive. He also provided Strickland with what he had written of the garden's fantastic forms before they were destroyed:

> On the rocks rest stalkless mushrooms, gills uppermost, which blossom as pom-pom chrysanthemums; rough nodules, boat-and canoe-shaped dishes of coral. Adhering to the rocks are thin, flaky, brittle growths resembling vine-leaves, brown and golden-yellow; goblets and cups, tiered epergnes, distorted saucers, eccentric vases, crazily-shaped dishes.[11]

The visitor wanted to see more of such writings, and Ted was delighted to oblige:

> To see the coral garden to advantage you must pass over it — not through it. Drifting idly in a boat in a calm clear day, when

the tips of the tallest shrubs are submerged but a foot or so, and all the delicate filaments, which are invisible or lie flat and flaccid when the tide is out, are waving, twisting and twining, then the spectacle is at its best. Tiny fish, glowing like jewels, flash and dart among the intricate interlacing branches, or quiveringly poise about some slender point — humming-birds of the sea, sipping their nectar. A pink translucent fish no greater than a lead-pencil wriggles in and out of the lemon-coloured coral. Another of the John Dory shape, but scarcely an inch long, blue as a sapphire with gold fins and gold-tipped tail, hovers over a miniature blue-black cave. A shoal darts out, some an old-gold, some green with yellow damascene tracery and long yellow filaments floating from the lower lip. A slender form, half pink coral, half grey, that might swim in a walnut shell, displays its transparent charms. Conspicuous, daring colours here are as common as on the lawn of a racecourse.[12]

Strickland insisted on seeing more and more, and was shown pieces ranging from leaders on pet subjects to pen pictures of the Aborigines, their ways, their beliefs, their folklore, their conduct. The visitor became increasingly intrigued and demanded to know what had prompted Ted to rebel against the uniformity of life, to shun the conventionalities of society, to indulge in his own caprices, to live in accordance with his own notions and to submit joyfully to the charms and wonders of the simple life.

As Ted answered, Strickland declared again and again: "You must write about *that* — put all *that* in a book." And as the original stay of a week was extended (to Bertha's silent chagrin) to a fortnight, Ted found himself being urged to marshal all his material and to shape it as a book. Carried away by encouragement from such an eminent authority, Ted even came up with a possible title — "The Confessions of a Beachcomber".

As a step towards publication, Strickland asked for samples of Ted's writings, together with a short outline of the proposed book; he would send this material to London to Critchell, who would pass it on to one of the publishers whom Strickland knew.

With his haul of land shells, snakes, scorpions, caterpillars, marine shells, beche-de-mer and other specimens safely preserved in formalin, the "queerly-arrayed, red-faced, fair-haired" man departed, never to be sighted again, but to be heard from intermittently — mostly from unheard-of places — as Ted settled down to his task.

His friends on the mainland came to hear about the book. To Adlam, who moved south to Sydney about this time, and Dodd Clarke and David Green, the Beachcomber had been bitten by the writing bug in no small way. Ted made no secret of it. On 20 December 1904, when he wrote to Robert Philp (now in opposition again) about the proclamation of the islands as sanctuaries, he mentioned what progress he had made, such as it was: "My book is practically finished; but whether it will ever be published is 'another story', unless I can discover a complacent publisher."[13]

Over another year passed before Ted considered the book ready for dispatch to London; but first he had to have all his handwritten bits and pieces with mazes of emendations, deletions and additions typed up from start to finish. As Bertha was to tell Alec Chisholm, when "The Confessions" was ready for typing Ted "got a young girl from Townsville — the sister of Capt. Robertson of the *Innisfail* — and it took all of three weeks to get it down. Ted dictated for none could possibly have read his manuscript, and I think they were both glad when the work was completed". The young lady must have brought a machine with her as Ted had yet to acquire his first Dunk Island typewriter. This typescript was sent off to London in March 1906.[14]

Even in those far-off halcyon days, it is highly doubtful that there was any such person as a "complacent publisher". It was a gentleman's profession to be sure, but those gentlemen were hard businessmen, as were most Englishmen in the mercantile world, so when, through the combination of Walter Strickland and J.T. Critchell, a publisher was approached, he gave very little away despite his enthusiasm for the book.

T. Fisher Unwin published tourist guides, maps, pocket dictionaries, phrase books, histories of nations, first novels, and, among other subjects, travel and natural history; Ted's book came under the two latter headings. His first reaction was that the book, for his requirements, was not yet finished. It needed certain specific revisions and expanding to bring it up to a total length of 150,000 words or thereabouts. The author would be expected to supply the publisher, free of charge or copyright fee, with about fifty pictures or photographs, a map of Dunk Island and its neighbours, and other material from which to illustrate the work.[15]

This was not all the author was asked to supply before an agreement could be signed — far from it. He would pay the publisher the sum of £150 ($300) on signature as a contribution towards the expenses of publication.[16]

Before Ted could protest that he was in no position to put up what in his case amounted to almost two years' income, the matter was solved for him. Walter Strickland, in conjunction with his solicitors and Critchell, agreed to advance the £150 — and, knowing that Ted would be unlikely to accept such charity, came to a business agreement on his behalf so that the sum would be deducted from the initial royalties of the book and paid to the solicitors who would see that Strickland was reimbursed. Once the £150 had been repaid, all profits would go direct to Ted, who remained bewildered by some aspects of the agreement, since there was a clause stating that the first fifty copies of the English edition of one thousand would be free of any royalty, quite apart from at least sixty copies which would be sent to the press for review purposes.[17]

More rewriting and revision followed, until finally he sent off the amended typescript in April 1908; and then, using his own copy, he set about drawing up an index.[18] However, this was never to appear.

The whereabouts of Strickland, who succeeded to the baronetcy on the death of his father in 1909 and became Sir Walter, were to remain shrouded in mystery. Ted was to contend that "so restless a spirit may be heard of at any odd moment in any odd corner of this all too little world", and in the weekly edition of that venerable newspaper *The Times*, which Ted received regularly, a paragraph appeared stating: "A York firm of solicitors, agents for Sir Walter Strickland, have published an announcement that Sir Walter has become a citizen of Czecho-Slovakia and desires to be known and designated as Walter William Strickland only."[19]

Ted knew that in his desperation to escape from the people and the society he abhorred, Walter Strickland was much drawn to other races, for "he has more than once mentioned his belief that the Orientals, especially the Chinese, are superior to the Occidentals and that they are destined to rule the world".[20]

He was also to write, after reading the paragraph in *The Times*: "That he should at last become a Slav seems to indicate consistency with long-nurtured ideals — wrong, undoubtedly, but irresistible. He, a derelict, deliberately adrift, was bound sooner or later to be beached in one of the backwaters of the world."[21]

This restless soul lived until the eve of the Second World War. Following his death on 7 August 1939, an Australian Associated Press dispatch from London reported:

> Sir Walter Strickland, who once lived in Australia, died today. He left the income from his estate, £16,000, to be used to promote Buddhism.
> He authorised that the boxes containing his manuscripts should be removed from Prague anywhere except in the British Empire.
> Sir Walter Strickland became a Czech citizen in 1923.
> He financed the revolt of Sun-Yat-Sen, which overthrew the Manchu dynasty and led to the formation of the Chinese republic.[22]

Such was the man who also financed the publication of *The Confessions of a Beachcomber*.

Chapter 17
Islands Ranger

In the closing chapter of *The Confessions*, Ted wrote: "Here I
came into my birthright — a heritage of nothing save the most
glorious of all possessions: freedom — freedom beyond the
dreams of most men".[1]

In the typescript he had included a number of detailed
excerpts from his diary, but in the final editing these were
deleted and only a general reference remained in the published
book:

> So tranquil, so uniform are our days, that but for the diary —
> the civilized substitute for the notched stick — count of them
> might be lost. And this extorts yet another confession. One
> year, Good Friday passed, and Easter-time had progressed to the
> joyful Monday, ere cognisance of the season came . . . A
> mechanical mis-entry in the diary threw all the orderly days of
> the week into a whirling jumble . . . Each day had been blue —
> radiantly blue — nothing more . . . But the steamer cuts a deep
> weekly notch. We jolted into it and became harmonised once
> more with the rigid calendar of the workaday world.[2]

According to Bertha, the diaries were:

> just the events of each day — Ted's own occupation, the coming
> and going of neighbours and above all the arrival of steamers or
> smaller boats. There is necessarily a good deal of almost repeti-
> tion in the entries, but for all that they have been most useful as
> works of reference . . . Ted was in the habit of copying into the
> diary, passages that he had read and appreciated.[3]

Her assessment was correct — as far as she went. As works of
reference the diaries proved invaluable to Ted many times, in
particular when he turned to the entries, as recorded in his
second book *My Tropic Isle*, for details of the arrival, the nesting,

the numbers, the habits, the comings and goings, and the final departures of the metallic starlings, whose yearly visits from regions near the equator almost coincided with those of the white nutmeg pigeons from Papua, Borneo, Java and the Malay Peninsula.[4]

Since the reprieve of the Australian bee-eaters and the white-rumped wood-swallows, the removal of the hives, and the declaration to make the island a sanctuary for all forms of bird life except the murderers and cannibals, Ted had single-handedly achieved remarkable results.

He carried out a Bird Census embracing "all permanent residents familiar to him, as well as casual visitors, and those which stay for a few hours or days, as the case may be, for rest and refreshment during migratory flights".[5] After excluding some which, with the aid of his telescope or field glasses he believed he had seen but not well enough to identify positively, he came up with a total of about 130, which was not far short of being a seventh of the known birds indigenous to Australia, and he was to name more and more as residents or visitors as time went on.

Under his patronage, there had been a striking influx to the sea-girt hermitage:

> Whereas in years gone by but two species of sea-birds nested on Purtaboi, now at least six avail themselves of that refuge. Birds that were driven to remote reefs and banks of the Barrier now make themselves at home for three months of the years within hailing distance. Tidings of goodwill towards the race generally are beginning to spread.[6]

When the space on Purtaboi became fully occupied, there was an overflow to the sand-spit of Dunk Island, and they became so tame in the presence of man that "they crowd me off a favourite promenade, mine by right of ten years' usage. They scold every boat, affront passing steamers, and comport themselves generally as if on the assurance of counsel's opinion on the legality of their trespass."[7]

The diaries recorded the comings and goings of many visitors, whether welcome or otherwise; and the letters written and received. Once, after the steamer had been held up for some weeks, 104 letters and parcels, including newspapers and periodicals, arrived together.[8] They also recorded something of the Banfields' own illnesses and those of friends and neighbours; while they had all the freedom they had ever desired, and shining blue delicious days at times seemingly without end, there was always that cloud, that threat brought about by their isolation, and it hovered however clear and perfect the days might be.

Among the arrivals and departures of people, and the

receiving and dispatch of letters, whether entered in the diaries or not, there had been contact with members of one of the bodies to which Ted belonged — The Royal Australian Ornithologists' Union. He was also involved with the Field Naturalists' Society of Victoria. Members were outraged at what was happening among the islands of Rockingham Bay. The white nutmeg pigeons, a species of the dove which was not only the symbol of peace and gentleness but also of the Holy Spirit, were being subject to massacre. The killers were somehow conspiring in the ultimate deed of desecration — the assassination of the Almighty.

Ted was asked if he would be prepared to undertake the office of Honorary Ranger in the area, as there was no provision for a paid ranger. He agreed, and with considerably more alacrity and enthusiasm than he revealed when he took steps to secure the office for himself by writing to Robert Philp in Brisbane.[9]

In this, the letter in which Ted informed Philp of the progress with his book, he wrote:

> May I ask your influence towards the adoption of a proposal that I will briefly explain:
>
> Since my coming here I have made the island a sanctuary for birds, and to develope [sic] the idea so that it may be really effective, find it essential that the restrictions against shooting must be extended over a prescribed area. On neighbouring islands birds (more especially the Torres Straits Pigeons) are shot quite regardless of the provisions of the Native Birds Protection Act.
>
> Torres Straits Pigeons are attractive birds to sportsmen, who do not, apparently, realise that they resort to the islands solely for breeding purposes and only during that particular period. Some who shoot are very thoughtless, some wantonly cruel; none who shoot Torres Straits Pigeons on these islands can avoid the destruction of nesting birds. It is obvious that if these birds are molested season after season while breeding, the species in no long time will be exterminated. Already I am given to understand that there are no Pigeons at the South Barnard Islands, "owing to the crews of vessels lying there having frightened them away". I quote from a casual remark in a recently received note. You have personal knowledge of the vast congregations that were wont to breed there a few years ago, and will remember the flights that took place that morning when the whistle of the "Ada Dent" gave the alarm as we steamed past from the wreck of the "Glaucus".
>
> What has happened at the South Barnards will happen elsewhere unless some secure retreats are provided, and I suggest for your favourable consideration the proposal that the named islands be proclaimed a perpetual reserve or sanctuary for all birds of whatever species:— Dunk Island, Mound, Kumboola (aboriginal name for an isle adjoining Dunk Island, but not named on the chart), Thorpe, Richards and the members of the Family Group — Wheeler, Coombe, Bowden, Smith and Hodson.
>
> Many years ago the late Walter Hill advised that the Brooke

Islands should be reserved for plants and birds, and possibly it might be wise to include the Group in order to safeguard the rights of birds at large.

Further, if I am gazetted Honorary Warden of the Isles so proclaimed sanctuaries for birds — though I do not seek the office nor desire it in any way — I will do my best to see that the provisions of the Act are respected.

So far I have found visitors most amenable to the restrictions I have ordained with regard to Dunk Island; and I feel sure that if my suggestions are enforced the birds will be permitted to breed in peace, otherwise certain species may become in a few years extinct in these parts.

Some time ago I casually suggested this course to a visitor who brought some departmental influence to bear through the medium of the Field Naturalists' Society of Victoria; but nothing was done.

If you think the proposal practical and well of it, I would very much appreciate your counsel in respect of the means by which it might be promptly adopted officially. Would it be wise to write to the Premier direct: I feel that he would be inclined to consider the subject the more seriously if you presented the arguments contained herein in its favor.

Walter Hill, a pioneer naturalist, director of Botanic Gardens, Brisbane, and selector of reserves, had been the official botanist in the Elphinstone Dalrymple expedition.

To his letter, Ted attached a list of the islands with both English and Aboriginal titles. Philp responded without delay and passed on Ted's proposal with a strong recommendation that it should be implemented, adding a personal comment: "I have known Mr Banfield for a great number of years and can strongly recommend him for the Hon. position he now seeks."[10]

The decision came under the jurisdiction of the Department of Agriculture and Stock, and the under secretary wrote to Ted on 2 February 1905: "The Department proposes to accept your kind offer to act as Honorary Ranger of these islands under the Native Birds Protection Act and I shall therefore be glad to be advised of your full name in order that the appointment may be gazetted."[11]

First, though, the named islands had to be proclaimed a Reserve for the Protection and Preservation of Native Birds, and this was done by the lieutenant-governor on 10 May 1905. Edmund James Banfield was gazetted to be an Honorary Ranger for the area on 24 June. Copies of the government gazettes were posted to Dunk Island, together with twenty-five calico notices: "The Shooting of Birds on this Island is Totally Prohibited". At the same time the under secretary informed the editors of "*Morning Post, Argus* and *Trinity Times*, Cairns; *Bulletin, Evening Star* and *Federal*, Townsville; *Sentinel*, Geraldton; *Northern Planter* and *Herbert River Express*, Ingham; and *North Queensland Register*, Charters Towers".[12]

In his acknowledgment, Ted wrote: "I will take advantage

of the first opportunity to post the notices up in prominent places on the several islands, and should any flagrant disregard thereof come to my knowledge will report at once to you."[13]

Although he made light of this appointment in *The Confessions*, and entered only a minor record of it in his diary, this was one of the major events in the life of Edmund James Banfield. No longer did he sail forth just to patrol the beaches for what the winds and the tides may have spread out for his inspection. Early in *The Confessions* he had written:

> Not to many men is permitted the privilege of choosing for his day's excusion from among so many beautiful spots, certain in the knowledge that to whichsoever he may elect to flutter his handkerchief is reserved for his delight; certain that the sands will be free from the traces of any other human being; certain that no sound save those of nature will break in upon his musings and meditations.[14]

Such musings and meditations were triggered by what he stumbled upon:

> A jolly red buoy, weary of the formality of bowing to the swell, broke loose from a sandbank's apron-strings, bounced off in the ecstacies of liberty, romped in the surf, rolled on the beach, worked a cosy bed in the soft warm sand, and has slumbered ever since to the soothing hum of the wind, indifferent to the perplexities of mariners and the fate of ships.[15]

Now, as he went about "policing the uproarious beaches", he was on the alert for alien footprints, discarded cartridges, the remains of slaughtered birds, or the sounds of gunshots. He had a mission against an almost invisible enemy — a role that well befitted someone whose mother claimed descent from the valiant Hereward the Wake.[16]

Essie McDonough was a member of the household again. She came from Townsville just for a change but stayed on.[17] She and Bertha watched as Ted made a little ceremony of putting up the first calico notices, nailing one to the trunk of a coconut palm near the thatched boatshed and erecting another on a signpost near the grass hut on the sand-spit — after moving some of the terns, who wheeled overhead, their screams a "blending of a cat's mieow with the squeak of a rusty key".[18] He could not help but recall how his father and the Banfields of Ararat owed so much to calico notices; when Jabez returned to his trade as a printer on the gold fields, he obtained some of his most lucrative contracts from a pioneer brewer for posters to advertise his beer.

Over the next few weeks, Ted posted identical notices on Purtaboi, on Timana and on Bedarra; and, before the wet season, on more distant parts of the domain which he roamed now both as Beachcomber and as Honorary Ranger. For the former there was no formal insignia of office, only his every-

NOTICE.

"The Native Birds Protection Act Amendment Act of 1884."

The Shooting of Birds on this Island is Totally Prohibited.

By Order,

D. F. DENHAM,

Secretary for Agriculture.

Department of Agriculture and Stock,
1st July, 1905.

BY AUTHORITY, G. A. VAUGHAN, GOVERNMENT PRINTER, WILLIAM STREET, BRISBANE.

day attire — rolled-up dungaree trousers, short-sleeved collar-less singlet, wide-brimmed hat and suntan, which, when on his own, was all he wore. For the latter, he had official documents, should they be needed, and was later issued with a metal badge to pin to his chest. While the occasions when this needed to be shown or jabbed with an authoritative forefinger were few, when he did so he made sure that his powers, such as they were, were well understood — but the most he could do was not all that much. As, for instance, on a day which he described

Twenty-five of these notices were posted to E.J. Banfield when he was gazetted as Honorary Ranger. An original notice in mint condition was found in the Queensland State Archives.
(Courtesy of Queensland Premier's Department.)

as "Deliciously calm and fragrant; brilliant, beautiful, fresh", he had to hasten over to Kumboola which, like most of Dunk's satellites, was a natural aviary, to warn off two men who were shooting nutmeg pigeons and other birds.[19] These and other intruders and desecrators were described or named in Ted's reports to the under secretary of the Department of Agriculture and Stock, but beyond being filed no other action was taken.

This then was the state of the Beachcomber's domain when Ted's first book started to come off the presses in London, "respectfully dedicated by one who owes to him much of his love for Tropical Queensland" to the Honourable Robert Philp, MLA, whose recommendation Ted considered to have been responsible for turning the self-declared sanctuary into an official reserve.

Chapter 18

No Hat Big Enough

On the September day in 1908 when *The Confessions of a Beachcomber: Scenes and Incidents in the Career of an Unprofessional Beachcomber in Tropical Queensland* was published in London,[1] the author E.J. Banfield went about life as usual on his island home on the other side of the world. It was a routine sort of a morning, much of it spent building a new fowl-house. In the afternoon his exploration of the high plateau brought a discovery. He had glimpsed small silent swiftlets on the wing without being able to establish where they nested. On this day, in the company of Tom, he found a small colony; but according to his Aboriginal friend, this was not their main hideaway.

He had two months yet to wait before locating this colony "close to the water's edge, on the weather side, where the birds had frequently been seen darting among blocks of granite almost obscured by jungle". Here "upon the exploration of a confined cave the excited flutterings of invisible birds betrayed a hitherto well-kept secret".[2]

As for his first copy of *The Confessions*, he had only a month to wait before it was revealed to him — although he was still to remain in total ignorance of how the work of over four years had been received. That night he had a spanking new "island" to explore and beachcomb, and he was ecstatic as he browsed through the book as he sat within the cone of light thrown by the kerosene lamp. All the strips of tropics, all inlets and coves contained herein were familiar to him, but now that they appeared in fresh print they took on that magic quality with which a luminous day could clothe them.

It was a thick volume, the cover black with resplendent gold lettering. The fifty-one illustrations all seemed fitting. Also the map which T.P. Adlam had revised, for wasn't it Robert Louis Stevenson who had said that "some island maps are just made to be filled in with an adventure story"?[3]

Having completed his preliminary survey of the volume, Ted was able to report to Bertha, who had to wait her turn to examine it, that it was an absolutely splendid example of the combined skills and arts of printer, blockmaker and bookbinder, to which she hastened to add: "*And* writer".

That he should have decided to precede his book with his favourite Thoreau quotation seemed entirely appropriate, since so many of those who featured in the scenes and incidents did not keep pace with their companions, perhaps because they all heard different drummers. These certainly included Walter Strickland, in whatever remote part of the world he might be, without whose generosity the volume would not have seen the light of that memorable Dunk Island day.

Sixteen more days were to pass before the steamer whistled and Ted rowed out to collect mail which contained a bunch of London reviews. In the case of *The Times*, the ultimate newspaper in Ted's estimation, the entire edition had been forwarded. It contained an historic story about aerial navigation:

Mr Wilbur Wright, having thoroughly overhauled his motor and provided it with a fresh magneto, made a flight this morning of 39 min. 18 3-5 sec. at a height of between 30ft and 40ft, thus more than doubling his performance of September 5. He was obliged to stop for want of petrol, but he covered the 40 kilometres and intends immediately to attempt to "break the record for distance".[4]

When Ted turned to the *Literary Supplement* it was as if Big Ben had chimed in his honour. Here was a lengthy review stating that while it was certain that beachcombers as law-abiding and cultured as Mr Banfield must be few and far between in Oceania, this was the work of a highly-cultured philosopher with no mean talent for word-painting, and that those who enjoy "strange and little-known happenings in remote corners of the earth will find here some very scholarly and pleasing specimens".

Other reviews were not as lofty but were equally, or even more, favourable. *The Daily Chronicle* stated: "This is a wholly exceptional book. It is a book which has been lived, and there are not over many books like that." On the strength of all this, Ted declared: "There is no hat in the Island big enough for me", and by this time he had a row of pegs and a hatstand hung with a wide selection of broad brims under which he could shelter from the sun. More and even better reviews followed in later mails, so much so that he was to declare swooningly that all the praise was becoming monotonous![5]

The Australian reviews were in the same laudatory strain as those from overseas.[6] Bertha was overjoyed for Ted and immensely proud; this confirmed him as a real writer, although she still believed that there were frequent occasions when his pen was out of control, like the luxuriant summer growth in the gardens when creepers, weeds and other swiftly-proliferating species all but smothered the blooms.

Ted modestly said that he might try his hand again, and he was well aware of the enormous amount of material that was accumulating now that he was turning out "Rural Homilies" for *The Bulletin* and *The Register* at a higher rate. While *The Times* review had been so generous and encouraging, it had at the same time dealt out a challenge to him when remarking that throughout his confessions he "carefully keeps his own personality in the background, and only by inferences aside and rare half-revelations may one gather what manner of man he is". It was suggested that more details of his daily life would have been welcome and that "a little less of impersonality, a few words on the homestead and the life there, would not be construed as egotism."[7]

Much the same complaint had been levelled at Thoreau who wrote: "I should not obtrude my affairs so much on the notice of my readers if very particular inquiries had not been made by my townsmen concerning my mode of life."[8]

Six months later, under the spell of lovely days of limpid serenity when the tea-trees were in bloom and the air syrupy with perfume, especially the scent of wattles, Ted wrote:

> since my life — and in the use of the possessive pronoun here and elsewhere, let it signify also the life of my life-partner — is beyond the range of ordinary experience, since it is immune from the ferments which seethe and muddle the lives of many, I am assured that a familiar record will not be deemed egotistical, I am scolded because I did not confess with greater zeal, I am bidden to my pen again.[9]

In *The Confessions* he had written:

> Many a time, home-returning at night — when the black contours of the island loomed up in the distance against the pure tropic sky tremulous with myriads of unsullied stars — has its tepid fragrance drifted across the water as a salutation and a greeting. It has long been a fancy of mine that the island has a distinctive odour, soft and pliant, rich and vigorous.

He also wrote: "English fields and hedges cannot be forgotten when one of our trees diffuses the scent of meadow-sweet, and one of the orchids that of hawthorn. 'Scent and silence' is the phrase which expresses the individuality of our island, and better 'scented silence' than all the noisy odours of the town."[10]

T. Fisher Unwin was keen to have a second book, so Ted began to make notes and sort out the most suitable articles, after both Dodd Clarke and David Green waived all claims. It was something to occupy him, as he missed Bertha intensely when she took a holiday break in Charters Towers after suffering a reaction to the tension and excitement of the launching of *The Confessions* into the world. The fact was that even though she was eminently balanced, practical and sanguine — and ever uncomplaining — there were times when the island life got her down, and she suffered attacks of nerves with distressing giddy turns. Although she kept it from Ted, she was to confess that the mosquitoes, for instance, "drove her mad".[11]

With so much already written and requiring only editing, Ted made swift progress with "Scented Silences", and had it in draft form by the time Bertha returned to Dunk, looking bright and happy and, in Ted's fond eyes, ten years younger. However, the break had done nothing to stave off the continuing deterioration of her hearing. Because Ted spoke up and shaped his words so that she could to an extent lip-read, she could understand him without the help of the cardboard tube; but with others, it had become essential to use it if she was to hear them — especially with Essie, whose quick quips in any event were often difficult to catch even by people possessing sharp hearing.

On her way back from Charters Towns Bertha stayed in Townsville for a few days, and on this visit she made a call which she had been thinking about for some time. At a medical agency selling appliances, she selected a somewhat sinister-looking hearing device which consisted of an earpiece which the user plugged in, a long rubber hose covered with black cloth and a shiny black trumpet at the end.

When first trying it out, Bertha fitted the earpiece into her ear and held out the trumpet to the shop assistant, one who was apparently as yet unacquainted with the diplomatic aspect of her job. Confronted with the gaping trumpet, the lady could think of nothing better to say than: "Can you hear me?"

Bertha, as people such as Walter Strickland well knew, could be terse or even tart when the occasion arose; and now she replied: "Of course I can hear you!"[12]

She heard so well that she purchased the device and took it home to the island with her. Realizing that the sight of it might upset Ted, she delayed showing it to him. He first saw it when he returned to the bungalow from the beach and found her extending the black trumpet towards the glowing red trumpet of a bloom on a hibiscus bush. It looked as if she was holding a dull-skinned black snake with a glossy frilled head, until, from the hibiscus bush, Ted heard the quaint, quick, whispering notes of a tame sunbird and realized that Bertha was listening to its song with the aid of a new hearing device.

Caught in the act of using it, she said to Ted, "I'm afraid we have an addition to the family — meet 'Black Maria'."[13]

The nickname stuck, and Black Maria became very busy being thrust this way and that when favourite friends visited and the talk flowed. For everyday use in the kitchen and about the house, she still used one of her cardboard tubes.

No doubt the state of her hearing had contributed to her recent malaise. Yet she stoically refused to allow her deafness to get her down, even though it did rob her of much, sealing her off within herself, increasing her isolation in the midst of isolation. Ted had developed a keen ear for the music of the island — the orchestrations of birds, insects and rummaging animals; breezes and winds on the sand, the leaves and vines. For Bertha to be denied all this, especially after having been of all things a music teacher, was a great hardship. She felt her deafness most acutely when with animals and children, all of whom she loved.[14] She was unable to hear the sounds made by animals and so gauge their feelings and reactions, nor could she hear the voices of children, who were frightened not only by being in the presence of someone who could not hear, but also by the sight of Black Maria.

Ted would come and go throughout the day, and unless he told her that he was going for a walk or a sail it was just as likely that he was in the office writing. It would seem that the deaf, unlike the blind, do not develop to the same degree a compensatory sense of perception. On one occasion she was quite certain that he was resting within the confines of the bungalow, because he was suffering from another outbreak of the nervous rash on his left eyebrow, creating a severe swelling and thus restricting the vision in his one sound eye.[15] This time the outbreak was so bad that he had been forced to abandon all writing and reading in connection with "Scented Silences" since he just could not see. When Bertha went looking for him, he was nowhere in the house.

Nor was there any sign of him in the kitchen, the workshop, the outhouses, the garden. He had wandered off. He could have stumbled. He might be lying injured somewhere in the undergrowth. As her fears mounted and multiplied, she saw him coming back from the forest, walking slowly yet surely, using a stick to locate a post, a tree trunk, also apparently finding his way by sound, as he kept pausing to listen before continuing again. In his second book Ted wrote:

> Often have I found myself as I strolled gloating over the exquisite absence of sound — enjoying in full mental relish the quaint and refined sensation. Yet when I have stopped and listened determinedly, viciously analyzing my sensations, have I become aware of a hubbub of frail and interblended sounds. That which I had thought to be distilled silence was microphonic Babel — an intimate commingling of analogous noises varying in quality and intensity.

Of silence, Thoreau had written: "Who has not hearkened to Her infinite din?"[16]

Ted had signposts everywhere to guide him — the fall of a blue quandong to the soft floor of the jungle, the bursting of a seed-pod, the patter of pink fruit from a fig tree, a faint familiar squeak where interlocking branches overhead fretted each other.

Besides sounds, there were other invisible signposts — "The pot herbs of the Gods", as Thoreau had described them. Scents. Those of the "native, untended, unpampered" plants and trees. And orchids — one with the subtle essence of almonds and honey, another with a perfume reminiscent of the violet. A putrescent fungus. The intangible but delicious scent of the wattle. And, nearer home, from the trees he himself had planted, the rich spicy odours of mangoes and the sweetness of lemons and oranges. All signposts of a kind to him.[17]

Bertha was so relieved that she proceeded to give Ted a good motherly scolding. Despite the persistent pain of his eye, he had to laugh. He had become fed up being inside the house and had gone for a stroll, and he had known all along precisely where he was. So she wasn't to worry. After all, between them they could muster a reasonably good pair of eyes and ears. And he must have been feeling that they could cope with the island life as well as ever since their Townsville house, which had been rented intermittently and had caused them some expense when white ants were discovered in it, was finally sold later that year in December 1910.[18]

T. Fisher Unwin had reservations about Ted's title, so "Scented Silences" became "My Tropic Isle", which the publisher felt was much more in keeping with the "Beachcomber" strain which Ted was continuing. Dedicated to "MY WIFE", the final typescript with photographs was forwarded to London in June 1910. In his covering letter, Ted wrote:

> May I say without appearing to brag that I fancy the book will do well out here, for I continue to receive letters of congratulation and promising a favourable reception to anything further from my pen. Several men of science have written in terms of approval. Indeed I myself have had intimations of a most hearty welcome from the literary men of Sydney if ever I visit that city. I mention these facts not because of the vanity they inspire but to induce you to have faith in the success of "My Tropic Isle".[19]

It could well have been the lure of the literary red carpet that persuaded Ted it was time he and Bertha made a trip south. In doing so Ted would be able to receive congratulations and adulations in person — and at the same time pave the way for his second major work.

They had been talking about visiting members of his family for some time. Besides, 1911 was a most important year; it marked the silver anniversary of their wedding and "My Tropic Isle" was due to be published shortly in London, so they decided to celebrate both events with a three months' holiday and left early in March.

Dodd Clarke, to whom Ted used to pass *The Times Literary Supplement* from London, presented his travelling friend with two volumes of Gibbon's *Decline and Fall of the Roman Empire* to help him to occupy "a week or more at sea". Bertha remained very nervous about the sea, and on this occasion she had another good reason to feel as she did. They left Townsville just in time to miss the cyclone in which the passenger steamer *Yongala* was lost with 120 people not far from Cleveland Bay.

In Sydney, where the windows of the big shops reflected the cavalcade of horse-drawn vehicles — buggies, wagonettes, sulkies, buckboards and runabouts, and the early English and American horseless carriages, such as Talbots, Silent Knights, Studebakers, Buicks, Singers — Ted saw *The Confessions* on sale in the main bookshops and made the acquaintances of at least two booksellers with whom he was to have dealings, Angus and Robertson and Dymocks.

In Melbourne, he and Bertha stayed with his sister Eva Strangward and her husband at St Kilda; at Wangaratta, near Albury, with younger brother Wally, manager of the local branch of the London Chartered Bank; and in Ararat with Harry, who was delighted with *The Confessions*, although his opening remark could have been taken two ways: "What a meal Dad would have made of it!"

Ted wasn't too sure whether Harry meant that Jabez would have been highly critical, since he still laboured under the impression that he had been a failure in his father's eyes. But Harry meant that their father would have been so proud that, like the articles from England, he would have used Ted's book as the basis for one of his recitals — and so Ted had grounds to feel that he had justified his withdrawal to the seclusion of his tropic isle.

Under the overall title "Southern Scenes Revisited", Ted wrote a series of articles about aspects of his trip for *The North Queensland Register*. They revealed a preoccupation with the fruit trade as he made inquiries about the marketing of tropical fruits in the south. His most striking article was entitled "The Age of Hurry", a subject about which Thoreau had written: "Why should we live with such hurry and waste of life? We are determined to be starved before we are hungry. Men say that a stitch in time saves nine, and they take a thousand stitches today to save nine to-morrow."[21]

Ted began this article by confessing:

until a few weeks ago I had never seen any form of self-propelled vehicle other than a sedate road-roller, with a cautious precedent man warning all on the highway to withdraw from the track of the Juggernaut . . . it has occurred to me that the sensations of one who has been self-banished from the street for very many years, and who suddenly finds himself in the heart of a busy city teeming with all manner of resource for the rapid transport of people and merchandise, must at least be novel.[22]

He admitted that he had heard all sorts of bad things about motor-cars, and had read that the great Melba had been inadvertently involved in a shocking experience in Paris when her chauffeur-driven limousine had knocked down and killed a man; that the pure country air of green England was being defiled by pestilential fumes; and that there was a new form of mental illness called "speedomania" which was causing havoc and disaster all around the world.

Despite all this, Ted arrived at a surprising conclusion about the advantages of motor-cars:

No man who is in any way an admirer of animals can say that a motor-car, however grand and up-to-date, has an effect as imposing as a carriage drawn by a pair of well-matched, up-standing, perfectly schooled horses; but when he reflects that the carriage horse is the aristocrat of the species and that in descending scale man exercises most arbitrary and often cruel authority over horse flesh, he will conclude that any condition which reprieves horses from the penalty of hard labor for life must necessarily be excellent.[23]

He had much to say in favour of the two great cities of the south. From Sydney, where he found "Everywhere flowers, hawked from the gutters and pavement, overflowing from the shops", he also wrote:

What a transformation! . . . the changes in respect of the frontages to the sea are not on the side of picturesque . . . But, after all, it is quite impossible to spoil the beauty of such a favoured scene, just as the extremities, yes, the absurdities, of fashion are powerless against the loveliness of woman. Man may impose acre after acre of red-roof, high pitched, squat domed and pinnacled where there was a universal sweep of grey-green vegetation, and yet not detract from the singular fascination of Sydney Harbour. Its excellencies are gloated over all the more enthusiastically after long years of absence, though in many respects individual scenes may have changed beyond recognition. The yachts nowadays are of more graceful form, clean cut, and as lithe as sharks; they seem to bear ampler and whiter wings and to behave more daintily than in the past. The motor boats are swift and noiseless; the ferry steamers are larger, more comfortably and completely fitted . . . the coastal steamers are on marvellously changed lines in every respect; and the great ocean boats almost diminish the effect of the huge buildings which stand back from the water.

The traffic that roared in "the pent-in streets" was "almost London-like in volume". He found very few shabbily or poorly dressed men, not the least appearance of poverty. The general tone of the male attire was most sober.

But on the other hand, the feminine portion of the community, which seems to be superbly ascendant in the streets between the hours of 11 a.m. and 3 p.m., blossoms, or rather bursts out in the bravest, boldest, and certainly the most successful of efforts to command notice . . . There are such endless droves — pardon the word — of fair girls in Sydney, and their clothes and hats are so extraordinarily becoming that the admiring but disinterested stranger must needs stand aside and let them pass, glad of the spectacle of such self-evident enjoyment of the glances of approval of sober-coated men. Just as the conglomeration of ruddy-roofed houses has failed signally to affect disastrously the charming precincts of Mossman's Bay, so no vagary of fashion is capable of smudging the prettiness of the typical Sydney girl. She may, on the whim of the moment, select a hat the size and shape of a bulged band-box, blue as the water of Middle Harbour, as coarse in texture as a coal-basket, and as ribbonless, and yet carry it off, partly on swinging shoulders, be it said, with triumphant success.[24]

Sydney had its fair women and harbour, Melbourne its street gardens and a noble avenue — St Kilda Road — extending four miles from Prince's Bridge:

Down the middle of the almost dustless thoroughfare is a double line for cable trams on each side of which is ample space for horse-drawn vehicles, from which wide ways for motors are separated by garden plots and rows of seemly trees. Thousands of fine houses front the busy scene, alike and unalike in variety of style and decoration. Terra cotta ornaments, griffins, cherubins, kangaroos, "shrill-clarion" cocks vaunting from peaked roofs and gable ends and chimney pots, out-scold neat, low-walled, red-roofed bungalows, and jeer at pompous, purse-proud mansions. There are houses in most of the disorderly styles of architecture, displaying individuality and colour from pill drab to pink, and white lolly-pop and mustard yellow, and mint-sauce green, semi-detached villas and cosy cottages behind gleaming flower-embroidered lawns, and frowning terraces with pocket handkerchief plots.

By day the famous thoroughfare was the scene of a continuous procession of vehicles. Then at night:

when all the arcs are blazing from one end to the other, and motor cars flash past with lamps of search-light power, and trams chase each other, and meet, and their head lamps, green, white and yellow, proclaim whither, away and whence, all in desperate impatience, and crowds swing off and on, and lights from the teeming bridge to the St Kilda Esplanade are sizzling in rivalry with the passionless planets, the scene is one to remember for the whole length of the illumination is stripped and edged with flowering plants and sombre-leafed trees.[25]

After returning to Sydney by train, Ted and Bertha boarded the *Cooma* and steamed north with a shipload of tourists escaping from the winter chill and mist. They disembarked at Townsville and transferred to the *Mourilyan* which dropped them off at Dunk Island on the way to Cairns.[26]

It had been a long three months for Essie and the friend Ted and Bertha had left in charge. The gardens were overgrown, but that was only to be expected — to Bertha it was as if Ted's long words had taken advantage of his absence and trooped out of his office and turned themselves into weeds and creepers. There was so much to be done to get everything straight again that Ted began to fret at being kept from the programme of reading that had become such an essential part of his life on the island. It had been wonderful seeing so many members of the family again, and meeting new grand-nieces and grand-nephews, but they were more than happy to be home; they had a greater sense of belonging here and felt that they would never wish to leave again.

On the actual day of their silver wedding anniversary, Ted was to declare in his diary: "our lives together have been extremely happy and contentful. How full of self-sacrifice Bertha has been . . . how industrious . . . how loyal to me . . ."[27]

Advance copies of *My Tropic Isle* arrived a few weeks later, another handsome black volume, this time with ivory embossing showing the head of a native. But soon after Ted had taken this "island" in his two hands to "explore", he was dismayed to find a number of blunders, one of which has already been referred to — the date they had taken up residence in the new bungalow. However, when the reviews began to arrive, Ted was able to see such so-called blunders for what they really were — no more than minor blemishes.

Again he seemed to have achieved the impossible. From this distant corner of the globe he received another favourable review in *The Times*. In the *Literary Supplement* the reviewer said that Mr Banfield has

> realized the dream of every boy who has read Ballantyne or Defoe, and, almost discarding the resources of civilization, has lived as a primitive man on the products of his own skill or on the random flotsam of the beach. He has been soaked by the salt sea, drenched with tropical rains, infiltrated by the purifying keenness of tropical light, invigorated by the sharp chemical odours of the uncovered reef, and soothed by the sweet scents of the tropical plants.

There followed a reservation, one with which Bertha found she had to agree: while the language was at times an echo of that of R.L. Stevenson, on occasions it descended to a strange journalese, but "none the less, Mr Banfield has reproduced many charming impressions of his enchanted island".[28]

The comparison with R.L. Stevenson appeared in a review in *Nature*: Ted's article on "Silences" was worthy of that master. And when the reviewer in the Sydney paper *The Daily Telegraph* compared him to Thoreau, Ted started sorting among his sun-hats again for the biggest:

Mr Banfield strikes us as being really as fond of solitude as Thoreau pretended to be. And he has one qualification which Thoreau lacked most emphatically, namely, a gentle and un-aggressive humor, which colors and brightens all the records of his observations upon the aboriginals of the Queensland coast, and the plants, birds, beasts, reptiles, and fishes of his tropic isle.[29]

A year later, Ted received a letter from Fisher Unwin saying: "The reviews still seem to come in very pleasantly", although one stingingly adverse notice had appeared in *The New Age*. Fisher Unwin had dismissed it: the paper was an "ill-conditioned one" and he set no store by it, particularly as the novelist Arnold Bennett wrote for it.[30]

One of the chapters in the new book, "The Death Bone" was the story described by Ted as "fact cemented with fiction". In this and other pieces, Fisher Unwin believed he detected a wider talent and wrote: "perhaps you may try another form of work, possibly fiction, why not?"[31]

While Fisher Unwin was to persist with this suggestion, in the opinion of probably Ted's greatest champion, George Barrymore, the Beachcomber's finest writing was going in another direction. Barrymore, who became editor of one of Ted's literary outlets, *The Northern Miner* in Charters Towers, believed that Ted was a poet and that "the quality of his prose shows this". In the chapter "His Majesty the Sun", for instance:

It being far more blissful to lounge in the sea than on the veranda, I sat down, steeped chin deep in crystal clearness, warmth, and silence, passively surrendering myself to a cheap yet precious sensation. Around me were revealed infinitely fragile manifestations of life, scarcely less limpid than the sea, sparkling, darting, twisting — strong and vigorous of purpose. Tremulous filaments of silver flashed and were gone. No space but was thickly peopled with what ordinarily passes as the invisible, but which now, plainly to behold, basked and revelled in the blaze — products of the sun. Among the grains of sand and flakes of mica furtive bubblings, burrowings and upheavals betrayed a benighted folk to whom the water was as a firmament into which they might not venture to ascend.[32]

Later in this same chapter, part of a similar paragraph can be set out in a different form, to become:

Shadows of fish
exquisitely framed
flit and dance.
I see naught but shadows,
dim and thin,
for I doze and dream again;
and so fantastic time,
whose footfalls
are beads and bubbles,
passes,
and grosser affairs
beckon me
out of the sunlit sea.[33]

Chapter 19
The Pleasures of Authorship

Concerning the financial side of his books, Ted did not go into too much detail with Bertha.

As she was to tell Alec Chisholm, the advance arranged for *The Confessions of a Beachcomber* by Sir Walter Strickland was the first item paid out of the returns from the sales:

> Beyond that and Fisher Unwin's share of the profits, there was very little indeed — I *think* some twenty odd pounds [$40]. I am not absolutely sure of the amount but believe that was it. As to the other two books the same holds good concerning them — there was very little profit to anyone beyond the publisher. Ah! well, it never worried him — the name he made was worth a lot more than money.[1]

Actually, at one stage it *did* worry Ted — and very much — because it smacked of what to him was an injustice. Regarding *The Confessions*, he was delighted to receive royalty statements set out in an immaculate copperplate hand which reminded him of those family treasures still held at Ararat — the letters written by his father from Australia to his children in Liverpool. They confirmed that the advance of £150 was steadily being paid back to Sir Walter's solicitors, and the discharge of his indebtedness was by far his primary concern.[2]

After receiving Ted's second manuscript in London, Fisher Unwin wrote to say that as it stood it would make a rather short volume. His reader suggested that any additional material should be more chapters on marine natural history which Ted did so well. This presented no problem as Ted had stacks of such material already written, mainly in the form of "Rural Homilies". But, when the publisher came to the question of terms, the author's hackles twitched:

it is a very great pleasure to say on this occasion we shall be very
happy to take up the book at our own expense and as our own
venture. If you desire it issued as it stands, we should have to ask
for a very considerable number of copies free of royalty, but if
you are prepared to add another twenty or twenty-five
thousand words on the lines indicated, so as to make the book
up to about eighty thousand words, we shall be happy to pay
you a rising royalty, commencing after the sale of the first two
hundred copies.

Fisher Unwin enclosed a draft agreement and ended his letter
by saying: "You will of course realize that in view of the fact
that on this occasion you will be making no contribution
towards the costs of production, the royalties must be propor-
tionately modified."[3]

This to Ted was being downright stingy. Among the additional chapters he had immediately envisaged was one on
marine novelties including a giant anemone which offered im-
munity to its deadly stings and so a sanctuary to one particular
little fish which, when threatened, shrank away out of sight
within the folds of the anemone's many tentacles. When
reading Fisher Unwin's terms, Ted felt that the anemone was
Dunk Island and that he was that little fish, so dependent upon
its host "as to be quite helpless apart from it".[4]

However, he braced himself and accepted the terms, and had
no further trouble with his hackles until the royalties from *My
Tropic Isle* began to appear, along with those for *The Confessions*,
on his periodic statements.

Early in November 1912, Ted received Fisher Unwin's letter
of 24 September in which the publisher wrote:

I have great pleasure in sending you the enclosed statement of
account, you will understand it and I expect will recognize that,
in accordance with instructions, we have paid to Mr Turner the
sum of £14.3s.11d. [$28.90]. So that the original payment has
now been returned and so that is satisfactory. I hope the
accounts on the whole are sufficiently promising to encourage
you to go forward with your work.[5]

Ted found little encouragement. The royalties from his second
book had been used to make that final payment to Mr Turner,
one of the principals of the law firm now dealing with this part
of Sir Walter Strickland's affairs.

Fisher Unwin went on to write that he had been in touch
with Mr Critchell, who acted as an agent for Ted and was shortly to leave on another visit to Australia; he had asked Critchell
to urge Ted to try his hand at writing a novel. Ted was only
moved to try his hand at what many disgruntled authors had
done before him, and are still doing, and no doubt will continue
to do. He complained that he was being unfairly treated. He
wrote that it "proves that one more literary labourer is not
worth his hire for it does not even reimburse the costs of photos

24/35

1, ADELPHI TERRACE,

LONDON, W.C., Sept 1911

E J Banfield Esq

In account with **Mr. T. FISHER UNWIN,**

Publisher.

Statement of Sales of Confessions of a Beachcomber

for Twelve *months ending* March 31st 1911

STOCK ACCOUNT.

1910			1911			
April 1	On hand		57	March 31	On hand	2037
	Printed		6	1	Free Copies	19
Dec 31	Since Printed	3000		1	Sales	1017
			3063			3063

By Royalty:

15% on 4 @ 15/-   15 -
10% on 30.8 @ 5/-   44
10% on 983 realised 9240   9 45

                                10 13 5

1911
July 18 To Goods as per invoice   2 13 3
Aug 21 "   "   17 9   3 11 -

Balance due to Mess E J Turner & Son £ 7 2 5

Royalty statement for *The Confessions of a Beachcomber* for twelve months ending 31 March 1911.
(Courtesy of Ernest Benn Limited, London.)

and typing". He said that he would be pleased to see his good
friend Critchell but that "he won't be able to convince me any
further work is not a waste of time" and that "My books have
involved a large amount of study and application" and finally
that "So far I am on the debit side very considerably. My means
are small, I cannot indulge myself in the luxury of writing".[6]
Besides, at sixty he felt too old to attempt a new form.

Fisher Unwin replied on 31 December.

> Let me acknowledge your letter of 13th November. I sincerely
> wish it was a more hopeful one. I think we ought to recognize
> that your first book was, so to speak, the foundation work and
> therefore could not be expected to be so remunerative. We,
> ourselves, had some doubt about it, but I am thankful to say that
> all the sum you invested in it has been paid back and now profits
> will come to hand.

This was galling enough, but worse was to come. "With regard
to your second book, it did not, in a sense cost you anything
and by this time you have received at least £30 [$60] for it."[7]

Enclosed was a further statement for *My Tropic Isle* to 30
December 1912 with a draft of £5.1s.9d. ($10.17) to add to the
£25.14s.1d. ($51.40) forwarded with the preceding statement.

By February 1913, when Ted replied to Fisher Unwin's letter
of New Year's Eve, he had calmed down. He was caught in that
dilemma common to authors who primarily wish to see their
work in print: "I quite see that my first book was in a sense a
preparatory work". Having said this, he could not restrain
himself from repeating that he was still out of pocket from his
two books. But with that off his chest, the irrepressible side of
his nature asserted itself. He admitted that "having once tasted
the pleasures of authorship" it was impossible to suppress the
urge to write, and then went on to outline the third book that
he had in mind, a further continuation of the Beachcomber
theme.[8]

On 11 April 1913, Fisher Unwin wrote expressing interest in
the proposed third book and stating that they were very sorry
that Ted was still dissatisfied with the "pecuniary results" of the
first two:

> We fear that it is the general experience of authors to be
> disheartened because their progress to public favour is not
> quicker. But it must always take time for a new name to become
> widely known, unless it is especially favoured by fortune. And
> good quiet work like yours which has to rest upon its own
> merits, has little chance of creating immediate sensation.[9]

By the time he received this letter, Critchell had arrived and
Ted had been to Townsville to spend some time with him; so
while the first two books may not have created what might
have been termed sensations, Critchell had been able to assure
him that in those circles where Ted would best wish to be
admired his work was regarded as unique.

As for T. Fisher Unwin, an important man in publishing circles, an alpine climber and traveller, an executive member of the Liberal movement, Critchell suggested that the publisher seemed, in Ted's eyes, to be like his policeman.

"What policeman?" Ted demanded, mystified.

"Your heron policeman."

Ted laughed, realizing that Critchell was referring to what he had written in *My Tropic Isle* about the common grey sand crab who has

> a special enemy in the bird policeman which patrols the beach. Vigilant and obnoxiously interfering, the policeman has a long and curiously curved beak, designed for probing into the affairs of crabs, and unless the "hatter" has hastily stopped the mouth of his shaft with a bundle of loose sand — which to the prying bird — signifies "Out! Please return after lunch!" — it will be disposed of with scant ceremony and no grace for the manners of the policeman are shocking.[10]

Ted had expected that Critchell would want to go butterfly-hunting and had reconnoitred several glades where flotillas of the iridescent blue Ulysses and green and gold Cassandras staged intricate manoeuvres; but to his surprise the visitor was more interested in another form of island life — the Barrier Reef crabs to which Ted had devoted a chapter in *My Tropic Isle*, one preceded with a quotation "beachcombed" from his father's small volume of the works of Milton.[11]

After being escorted to reef pools and rock corners, Critchell well understood why Ted could write: "Unless a crab is a giant in armour, or is endowed with almost supernatural alertness, or is an artist in the art of mimicry, or unless it cultivates some method of rapid disappearance, it has little chance of holding its own in the battle raging unceasingly over vast areas of the Great Barrier Reef."[12]

Chapter 20
Lifelines

Although Ted Banfield had called himself "Rob Krusoe" and had written: "Who would not thrill at the chance of visiting Robinson Crusoe's island?", the link between the Beachcomber and Daniel Defoe's castaway was a slight one.[1]

Crusoe had been marooned and wrote in his journal: "I, poor, miserable Robinson Crusoe, being shipwrecked . . . came on shore on this dismal unfortunate island, which I called the Island of Despair". Ted Banfield's isolation was voluntary, and of his island he wrote: "It typifies all that is tranquil, quiet, easeful, dreamlike, for it is the Isle of Dreams."[2]

However, in the case of the English reviewer H.J. Massingham, who belatedly discovered Ted's writings, the link enabled some pertinent observations to be made.

After calling Ted "A Modern Crusoe", Massingham wrote that it was good for men that such "isolated figures as Banfield should exist or have existed, not exactly among them, but of their kind. They make one see our self-absorbed modern life from a new angle of vision". How many people, he wondered, might murmur to themselves after reading his books: "Ah, would that I might go and do likewise?"[3]

Massingham's conclusion provides an answer to those who questioned or criticized Banfield's motives. *The Athenaeum*, for instance:

> The author prides himself that he has "returned to nature", but that is impossible; he has returned to solitude, to poverty, to freedom, and many other things but he has not accepted the conditions of nature. He has rejected the burdens of civilization, and gone off with the loot into the wilds; extirpated the native vegetation, and planted the trees that feed him agreeably.[4]

The first reviewer in *The Times* had raised much the same point:

> Whether Mr Banfield is ethically right in withdrawing himself from the fever and fret of the world is a larger question which is bound to suggest itself; he seemes to be in no doubt about the answer, and a man of his temperament is sure to have considered this aspect of his enterprise carefully.[5]

It was largely to people who wished that they could do as Ted had done that he and Bertha owed their lifelines with the outside world, a world from which they could not entirely escape, even had they wished for such a total break. Without the weekly visit of the steamer, their isolation could well have been unendurable. It was true that the products of the island could if necessary suffice for all their bodily needs, but Ted was dependent upon an inward flow of books, newspapers, periodicals and letters for the good of his mental health. Without all this printed matter, he would have been hard-pressed to continue writing — and in the years from 1911 to 1914 as many as 123 of his "Rural Homilies" appeared in print.[6]

Members of the Howard Smith family, whose company controlled much of the shipping on the coast, saw to it that Dunk Island remained a regular calling point. Among the passenger and cargo ships were the *Palmer*, 267 tons; the *Lass O'Gowrie*, 244 tons; the *Kuranda*, 928 tons; and the *Innisfail*, 399 tons, named after the nearby town which, until 1910 — the year in which

S.S. *Kuranda* berthing in Townsville in the horse cab days.
(Courtesy of Townsville Harbour Board.)

Halley's Comet appeared like a plume of sparks in the sky over Dunk — had been called Geraldton, the change being made to avoid confusion with the town of the same name in Western Australia. A bag of fresh meat would sometimes come over the side of the steamer with the mail, as the Howard Smiths knew the Banfields often went short of it.[7]

Increasingly, as the years went by, Spenser Hopkins became a one-man lifeline. The son of Thomas Hollis Hopkins, founder of Hollis Hopkins and Co. Ltd, Townsville, warehousemen and manufacturers of drapery and men's clothes, Spenser McTaggart Hopkins had been educated at the Townsville Grammar School where he was a foundation pupil. After training in business management in London, where he had worked in the London branch of his father's firm he returned to Townsville in 1905 to take over from his father. Three years later in Melbourne, he married Rosa Sykes, whom he had met in London. He had much more in common with Ted Banfield than an English bride, for he also shared Banfield's love of outdoor life and literature. While Spenser Hopkins, a man dapper in appearance and an excellent tennis player until late in life, perhaps in a sense hero-worshipped Ted Banfield for what he had achieved and what he stood for, they got on together as kindred spirits despite the fact that there was a generation of more than average length between them. As time went on Ted and Bertha came to have a parental attitude towards Spenser, as if he had taken the place of the son they had never had.

As the First World War loomed and broke, Spenser became more and more their mainstay in Townsville, and some of their needs came direct from Hollis Hopkins and Co. As Spenser's seven children began to come into the world, he took family breaks and holidays on the island. More often, though, he came on his own and spent an energetic few days, or even a week, helping Ted with the general maintenance and construction — cutting down overhanging trees, erecting fences, building outhouses for horses (and cows when they came), clearing land, weeding, mowing. When the fruit trees reached the stage at which Ted started to earn some income from them, Spenser assisted in the making of the wooden cases and in picking oranges, mangoes and mandarins to fill them. While most cases ferried by rowing boat to the steamer were for the markets in Townsville, many went to friends there such as Ted's newspaper colleagues, to whom he was still "Our Man in Eden".

Spenser accompanied Ted in days of "fossicking, bathing, beachcombing and botanising" on and around the island. Many of the shells they collected came to be displayed in the handsome wooden cabinet which Spenser designed and constructed. Other specimens were carefully packed and sent to collections and museums within Australia and overseas.[8]

In Ted's first *Nee Mourna*, the Aboriginal equivalent of the Red Indian "Minnehaha" for "laughing water",[9] a sturdy whaler-type of boat with an inboard engine, the two would set out on a voyage around Ted's little world, circumnavigating Dunk, and then ranging further afield to inspect other islands and islets. They might replace a weathered notice prohibiting the shooting of birds, or, when the Native Birds Act came to be amended, replace the old calico notices with new ones, the sharp black lettering on the speckless white cloth making them as fresh as newly-minted coins.

During one of Spenser's visits, Ted had to go to the mainland for a few days, so it was left to Spenser to write up the day's events each evening in the diary. This alone is an indication of how intimate he had become with the two islanders.

A.J. Hordern, a head of one of Sydney's major stores, came to be a staunch friend. He brought his family on holidays, starting before the "Great War", as newspapers referred to it during the conflict. Caroline Hordern took some of the finest photographs of the Beachcomber in his domain, a number of which Ted used for his article of 1 January 1913 in *The Lone Hand*. Bruce Hordern brought his bagpipes and, after practising in one part of Australia where it was highly unlikely that he could cause a nuisance, started a rumour that a weird new bird had taken up residence in the reserve.[10] When the goats had to go, because of the foot rot to which cloven-hoofed beasts are subject, A.J. Hordern sent up some beautiful little fawn and yellow Jerseys from his country cattle stud, and thereafter Ted claimed that while Dunk was noted for many things its milk and cream were the finest in the north. He purchased a churn, and he and Bertha made their own butter; when there was an excess, they shipped it to the mainland in exchange for groceries.

Meanwhile, by publishing *The Confessions of a Beachcomber* and *My Tropic Isle*, Ted had lifted the veil off Dunk Island and advertised its many charms to the world, so it was not surprising that it should attract those with a hankering for the romantic tropical island life. He received requests from would-be beachcombers in Great Britain, America and elsewhere, wanting to visit or stay, or even purchase part of the island. To almost all of these, Ted was able to write polite, tactful and firm refusals, but on a number of occasions he relented — usually to his eventual regret, as relationships became difficult. Such escapists and romantics just did not realize that to succeed in this sort of life meant exerting strict personal discipline, not lolling about in the sun and postponing until tomorrow what should be done today. Bertha put it in a nutshell to Alec Chisholm: "this is a place to be *lived* in, not for the mere dreamer, or Mother Nature will smother him".[11]

Many came unheralded and uninvited — by frail open boat, by yacht, by the steamer, by luxury cruiser. There was for instance the titled man who had observed that if the exile here happened to be a descendant of the King of the Beggars, this is just the life he would choose. Recalling how his father Jabez had claimed that they were descended from the family of the scallywag Bamphylde Moore-Carew, Ted was delighted to be able to admit kinship.[12]

Some of the uninvited were brother beachcombers, such as the one-armed Yorky who could sail his boat anywhere and under any conditions, through ragged reefs and raging storms; and Hamed the Arab who could tell a spellbinding tale in fractured English which Ted expertly retold; and George the Greek — surname Cilicardikis — who ran into problems transferring his oyster lease in the Hinchinbrook Channel to the tidal area between Dunk and Kumboola. Ted took this up with his usual ardour in the face of what he believed to be bloody-minded officaldom and therefore a glaring injustice which had to be remedied. To such as these, all of whom walked to the music they heard, Dunk was always an open house.

Hamed could neither read nor write, and while the main reason for his visit might be to ask Ted to pen a letter for him, like the others he always had the Banfields' welfare at heart. When in Europe, Hamed had been initiated into the mysteries of making Irish stew. In an outburst of gratitude to the Banfields for having entertained him at their dining table

> he let out the secret in these terms: "Eerish sdoo you make 'em. Four potats, two ungin, hav-dozen garleek, one hav-bucket water." At first it appeared that he had obtained his knowledge from a passionate vegetarian, but upon reflection we concluded that in his opinion meat was so essential an item that it was to be taken for granted. Anyone wishing to try the recipe would be safe in adding "meat to taste".[13]

The same concern for the couple prevailed among those of Ted's colleagues who worked by gaslight far into the night in the newspaper offices in Townsville and Charters Towers, in particular David Green of *The Bulletin* and George Barrymore of *The Northern Miner*. If word came ahead that Ted was due in Townsville for a day or two, David Green would phone Barrymore and say that he had better come down.[14]

Like Green, Barrymore had been a sportsman and had started his newspaper career by writing about boxing — under the pseudonym "Cestus", after the loaded leather glove worn by the Romans when they boxed — and then horse-racing. Under the Beachcomber's influence he had taken to watching birds and writing about them, too, and no doubt it was through Ted that he had come to have a greater love for "the old aboriginals, with their soft spoken words and their bush lore".[15] He and Ted had the same literary enthusiasms and shared a special delight in the works of Lewis Carroll; on Barrymore's visits to Dunk, they would roam the reefs and parade the beaches, reciting chunks from *Alice's Adventures in Wonderland* and *Through the Looking-Glass*. At times, in Bertha's eyes, "E.J.B." and "E.G.B." must have been counterparts of Tweedledum and Tweedledee.

Both David Green and George Barrymore made it plain to Ted that if ever he wanted anything done he had only to mention it. Green also had an abiding admiration for Ted's skill as a writer, and through the paper he edited he helped to promote some of the finest writing about North Queensland and its neighbouring areas, and the people who lived there, as the Queensland newspaper historian, James Manion, has recorded:

> The northern goldfields, the western cattle stations and the Pacific Islands and, less frequently, South-East Asia provided the settings for many of the stories published in *The North Queensland Register*. The characters hinted at former lifestyle in Europe, drank whisky, and were frequently involved in fierce battles with Chinese and Aborigines. Mining frauds and wildcat schemes were acknowledged. Descriptions now and then reflected the severe climatic conditions, the despair of the failing squatter and the laconic humour of the outback. International implications were not entirely forgotten as the shadows of the looming struggle in Europe were depicted some 21 years before the actual event.[16]

Among the talents this "visionary editor"[12] promoted were those of the novelists Louis Becke and Stefan Von Kotze, whose contributions to the special Christmas editions of *The Register* helped make its annual appearance a literary event. Some of the Beachcomber's best articles appeared in these editions. He was *The Register*'s most regular contributor, its star writer, David Green's favourite. However, there was a time when Ted decided that he was written out and that there would be no more "Rural Homilies" — or, as he himself put it, "Rural Abominalies". And so he laid down his pen, but not for long. Barrymore recalled what happened:

> A year or so afterwards there was a tropical disturbance, and Banfield wrote a particularly graphic thing. It just told of the vagaries, whims and fancies of the barometer, what it foretold, what ominous messages it sent out, and then, as the glass rose, the joy and promise emanating from it. It was really clever fancy, concise and charming. Mr Green, placing his article on my desk for me to read, said, "And Banfield says he is written out! I do not know of another man who could have written that."[18]

Barrymore believed that another of Ted's best pieces was the chapter "A Tropic Night" in *My Tropic Isle*, one with a direct link to the Banfields' lifelines as it described how Ted settled down on the sand-spit to await "the smoky messenger from the stuffy town". What was presented as prose became in Barrymore's eyes poetry:

My solitary watch gives the rare delight of analyzing the night
thoughts of the ocean, profound in its slumber though dreamily
conscious of recent conflict with the winds.
All the frail undertones
suppressed during the bullying day
now have audience.
Sounds which crush and crowd
have wearied and retired.
The timid and shy venture forth
to join the quiet revelry of the night.[19]

Members of the crews of the steamers became good friends
— not only of the Banfields but also of their dogs, one of whom
always received half a leg of mutton from the cook. In the
words of a crew member who had called many times at Dunk,
"If we couldn't get into Innisfail because of slack water there,
we'd run the steamer into the bay and come ashore for a few
hours, to have a cup of tea and a yarn up at the bungalow."[20]

Opposite on the mainland, the Banfields had friends among
the settlers such as the Cutten family, with whom they spent
many Christmases, and Chris Wildsoet who was always willing
to come to Ted's aid when there was a big or tricky job on
hand, such as the time the Hordern Jerseys were landed late at
night and had to be rounded up the next morning.

There was also the man in charge of the Hull River Aborigine
Settlement, Superintendent John Martin Kenny, "a native of
New South Wales, one of the big-framed, big-limbed men that
the Northern Rivers produce, a man of varied experience
ashore and afloat, who knew Cape York Peninsula to its ter-
minal rock". He was liked by the Aborigines; he often acted as
doctor to them; he had a widespread knowledge of their
dialects, customs and folklore; he understood how they felt and
how they reasoned.[21]

Ted Banfield learnt much about the original inhabitants of
this part of the world through Kenny, and so was better able to
deal with them during the years of his occupation of the island,
when they provided one of the major lifelines. Without the
help of the Aborigines, it would not have been possible for Ted
and Bertha either to have established their little outpost or to
have remained there.

Chapter 21
Original Inhabitants

In *The Confessions*, Ted wrote of his experiences with the Aborigines as labourers: "when in the humour [they] will work steadily and consistently. When not in the humour, it is well to accept the fact cheerfully."[1]

The fact was that Ted had little choice in the matter. Since he could not afford white labour, except on a few rare occasions, he had to make do with the help of the Aborigines or try to fend for himself.

Like many who had come to the north, he had preconceived views about the Australian Aborigines in general. In his case, such views dated back to his boyhood in Ararat where he had first encountered members of the race which had originally inhabited the continent; unfortunately, they were drifters and derelicts, dark-skinned counterparts of the tramps who hung about old diggings, combing through tailings where there might be a little golden dross to be found. Some of them had been brought before his father at the Court of Petty Sessions, sometimes when Ted was there as a reporter, and he had fallen into the way of regarding them as remnants of an inferior race.

This, of course, was at at time when the British Empire was at its zenith of power, when its members — Britons, wherever they might be — regarded themselves not only as a higher form of human species than coloured peoples but also superior to other white nations.

A charge aimed at the natives was that they failed to cultivate the land and took "no heed of the morrow, but accepted the fruits of the earth without thought of inciting Nature to produce better or more abundantly."[2]

They had feasts waiting for the taking. A choice of three or four varieties of oysters; numerous other shellfish such as periwinkles, cockles, mussels, scallops; a selection of many fish, including whiting, bream, flathead, mullet, rock-cod, eels, perch; crabs, prawns, crayfish; seabirds' eggs, pigeons' eggs, scrub fowls' eggs; roast scrub fowl and pigeons; entrees of turtle cutlets; a huge piece of dugong or perhaps a luscious carpet snake as the roast of the day; for vegetables, sweet yams, the hearts of palms, the cores of fern trees, the broad beans of the white mangrove; for sweets and dessert, bean-tree nuts with honey, and fruits with the flavours of red currants, cherries, raspberries, strawberries, and a variety of figs, plums and bananas.

Why cultivate them when they could wander off to another place where another such feast awaited? When they returned to former sites, nature had done the cultivation for them and replenished the stocks. Surely Thoreau would have approved of this, for he had written that men "take a thousand stitches to-day to save nine to-morrow".[3]

The gifts bestowed on the natives were so great that Ted was moved to make a certain culinary comparison: "The menu of the Chinese — with its ducks' eggs salted, sharks' fins and tails, stewed pups, fowls' and ducks' tongues, fricasseed cat, rat soup, silkworm grubs, and odds and ends generally despised and rejected — is pitifully unromantic when set against the generous omnivority of Australian blacks."[4]

Ted may have taken a little time to come around to a comprehensive appreciation of the philosophy of the Aborigines, but even in *The Confessions* he went on to express, as few men before him had ever done, a great love for them and a delight in their humour, whims, fancies and their wildly imaginative explanations for such phenomena as the presence of stars in the sky. He could not help but treat them as wayward children, and it is possible that the few with whom he was in touch, after the widespread hunting, killing and harassment by the "wonder-working whites",[5] were less disciplined and *possibly* less intelligent than their fellows and forbears who had stood up to the intruders and, by doing so, had perished.

Tom was the first of the survivors of the Dunk Island tribe Ted had met; and it was through Tom that he was to gain so much of an insight into the Aborigines, and discover so much about them, that this aspect of his writings was one of the main appeals of his books, and one of their greatest achievements.

Whatever Tom's failings — and he could become magnificently paranoid and imperious — it would be difficult to imagine Ted Banfield writing about any person with such admiration and affection. Although, like many of his people, Tom was terrified

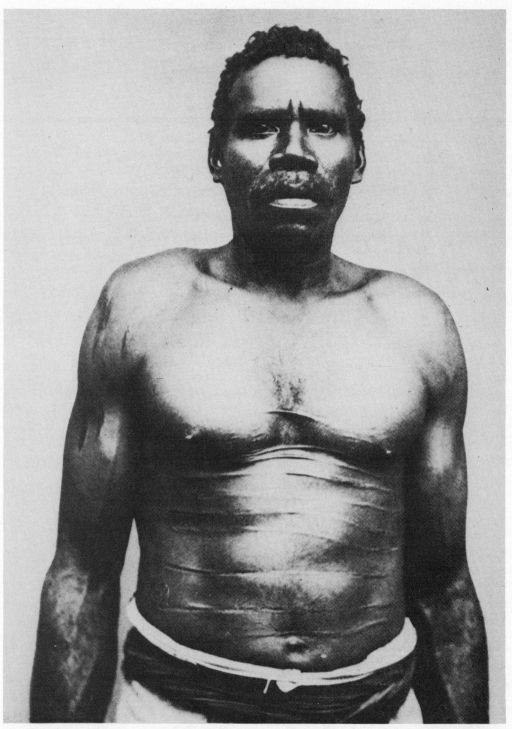

Tom the Aborigine, E.J. Bandfield's friend, helper and teacher. First edition *The Confessions of a Beachcomber*.
(Courtesy of Queensland State Library.)

of the dark, believing it to be swarming with sinister "debil-debils",[6] he was still the bravest man Ted had ever seen.

He could calmly spear fish "in a frail bark canoe among the sharks on the skirts of a shoal of bonito"; "all the ways and habits of fish, and their favourite breeding grounds, are to him as the pages of an open book"; he "would go to sea on a chip" using sucker fish to catch an immense bull turtle. Nothing was caught or killed just for the excitement of the hunt, but always for food. He introduced Ted into the mystery of "wild dynamite" — not the explosive used by the dynamiters who sneaked in "like shame-faced spies, carrying death and destruction into almost every river, creek and lagoon, and even into the deep blue sea, as far as the Great Barrier" — but a plant which, after being crushed on a rock, was shaken in the water, thus merely stunning the fish with narcotic; only those needed for the table were scooped out, and the rest were left to recover.[7]

Of his wives, with all of whom he had some monumental rows, his favourite was Little Jinny. Relatively early in the Banfields' occupation of Dunk, Little Jinny became desperately ill with agonizing stomach pains. Ted and Bertha tended her with brandy, blankets and kind words of encouragement, but she failed to respond. Tom had the answer. She had a debil-debil inside her, and as she lapsed into unconsciousness, he filled his lungs and blew gusty breaths into her big black eyes to try to revive her, but at sunset Little Jinny died.[8]

After they buried her in the smoky hut where she had lived, digging a shallow grave in the black sand, Tom put on the mourning of his tribe. He could not bear to be reminded of his lost love. He spent the hours between daylight and sunset wandering around wherever Little Jinny had been, obliterating the tracks made by her feet, and with the keenest of sight "which is one of the superior qualifications of the race", he identified the tracks she had made on the ground and rubbed them out with his foot. Tom's grief "drove him remorselessly, until no outward and visible sign of the dead girl remained to challenge it".[9]

It was from Tom and some of the other native boys that Ted came to hear about the wonders of certain caves and caverns on the island. Although approachable only by boat, "Falling-Star" cavern was easily located near Brammo Bay. From Tom, the Beachcomber learnt that it was supposed to have been bored out by a meteor; another version of the legend claimed that a giant debil-debil had taken out a plug of rock with his mighty fingers and placed it in a hole on the top of one of the highest peaks on Hinchinbrook Island, about thirty kilometres away, to trap winds and rain there. Ted found it some nine metres in depth and a delightful place to take visitors as its entrance was hung with creepers and its rocks decorated with bronze orchids.[10]

He was also told about caves high up in the island, used as galleries by native artists, although no one had ever actually seen them; knowledge of their existence had been handed down by their forefathers.

With Tom as his main companion, Ted set about trying to locate the caves. He discovered what he termed the "lower studio" on the eastern slope of the island about sixty metres above Panjoo, a natural harbour just large enough for a small dinghy, provided the sea was calm. Otherwise it was a hard climb and struggle through tortuous jungle, and a descent among massive stones and boulders. Either way it was worth the trouble, for here crude and grotesque human figures were to be seen in fading red clay on smoothed grey rock.

A second gallery, the "upper studio", lay close to the backbone of the island "in the heart of a bewildering jumble of immense rocks overgrown with jungle". Its whereabouts, three times higher than the first studio, was marked by a broad horizontal white streak made by the bleaching of stag's horn fern. As the natives were reluctant to crawl into dark places, Ted ventured in first alone and had to lie on his back beneath a great granite rock, as the Aboriginal Michelangelo must have done to execute what Ted now saw — designs incorporating animals and weapons, in his opinion resembling "those fantastic interwoven shapes that some men in fits of abstraction or idleness sketch on their own blotting-pads, and which signify nothing". To one who had seen some of the works of the great Turner (and tried his hand at matching that master's amazing pictures in words) here was "the sheer beginning, the spontaneous germ of art".[11]

Visits to these galleries by outsiders were confined to a few favoured guests, such as T.P. Adlam, who made drawings of each of them. From Tom and the boys, Ted gathered that there was a third such gallery, and so all expeditions were enlivened by the possibility that this one, too, would yield up its secret; but Ted never found it.

From observations recorded in *The Confessions*, Ted came to a realization that the rough, rude, stone-age savage was well able to feel what the superior whites called love and to have the desire to express himself aesthetically. Although it was still qualified by the assumption of white supremacy, in *My Tropic Isle* Ted revealed an even greater sympathy towards the natives: "Whosoever has seen (himself unseen) an unsophisticated North Queensland black parading his native strand has seen a lord of creation . . . His bold front, fluent carriage, springy step, alert, confident, superior air proclaim him so, innocent though he be of the frailest insignia of civilization."[12]

Almost certainly, Ted had Tom in mind; but his loyal native friend and companion was being sadly led astray during his absences from Dunk. He was even more vulnerable than Ted had yet realized to the intensity of the emotions he could feel. When one of the boys close to Tom died of heart failure, an after-effect of rheumatic fever, Tom was so distressed that he found his grief unbearable. The only way he could escape from it was to go to the mainland. As Ted wrote, Tom murmured: "Carn help it. Must go away one month. I bin think about that boy too much."[13]

Three months passed, but no sign of Tom. Word was received that he was north of Clump Point at Maria Creek, so Ted sent a message there, asking Tom to come back and saying that he was welcome, that there was work and tucker and pay for him; but still the wanderer did not appear, so Ted went in search of him and found him further north in a settlement at Mourilyan. He pleaded with Tom to return, but the black man was in a sadly degenerated state due to the combination of white man's rum and yellow man's opium, so deranged that he could not comprehend what was being said to him. Ted returned home alone, deploring "the unfitness of the aboriginal in the battle of life" when exposed to intruders' evils.[14]

Ted himself had fallen by the wayside in the battle of life. Bearing in mind how the town had almost suffocated him to death, Ted might have been writing about himself.

A few months later, still in the same drunken and drugged state, Tom quarrelled with a half-brother who rammed a spear between his ribs. The police came and Tom was taken to hospital by steamer, but not long after he passed away. Ted had prepared a chapter "Tom and His Concerns" for "My Tropic Isle"; following Tom's passing, he added a moving tribute:

> Although he was "only a black fellow", yet was he an Australian of the purest lineage and birth — one whose physique was [an] example of the class that tropical Queensland is capable of producing, a man of brains, a student of Nature, who had stored his mind with first-hand knowledge unprinted and now unprintable, a hunter of renown . . . Serene in the face of the perils of the sea, with all of which he was familiar, he was afraid of no man in daylight, though a child might scare him after dark . . . Among his mental accomplishments was a specific title for each plant and tree. His almanac was floral. By the flowering of trees and shrubs so he noted the time of the year, and he knew many stars by name and could tell when such and such a one would be visible . . . Given protection from the disastrous contact with the raw, unclean edge of civilization, he and others, his fellows, might have lived for a score of years longer, and in the meantime possibly the public conscience of Australia might have been aroused, and his and their last days made wholesome, peaceable, and pleasant.[15]

Steps were taken to give the natives some protection, although these seemed to Ted to be too late and too harsh.

Many times, recalling how Tom was "ever a free man, given to the habit of roaming",[16] he was thankful his friend was no longer here, for a decision was made to round up all Aborigines and place them in settlements under government supervision. This was like placing them in prisons, and the nearest one — across on the mainland — was well within everyday view, near enough, were a telescope to be used, to count them as they pottered or sat about.

They were shipped to this settlement via Dunk, and it upset Ted deeply to see them coming ashore from ketches and steamers to be herded on the sand-spit before being taken across by smaller boats to the home none of them seemed to want. When they were forced to wait in gales until the boats could cross for them, Ted was so concerned that through Spenser Hopkins he provided blankets for them at his own expense.

Even if it can be said that Ted Banfield by words and actions later compensated for his earlier lack of understanding of the natives, to a degree they still remained children in his eyes. He spoke to them as children, and with his gift for dialect and vernacular he became adept at "pidgin", although it could have been disconcerting for a visitor to hear Ted using that same pidgin when talking to one of his well-loved dogs after it had come to him with something it had just caught: "What you got there? Snake? Go on silly fellow. No snake. That one only lizard, that no snake."[17]

In *The Confessions* Ted summed up the dilemma imposed upon the indigenous inhabitants by the intruders: he related the poignant tale of the simple Aboriginal girl who had stolen a tiny gold crucifix and worn it overnight in the hope that it would work a miracle, and she would wake up to find herself white-skinned. By the time he came to prepare a third book for publication, he was somewhat bemused by his fellow whites who seemed to be trying to do just the opposite, by excessively exposing their bodies to the sun and making themselves as dark as the Aborigines.

By this time he had also managed to observe the inland cousins of the coastal Aborigines who had hitherto been his main study. He made contact with some of them when he and Bertha crossed to Mission Beach to be guests at a corroboree.

From among mountains two days' journey from the coast, some of the performers came through unknown country. The days of tribal feuds were past, so the only weapons the visitors carried were talismen to ward off spectral enemies of appalling shape, cunning and ferocity said to dwell in the jungles.

Most had never seen the sea before. As they gazed with mute astonishment at what confronted them, the sea was "almost as incomprehensible, and therefore almost as fearsome, as the phantoms of the bush. Mysterious, vast beyond the range of vision, here grumbling on the sand, there mingling with the sky, the strangers peered at it through screens of whimpering casuarinas and trembled". The big salt water was alive while their own sleepy lagoons were silent and tame.

"That b-i-g fella salt water," one of the newcomers cried. "Him sing out plenty. Mak'm b-i-g fella row."[18]

Watching and listening, Ted witnessed the communion of the inlanders with another entity, one so big that they could not see where it ended:

> They sat and watched its enticing gestures, and, gathering courage, stood tremulously while the tide splashed their feet and retreated. The boldest walked in ankle-deep and danced in daredevilry, and soon young and old were gambolling uncouthly, tasting the sea's quality, shouting and splashing. None ventured more than knee-deep; some crawled and wallowed in the wet sand, too fearful to trust their lives to so big a thing which showed itself to be alive by breathing and moving.[19]

The corroboree began in the late afternoon. Those taking part had spent hours preparing their costumes, plastering down feathers with grease and mud. To the clapping of hollowed hands and the clicking of boomerangs on resonant logs, the dancing began.

If ever Ted had found occasion to apply that key saying of Thoreau's, this was it. These natives certainly did not keep pace with their white companions; they certainly heard a different drummer; and here they were joyously stepping to the music which they heard.

Chapter 22
Home Front

Following the outbreak of war in 1914, none of the shots fired on Dunk or within hearing of the island had any connection with the hostilities — except when the big guns of an Australian cruiser opened up, but even then it was only firing practice.

Ted himself was obliged to fire a number of shots. A brown goshawk made it impossible for the fowls and chickens to have a free run unless someone stood guard, so the marauder had to be destroyed. An aged sick horse had to be put down. Pythons and other snakes had to be dispatched, as well as flying foxes spoiling fruit and sharks disturbing fishing spots. The only other shots were fired by intruders violating the sanctuary; these Ted tried to confront, although usually by the time he reached the scene the shooters had slipped away.

Naval vessels began to appear in Brammo Bay more frequently, and due to an unfortunate incident a number of years earlier Ted was very much on the defensive. He had come out one morning to find a survey ship anchored off Purtaboi. As he looked the ship over, he liked what he saw — a steam vessel with masts for sails, an obsolescent type but one that brought back memories of the *Chyebassa* and his trip to the Old Country; and had he not gone on that journey he certainly would not have had Bertha here now to help him lay "pedal autographs" on the tide-swept morning sands. His cogitations were rudely interrupted by a rifle pumping out shots on Purtaboi. Terns and other birds went shrieking into the air as Ted raced to a dinghy on the beach. He launched it and rowed hard over the three-quarters of a mile gap between the beach and the islet, as

The Beachcomber with
his dog on his favourite
strip of the tropics,
Brammo Bay, Dunk
Island, 1912.
(Courtesy of Mrs L.
Webb, Winchester,
England.)

further shots kept the birds milling aloft. He expected to find some hardened poacher at work, so was shocked when the offender turned out to be a fair-haired, fresh-faced and very young-looking naval lieutenant blithely blazing away at pigeons. A score of them already lay dead on the sand and among the coral chips and rocks.

Ted was in such a fury that when he tried to express his disgust he was almost incoherent. In the face of such uncontrolled remonstration, the young lieutenant decided to question Ted's right to interfere; since the Honorary Ranger had not taken the time to return to the bungalow to collect his metal badge of office, he had to try to make do with the nearby calico notice, which stated in simple straightforward English that shooting was forbidden.

The lieutenant withdrew by dinghy, rounding the side of the islet on his way back to the survey ship — but not before he had picked up several dead pigeons.

There had not been the shadow of an apology, which made Ted all the more outraged. He stormed back to the bungalow and went straight into his office, ignoring Bertha's attempts to calm him down as he started to scrawl a letter to the under secretary in Brisbane, reporting this appalling violation of the sanctuary — and by a uniformed officer of the naval forces. As with many letters dashed off, whether in the white heat of indignation, inspiration or euphoria, it was one which would have to be blue-pencilled and rewritten, but he was determined to have it on board the next ship calling for mail.

That afternoon the captain of the survey vessel came ashore to pay his respects to the celebrated Beachcomber. With him he brought a contrite and red-faced young naval lieutenant who, having thought over what he had done, realized he had been guilty of a serious transgression, so had made a clean breast of things to his commanding officer who had escorted him ashore to express his regret in person.

The young man did so with such grace that Ted overflowed with forgiveness — much to the relief of Essie and Bertha.

"Now, really, Captain," said Ted, "I'm delighted to see you and your junior officer. It — it is remarkable that I have never heard of the incident you mention. No, really I haven't — or, if I have — most surely have I forgotten all about it. I'm so glad to see you both. Now come in, and we will give you some tea with Jersey milk. It is nice of you fellows to come ashore to see me."[1]

He also gave them fresh mangoes, and since he had what amounted to a captive audience, he took yet another opportunity to expound on the marvels of this fruit, one which in his opinion was the "unspeakable eatable", with fantastic flavours which were beyond the ability of mere man to analyze — although in *My Tropic Isle* he made a heady attempt:

Take of a pear all that is mellow, of a peach all that is luscious, of a strawberry all that is fragrant, of a plum all that is kindly, of an apricot all its aroma, of cream all its smoothness. Commingle with musk and honey, coriander and aniseed, smother with the scent of musk roses, blend with cider, and the mixture may convey a dim sense of some of the delectable qualities.[2]

Crews looked forward to dropping anchor in Brammo Bay. After drilling on the beach, there was time for games — football and basketball — and it was a wonderful spot for swimming. Fruit and coconuts were plentiful. Ted made it known that the sailors had but to ask and bananas, oranges, mandarins and other fruit would be made available; only the odd vandal went off picking mangoes or knocking down coconuts without permission. The officers enjoyed the stops here and visits to the Beachcomber up at the bungalow. After listening to his rich, informative talk, they invited him and Bertha on their ships for meals — and on the decks at night under the stars they saw some of their first moving picture shows.

As well as literary heroes such as Shakespeare, Dickens and Thoreau, Ted had others — and Nelson was one of them. No word of criticism could be levelled at this man, so it gave Ted an immediate bond with naval officers who thought likewise, especially Englishmen serving on the Australian station. However, he loved to try pulling their legs, and he claimed that James Cook was indeed fortunate to have arrived in time to chart the east coast of the continent and to claim it for Great Britain. The fact was that Cook was still fitting out the *Endeavour* in the Thames when de Bougainville approached the coast from the east. Had the Frenchman held his course instead of deciding that the roar of the Pacific Ocean striking the great wall of the Barrier Reefs was the voice of God warning him to turn away, the island would probably have the name of some noble French family rather than the English name of Dunk. And speaking of that name, Cook had made a mistake. Yes, a mistake. One which Ted himself had been a party to disseminating in *The Confessions*. He publicly acknowledged his own and the great mariner's mistake in a "Rural Homily":

By unfortunate fault in hearsay evidence a blunder was made some years ago in a statement having reference to the origin of the name of Dunk Island, and since the error has been made in good faith in publications, the contributors to which have been thrown off their guard by a deeply regretted slip, it seems to be a duty to make amends by details obtained from authoritative sources.

Trusting to what at the time appeared to be a statement that did not need verification, I mentioned that the name had been bestowed by Captain Cook in honor of his patron, 4th Earl of Sandwich, who was the First Lord of the Admiralty of his day. This was correct as far as it went; but it was added that his family name was George Montagu Dunk, and therein lies the mistake.

173

> Halifax Bay, Hinchinbrook Island, and Cape Sandwich do
> commemorate Captain Cook's patron, who had previously
> named the Sandwich Islands, a desolate group within the range
> of the drift ice of the South Atlantic Ocean, with like intent.
> His son, John Montagu . . . inherited a large estate from Sir
> Thomas Dunk, of Tongs, Kent, and assumed the name . . . it is
> evident that it was in Captain Cook's mind when he passed this
> island on 8th June, 1770.[3]

This could not be argued, but then Ted would go further —
after claiming that he did not wish to appear to denigrate the
achievements of the great navigator — by suggesting that
Cook's long northward voyage unknowingly *inside* the Great
Barrier Reef was no accident. To have entered the inner passage
so far to the south, surely Cook must have had some prior
knowledge, some secret naval intelligence, perhaps an early
Portuguese chart, for the world's largest coral structure had
appeared on maps early in the sixteenth century. His good
friend, Critchell, a contributor to the *Encyclopaedia Britannica*, had
started his summary of the history of Queensland by stating:
"The Portuguese may have known the northern shore nearly a
century before Torres, in 1605, sailed through the Strait called
after him."[4]

As for the maps, Critchell had seen them with his own eyes.
On them were strings of crosses where the Great Barrier Reef
lay, and near the crosses, ranging from Portuguese to Spanish to
French, the words "Coste Dangereuse", "Coste Dagerose",
"Coste Perilleuse", "Costa Peligrusa".[5]

There would be loud protests that this was sacrilege, and
Bertha would hasten in with Black Maria to make sure that Ted
was not overdoing the leg-pulling.

Some of the visiting warships were camouflaged in jagged
patterns of tropical grey and aquamarine, but even though they
kept passing and calling in, the actual war continued to remain
so remote that it might have been a storm hammering away on
another planet. The drive in Townsville for the Soldiers' Sock
and Comfort Funds, to which Ted donated cases of fruit and
bags of oysters, did not make the conflict more real. Nor the
departure of mainland neighbours headed for the front in
France. It took a doll to bring it home.

Children came to the island with their parents, and it was not
unusual to see them blowing tin trumpets and parading on the
sand. Small boys sailed wooden gunboats in the calm water of
Brammo Bay while the girls played with rag and celluloid dolls
under the trees at the top of the beach. Tin trumpets, model
warships and dolls had been around for a long time, but not a
Nurse Cavell doll, a replica of the defiant British nursing
matron who had been shot by the Germans for harbouring
wounded and fugitive British soldiers in occupied Brussels and
assisting them to escape to Holland.

⋙ ⋙ ⋙

Between the beginning of 1915 and the end of 1917, Ted wrote over one hundred articles for *The North Queensland Register* and *The Townsville Daily Bulletin*.[6] As before, these pieces reflected his many social and natural history interests, the development and potential of the north and the welfare of its people; but he became more and more outspoken in his criticism and attacks on wanton shooting of birds, collecting of eggs, trading in birds' skins and looting of coral and shells, as he, as Honorary Ranger, took a more determined stand.

Behind his back on the island, someone had crept in and ravaged the swiftlets cave. The number of nests built on the cave walls had grown to almost a hundred, but Ted found fewer than twenty left.

He reported this to the Department in Brisbane, but did not expect any action to be taken. He could furnish no information about the identities of the desecrators. He became more critical of the Department, drawing its attention to a gross inconsistency: on the one hand sanctuaries were proclaimed, but on the other general permits were given to collectors to operate in these areas. In a "Rural Homily" entitled "The Ruthless Collector", Ted called for action against so-called professional collectors:

> I would urge on settlers to give all such privileged individuals the cold shoulder. They are very often nice men as individuals, and apart from their trade desirable visitors ... But being destroyers of birds they should be regarded as the most direful pest the country breeds. No method short of physical violence is too strong to adopt to scare them from the land. We must be rude, inhospitable, boorish, defiant, for the birds do work in our interests all the hours of daylight and some of them from dark till dawn. Their unreflective ways counsel us to wisdom, and their gay feathers and gladsome notes are universal property and not to be bartered for the sale of those who ply a profitable trade.[7]

At the same time, he moved in the direction of a third book for Fisher Unwin. He did not feel that a longer sustained book such as a novel was something he could tackle with confidence, although he had been flattered when another publisher had approached him to write the biography of Sir Robert Philp; his main reason for declining had been that it would mean leaving the island to carry out the research. Besides, after so many years in journalism, he had become a short distance writer, a sprinter if you like. This did not mean that Fisher Unwin had been wrong in perceiving in Ted's writing a gift for fiction. George Barrymore realized this too. Ted had already written a number of pieces that were almost entirely fiction, and a good many years back, so he dug out several of these for the new book, including "Passeth All Understanding" which he had written for the 1914 Christmas edition of *The Register*.

It was about the rise and fall of a solitary Chinaman on the northern gold fields and his deception and exploitation by a scheming policeman. It is a fine piece of narrative writing, worthy of R.L. Stevenson, having moments when it could be compared to Joseph Conrad for its perception of human nature and Somerset Maugham for its atmosphere and story.

Fisher Unwin was again eager to have a new book and Ted proposed to call it "Sun Days": "All my days are Days of the Sun. All days are holy."[8] Ted had recently been more bemused than disappointed when a royalty cheque arrived for the astronomical sum of £1.2s.0d. ($2.20) — although this was not a true reflection of sales as he had ordered so many free copies to be sent to friends that their cost had cut into his payment. Even though he might now be considered an established author of world renown, he was prepared to accept that this was no guarantee of financial success. His share of the rights for the Dutch edition of *The Confessions — Bekentenissen Van Een Strandvonder* — had been also monumental — £2.7s.6d. ($4.75).

Ever since J.T. Critchell had suggested the comparison, Ted had envisaged Fisher Unwin as looking like his "heron policeman", although he was also one of those individuals Ted classified as nice men as long as they weren't professional collectors. Fisher Unwin decided to be magnanimous and remove future grounds for complaint by offering the author £100 ($200) outright on delivery for the full copyright. He had not been too seriously stricken with charity, however, as he wanted all future royalties on *The Confessions* and *My Tropic Isle* thrown in for good measure. Again, he felt that Ted's title was not quite right and suggested "Tropic Days".

Life on Dunk Island for "The Master", as Bertha called Ted, and "The Lady of the Isle", as he called her, had reached a plateau of fulfilment and content:

> The sun rises, travels across a cloudless sky, gleams on a sailless sea, disappears behind purple mountains gilding their outline, and the day is done. Not a single dust-speck has soiled sky or earth; not the faintest echo of noisy labours disturbed the silences; not an alien sight intruded. What can there be in such a scene to exhilarate? Must not the inhabitants vegetate dully after the style of their own bananas? Actually the day has been all too brief for the accomplishment of inevitable duties and to the complete enjoyment of all too alluring relaxations.[9]

So Ted accepted, although he told neither Bertha nor Spenser Hopkins of the outright sale of copyright. In June 1917 he sent the typescript to London, done on a Corona which had been presented to him by the captain of one of the visiting warships, the *Parramatta*.[10] There were some problems due to wartime regulations regarding the posting of photographs, but after this hitch had been sorted out, the book — dedicated to "My Brother Beachcombers; Professing and Practising" — was on its way to the publisher, who had warned that because of staff and paper shortages and printing difficulties caused by the war, there would probably be delays.

Why worry, Ted could wait. He and Bertha were as remote as ever from the never-ending war, but closer to other things: "Those who are out of touch with great and dusty events may, by way of compensation, be the more sensitive to the processes of the universe."[11]

Despite the serene spell the island exerted over their lives, Ted and Bertha could not help but be disturbed at what they saw in the newspapers and journals arriving from the outside world — lists of the killed and the wounded, and pictures of the desolation on the Western Front — even though they had little personal connection with any of the casualties or their families.

They did lose one friend at this time. In November 1917 the flag was flown at half-mast on the sand-spit in honour of their "gentle, kind and good" friend James Troubridge Critchell who had died in London at the age of sixty-seven.[12]

The year 1918, a crucial one for the world, began with the island shrouded in rain. Not that Ted loved his Isle any the less: he still revelled in the scene even when "my trees are tempest-tossed, and the grey seas batter the sand-spit and bellow on the rocks, and neither bird nor butterfly dare venture from leafy sanctuary".[13]

In January, Essie left for her annual break on the mainland. In February a dynamiter had his hand blown off, and Japanese boats anchored in the channel before starting out to pillage the reefs. Shots were heard on Purtaboi, cartridge cases and dead birds found, but again the shooters crept away unseen. Another generation of white nutmeg pigeons had come into the world. They and the metallic starlings were preparing to leave for regions near the equator, training themselves for

> the long Northern flight and its perils, dashing with impetuous speed through the forest and wheeling up into the sky until they disappear, to become visible again as black dots hurtling through space when the sunlight plays on their glossy feathers as the course of the flock is changed. With a rush of wind of small measure but immense velocity, the flock descends earthwards, manoeuvring among and over the trees, perfecting itself by trials of endurance and intricate alertness.[14]

Fine weather followed the early rains, sublime weather, with one special day calm and transparently clear beyond all others, a day when the scene was magically transformed:

> In a sea which shone like polished silver the islet was a gem — green enamel, amethyst rocks, golden sand. The bold white trunks of giant tea-trees glowed; the creamy blooms of bloodwoods were as flecks of snow; the tips of the fronds of

177

coco-nut palms flickered vividly as burnished steel; the white-painted house assumed speckless purity. All light colours were heightened; ruddy browns and sombre greens seemed to have been smartened up by touches of fresh paint and varnish. An idealistic artist had revealed for once living tints and uncomprehended hues.[15]

Such was the intensity of the calm before the storm.

Of all the papers reaching the island, *The Register* and *The Queenslander*, which was published in Brisbane, had the fullest coverages of the war with pictorial sections on glossy paper carrying high definition photographic reproductions of war zones and battle fields, while the main dispatches appeared under tiers of headlines set in various sizes and shapes of typeface, reminding Ted of the way his father had set out the advertisements for the annual Ararat Easter Festivals:

FRENCH BALLOON SHOT DOWN
TANKS — WESTERN FRONT
CREEPING BARRAGE OF ALLIES
POUNDING THE WAY TO VICTORY
HELLING THE HUN

Such headlines boosted the public's expectation of victory; but at the end of March and the start of April 1918, they became deeply alarming as the enemy fought back:

HEAVY GERMAN ATTACK
BRITISH LINE BENT, BUT UNBROKEN
HEAVY TOLL EXACTED FROM ENEMY
TREMENDOUS AERIAL ACTIVITY
HUN CENTRES BOMBED
A GERMAN WONDER GUN
PARIS BOMBARDED FROM 75 MILES

While the Battle of the Somme got under way and more square miles of France were laid waste, suddenly much closer to home there were reports of shattering desolation:

CATASTROPHE
DISASTROUS CYCLONE
INNISFAIL WRECKED
FIFTEEN LIVES LOST
GORDONVALE HALF DEMOLISHED
DAYS OF HORROR

What had happened to Dunk Island and the Beachcomber's little kingdom as nature subjected those so long seemingly safe and remote in their sanctuary to an outburst of violence which more than matched that being inflicted by the bombs, shells and bullets of the man-made storm on the other side of the world? One of the first reports was published in Townsville:

According to information which has reached here by the Lass O'Gowrie, the hurricane started at noon on Sunday, and at dusk the roofs began to go ... the new wharf at Clump Point has

gone and all the buoys are apparently swept away ...
"Beachcomber" wires that his house on Dunk Island was
damaged and his motor boat has been destroyed. No such
devastation has occurred for half a century. The coastal scrubs
look as if they have been burnt.[16]

Side by side in *The Register* and *The Queenslander* were scenes of
cyclone and flood chaos in North Queensland and the ruina-
tions of war in France, while the tiers of headlines continued:

BACKS TO THE WALL
BRITISH HARD PRESSED
GERMAN ADVANCE STOPPED

And finally, as the tide began to turn, the one-word headline:

HELD

But what of the situation on Ted Banfield's "adorable Isle"?

Chapter 23
The Clocks Have Stopped

Two days after the cyclone, Ted sent George Barrymore a "Rural Homily" entitled "The Tempest".[1]

There had been portents ahead of it: exceedingly close and oppressive days; snakes lurking near the homestead; fires running along the ridges on the mainland; and sightings of lesser frigate birds, which rarely visited except in advance of bad weather: "Ten days prior to the event a large flock appeared, wheeling high up in the sky. These, or others of the species, were seen each day until the morning of the outbreak."[2]

That day began with swiftly mounting seas and a wind which rose steadily until, shortly before dusk,

> it was travelling at a furious speed, twisting branches from trees and thickening the now gloomy skies with leaves. Consistently with the strength of the wind the barometer fell until between 9 and 10 p.m., when, with a conglomeration of terrifying sounds varying from falsetto shrieks to thunderous roars, the centre of the cyclone seemed to bore down on the very vitals of the island.[3]

Although Ted described the extent of the destruction in sufficient detail to present a picture of appalling upheaval, he did so with a sort of nonchalant forbearance, shrugging it off. However, in his letter accompanying the article, Ted gave Barrymore a much different account of the event and admitted that he had "passed lightly over its destructiveness". He wrote from his office, the only part of the bungalow where the roof remained intact:

> We have passed through a terrible experience . . . Kitchen gone, spare room flattened out completely, house proper minus a

good deal of its roof; all belongings saturated; every other
building crazy with palsy and generally broken-backed; boatshed vanished, only indication of the site being the broken
winch; Nee Mourna a battered skeleton fifty yards from where
she reposed at sundown on Sunday safely upon her trolly [sic];
the dinghy vanished; all equipment, oars, etc., gone; the whole
outline of the beach transfigured; the very hills changed; not a
tree or a shrub or a blade of grass that does not show signs of
awful buffeting. The Isle is badly soiled. We do not know what
to do. May be that we shall have to leave it, for it would cost
close on £500 [$1,000] to re-establish the dear spot as it was on
Sunday afternoon. It is too late in life to undertake such work.

As for themselves, in what shape were they?

Bertha is well, I am thankful to say and is working like a demon,
as she always does, on such occasions. I am first-class, too,
although we had 24 hours of extreme dampness and no trifle of
mental strain. The place looks pitiful. All Bertha's nick-nacks,
brooches, rings, pins etc. and her raiment were scattered in wet
masses on the bedroom floor and are there now. We are sleep-
ing in this office on the floor in not over dry things and on a
strip of rubberoid to keep off the moisture of the floor. The
clocks have stopped, the fowls are silent — some must have
been killed, the birds have been killed, and only the cow-bell
forgets to be quiet.

Would Barrymore kindly tell Spenser Hopkins of their plight?
And could Spenser ask a friend, a contractor, if he would care
to give an estimate of the cost of repairs? Although, as Ted
added: "we may yet decide to leave the adorable Isle now that
it is so sadly soiled".[4]

Ted and Bertha were not alone on the island. A native boy,
Pompey, from the settlement across on the mainland, had been
working for Ted. In Essie's absence, the settlement superintendent, John Martin Kenny, sent across Pompey's gin and two
children to help with the housekeeping. During the most
violent phases of the storm, separated by a brief but sinister lull,
Ted had stationed Bertha and the natives in the office, which
was on the lee side of the house. Here he crouched down with
them as the trees outside splintered and crashed, and the iron
from the roof was ripped off and whisked away, adding whin-
ing sounds to the tumult of the night. The natives were
petrified with fear. As for Bertha, she could not hear these
sounds in full, but she experienced them in a different and
perhaps more terrifying way because she "felt" them — the
impacts, the rendings, the crashings being relayed through the
ground and through the timbers of the disintegrating dwelling.

In the seething darkness, books tumbled down over them,
shaken and wrenched from the shelves. Folders were blown
open and papers whirled around as if the room was crowded
with ghostly bats. Water poured in and blasts of wind made
waves which splashed about their hands and feet.

Above: Dunk Island, looking towards Purtaboi Islet, March 1918, following cyclone. *Below:* The same scene three and a half years later. Photographs by Spenser Hopkins.
(A.H. Chisholm Papers, courtesy of Mitchell Library.)

With the first glimmer of daylight, Bertha was less concerned about what had happened to her things in the bedroom than to Ted's books and papers, which lay in sodden piles on the office floor. As the light strengthened and they peered out through the frames of doors and windows, they saw a leafless wilderness. In every direction were scenes so much like those pictures of the battlefields of Europe that Ted could not help but feel that this was some form of retribution meted out to them for having enjoyed such an idyllic life while so many others had suffered.

Tremendous seas still ran on all sides. The fence around the house had vanished and the Jersey cows and horses wandered bewilderedly among the tattered remnants of the uprooted crotons. The mango trees, over whose growth and well-being Ted had watched for so long, mostly lay prone — the few that still managed to stand had been torn to pieces. Cart-loads of fruit gathered on the Sunday to be boxed and shipped were strewn about, already rotting. Sand, shells and broken coral covered acres of cultivated grounds, superimposed by a moving layer of millions of aimless insects. The loveliness of the island was of the past.

In his letter to Barrymore, Ted also wrote: "Perhaps one is inclined to feel a trifle desperate and our case may not be nearly as bad as that of others." He soon came to a realization of this. Looking towards the mainland Aborigine settlement, it appeared that no building was left standing. Natives could be seen — sitting or wandering about — but there was no sign of Superintendent Kenny. Flashes of Morse Code were seen, and from them it was gathered that there had been a great disaster over there and that help was needed urgently.

As Ted had no boat — even if he had dared face that tumultuous sea — he had to wait until the *Lass O'Gowrie* appeared on a northward course. On board was Ted's friend Chris Wildsoet who had come up from Townsville to find out how his relatives had fared at Mission Beach. After taking a vote from the crew, Captain Stewart agreed to lend Chris and Ted one of the ship's two lifeboats. As the steamer proceeded north, Ted and Wildsoet rowed across to the settlement and learned that John Kenny had been killed at the height of the cyclone by a heavy piece of wood when he had gone from shelter to try to help his daughter Kathleen, who had been speared by a shaft of flying timber and was herself already dead. Mrs Kenny was badly injured, and so the *Lass O'Gowrie* was intercepted as it came back south and she was taken on board for the hospital in Townsville after Ted paid her fare. He saw to it that the authorities would be immediately notified of the plight of the Aborigines in the settlement, two hundred of them, three of whom had been drowned in a tidal surge following the storm.[5]

As to Ted's own plight, the response of friends was immediate and overwhelming, so much so that a week after sending off "The Tempest" to George Barrymore and that despairing letter, he wrote that he and Bertha were going to attempt to get everything in order again: "The Big Man is financing me for the present. Mr Hordern says he is ready to reinstate everything when I say the word." The "Big Man" was of course David Green. Ted finished this letter by saying: "when you next come perhaps the soiled Isle may hand you back one of your good sister's roses".[6]

Barrymore remained a bachelor until late in his life when he married Freda Sternberg who, years earlier, had been Dame Nellie Melba's secretary. After a visit to Dunk, Barrymore's sister, Mrs J.B. Wood of Brisbane, had sent the Banfields a dozen rose plants with a note which said: "I have thrust open the gate of Paradise and thrust in a rose."[7] Ted had thought that these bushes would also have to be numbered among the losses; but one of them had survived and he decided that it could well bloom again.

He had been reassured in other ways. When he took out this second letter to Barrymore, Spenser Hopkins was on board the steamer, accompanied by a carpenter who had been brought along to inspect the damage and to work out the nature and cost of repairs. Believing Ted to be without a boat, Spenser had also brought along his boys' flattie. In the diary, Ted wrote of Spenser that he "has proved himself a true and most practical friend".[8]

Nevertheless, in the aftermath of the "storm wind", Ted had been genuinely convinced that their occupation of the island had come to an end. At the age of rising sixty-six, he did not feel capable of rebuilding from scratch; nor did he feel that he could subject Bertha, sixty, to going through it all again.

She sensed what he was thinking, and after a few days she found an answer to it. Taking Ted by the hand, she led him across what had been a garden, flies and beetles rising like dust puffs from the overlay of sand, broken shells and coral chips, to where a few ragged trees stood broken but unbowed. She pointed to something that had caught her eye like a flash of emerald when she had been rounding up some of the cows.

"There!" she said, directing Ted's gaze to the new green shoot bravely trembling on a ragged broken branch. "Soon it'll be breaking out everywhere, so let us get the clocks going again — and no more of this ridiculous talk about leaving."

The sun was already at work: "So commanding his rule . . . so influential his presence, that I have come to look up to him as the transcendent manifestation of that power which ordains life and all its privileges". And had not Ted himself owed to the sun "salvation from that which tributary friends in their meed of tenderness predicted — an untimely grave".[9] The strong rays reached down through the tangled debris and germinated the seeds lying there, so that a thick new undergrowth rapidly rose, with types of grasses never in fact seen before on the island, but which the cows obviously found much to their liking.

Even so, between moods of hope and optimism, Ted remained shaken and depressed. Purtaboi had been reduced to a bare rock with a frayed crest of seared shrubs, and he had to remind himself that given a little time it could be a sort of floating garden again. The whole island had been seared, the secrets of its valleys and ravines laid bare; although secure in their fortress of granite rocks, those remaining swiftlets had survived totally unscathed. Bedarra and Timana were as sorely ravaged as the mother island of the group; yet on the latter, as he passed in a boat, Ted heard the contented call of a swamp pheasant, a species which had hitherto been only on Dunk, its migration due to the storm wind.

Ted's promenade in Brammo Bay was obstructed by heaps of seaweed and lumps of coral torn from reefs, which had suffered their worst battering for hundreds of years. The sand-spit was minus the flagstaff and the grass hut, and where a few days previously a great flight of terns had settled, he now saw one lone bird, a "wind-wearied gannet" asleep with its head under its wing.[10] His other strips of the tropics had become Beachcomber's nightmares, crowded as they were with flotsam and jetsam from his own domain: part of his splintered flagstaff, broken oars, fence posts entangled with wire — but nowhere any sign of the sailing ship grating which had served as his welcoming gate for so many years.

From Dunk, Purtaboi, Bedarra and Timana — and undoubtedly from all the islands under his jurisdiction — the notices forbidding shooting had gone, some with their posts and trees, others without leaving a shred of cloth behind them. He had replacement notices stored in his office, and they had come through the cyclone in mint condition, but it hardly seemed worth going to the trouble of putting them up. So many birds had been killed that it was as if half the guns of the Western Front had been swung around to rain their shells upon the island. With so many thousands annihilated and their habitats destroyed in a matter of a few hours, it made all his efforts over the previous thirteen years as Honorary Ranger seem somehow pathetic and puerile.

In his vacillating moods, he still could not shake off a feeling of guilt, that by indulging himself here on Dunk while so many others had to endure the horrors of war, he had brought retribution upon himself — and, in doing so, had brought calamity upon the island, and upon its creatures and adornments. It was as if the sanctuary, the sea-girt hermitage, no longer existed.

⋯   ⋯   ⋯

With the tank wrecked and the pipes broken, the vaunted system that brought running water to every room in the bungalow had completely broken down. But in the wake of the carpenter came a plumber to get the system working again. Spenser Hopkins managed to spend a great deal of time lending a hand as the repairs got under way, to the roof and other damaged parts of the house, the kitchen and outhouses and sheds, while a new boatshed was necessary after the complete disappearance of the one that had housed the first *Nee Mourna*. David Green had earlier offered Ted a hut from the garden of his Townsville home, one which was used as a playhouse by his daughters and was dubbed by him "The Rats' Palace".[11] Ted now took up the offer, and the hut was shipped to Dunk and re-erected up behind the bungalow. Work often went on well after dark. At the same time, the scars on the island itself began to disappear as trees recovered and shrubs grew. The tides were at work, too, sweeping and moulding, restoring the strands of Dunk and its satellites to their former outlines. And the grating gate had weathered the storm after all; it was salvaged from under a heap of debris, ready to swing on its hinges again.

Throughout all this, as Bertha was well aware, Ted continued to be up and down. Very much up indeed when advance copies of *Tropic Days* arrived, and up even further when he received the first batch of reviews. Once again *The Times* had done him proud. The *Literary Supplement* stated: "If Mr Banfield does not know the coast of Queensland well he must be one of the greatest of imaginative artists. He gives the impression of having absorbed its sunshine and sea-water until he has become part of it". But on this same tropic day, down he went again as the same mail brought the sad news of the death of his long-time friend Dodd S. Clarke who had written: "North Queensland is my country. I love it. I live in it. I would die for it."[12]

In August Ted and Bertha celebrated yet another wedding anniversary, their thirty-second. Since the restoration of the domain had advanced so well, as in the past Ted felt free to declare the day a holiday. The time when the white nutmeg pigeons and the metallic starlings were due from the north was close, and he was afraid that the March cyclone might have caught them as they were leaving and that they would be added to the lost creatures the island had to mourn. To his relief they appeared on time, although there were fewer of them. Old nests, old haunts and old trees, which had provided tiers of dormitories, were no more, so they set about building new abodes and raising new families as if nothing untoward had intervened.

The birds were followed by a few less regular migrators from other climatic zones — the Horderns from Sydney. Ted was most anxious to see their reactions, since landmarks they had known, trees that had become as familiar as old friends to them, had vanished. They arrived prepared to be dismayed by such dramatic changes, and so were amazed to see the island looking serenely beautiful, arrayed in a mantle of bright new green, still filling the air with the same delectable scents and fragrances. Ted was happy — the island was blossoming again.

One of the losses both Ted and Bertha greatly lamented was that of the sunbirds, the tiny creatures "sired by a sunbeam, born of a flower". As weeks went by without a glimpse of a single member of this divine species, they came to accept that their absence meant a permanent loss. To their joy, "in the quiet of a lustrous and lazy afternoon, one of the living jewels came to feast among the red hibiscus blossoms".[13]

Thus the island recovered from the pulverizing impact of the storm wind. However, its full effect on Ted was delayed for nearly six months, until shortly after the *Innisfail* delivered his new motor-boat, the second *Nee Mourna*. Before he could really get to know how she handled and behaved — and her engine was to continue to misbehave badly — the combination of shock, worry and overwork on reconstruction overtook him, and he began to show symptoms which reminded Bertha of his condition prior to his breakdown all those years ago in Townsville.

Bertha, who had had some trouble of a nervous nature herself, took an immediate and determined stand. Ted must have proper medical attention without delay, and since their friends were returning south they escorted him to Townsville, where he was admitted to a private hospital room with what was described as a nervous collapse.

Five days of tender care magically restored him, although there was another vital factor in his recovery. He had been understandably fretting about financial matters, not only those involving the restoration of the island but for the future. Spenser Hopkins had a suggestion to make. As he saw it, Ted and Bertha had many, many years left; but would it make it easier for them if they were to be guaranteed a fixed income over, say, the coming fifteen years? Out of this came a business arrangement between Ted Banfield and Spenser Hopkins and handled by a firm of Townsville solicitors. Spenser would guarantee that income in return for a half share of Ted's Dunk Island land.[14] Within a week of being taken to Townsville, Ted was back on the island, reading and writing, and putting up new notices as he patrolled his domain in the second *Nee Mourna*.

In November the hostilities ceased on the other side of the world, and by this time Ted was making light of the great "debil-debil" of March, which had loomed so large in his diary, by calling it "that inordinate puff of wind".[15]

A mainland neighbour had also recorded the event in his diary. George Webb, a man of notably few words, had written: "Cyclone".[16]

Chapter 24

Ancient Order
of Beachcombers

While Ted and Bertha enjoyed the company of most of their visitors, whether invited or impromptu, they were more than content to be left on their own for spells. It was at such times that the creatures of the island gave them endless joy. A certain magpie, for instance, a bird that

> spent many wayward hours endeavouring to sing. No cultured relative was present to teach the notes of its kind, so that in default it learned the complete vocabulary of the domestic poultry, besides the more familiar calls and exclamations of its mistress, the varied barks of two dogs, the shrieks of many cockatoos, the gabble of scrub fowls. The bird also began to play in semi-human style, performing marvellous acrobatic feats on the clothes-line, and lying on its back juggling with a twig as some "artists" do with a barrel in the circus.[1]

There was also a lorikeet that established a special relationship with their fat yellow cat, Sultan. This bird would "fill its lower mandible with water from a drinking dish and tip it neatly into the cat's ear, and scream with delight as Sultan shook his sleepy head. To dip the tip of the cat's tail into the water and mimic the scrubbing of the floor was an everyday pastime." The bird went on to play an even more dangerous game. It would climb into a low bush and appear absorbed inspecting young shoots and tender leaves, while

> Assuming a ferocious mien, Sultan approached ... His eyes glittered as he crouched, his tail thickened and swayed, his ears were depressed, his whiskers and nose twitched, his jaws worked, his claws were unsheathed and sheathed spasmodically as he crept stealthily towards the apparently unconscious bird. After two or three preliminary feints for the perfect adjustment

of his faculties and pose, he bounded into the air with distended talons well over his screeching playmate. The scene would be rehearsed several times before Sultan, tired of the mummery and eager for actualities, slunk yawling into the bush.

The bird "whimpering in the dusk, waddled home to be caged".[2]

It was the publication of such incidents, as much as the descriptions of strings of bays and blazing beaches, that made Ted's readers eager to share the island life, and he received a warning about this from a very old friend.

On one of his rare visits to Townsville, Ted had crossed to Magnetic Island with George Barrymore to visit Dodd Clarke, who had been living in retirement in a "quaint little tropic residence" by the sea at Nelly Bay. Dodd Clarke's parting words to Ted had been: "Now, look here, you are writing too much and too well about that island. You'll bring people about you. Stop it! If you don't you'll be over-run."[3]

Ted had laughed. "Goodbye Clarke. Have no fear."

As the ferry had slipped away, Dodd Clarke had remained on the wharf, sadly shaking his head. He himself had already experienced something of what he had warned Ted about: as this island had become more popular his "long desired exclusiveness and beloved isolation was interrupted", and eventually he had moved to old haunts near Cardwell.[4]

Clarke had not been altogether wrong. In *The Confessions* Ted wrote: "A strange sail brings out the whole population, staring and curious" — all three of them, provided Essie was not away. But as the island became better known, mainly because of its celebrated inhabitant, the situation changed, and in one of his letters to Alec Chisholm, Ted wrote:

> You might imagine that living on a desert island would be an insurance against visitors; but we have got into the habit of expecting our daily visitor even if we do not offer special petition for him, and when the visitors come by the half dozen or even two dozen, time flies with talk and walk and idle dreaming. The other day my wife and I glanced through my diary and found that a few years ago we spent over three months without seeing a strange face. It is rare now that two days pass by without a caller.[5]

Not only were there callers arriving in cruisers, destroyers, survey ships, steamers and private vessels, but the pleas had increased — from young people and old, from Great Britain, Europe, America, as well as from within Australia — to be allowed to come and sample the island life.

Ted continued to try to be firm, and Bertha encouraged him to be so, but he had a soft heart, and from time to time he relented. As in the case of the naval man Hough, who had visited the island on one of the warships. He was invalided out of the navy in 1918; so partly as a gesture towards the general

Above: The second *Nee Mourna* on trolley.
(Courtesy of Helen Dyer, Townsville.)
Below: The replaced boatshed with tramway down to water.
(A.H. Chisholm Papers, courtesy of Mitchell Library.)

war effort, Ted invited him to try Dunk's vaunted recuperative powers. Hough came with his wife and two children.

Years later, Elinor Hough wrote nostalgically of the time they had occupied the hut above the Banfield bungalow, the one that had been in David Green's backyard. They also had use of an old slab hut as a kitchen with "a floor of broken coral, kept clean by means of a rake instead of a broom". Their living expenses were very low as they had all the fish, oysters, fruit, vegetables, milk, cream and eggs they needed.

> We were never bored; there was always something fresh and interesting to do and see. I gave the children lessons on the beach, as before my marriage I had been a teacher. We swam, fished, hunted for shells and corals, gathered orchids and lovely wild flowers, watched birds, crabs etc. We collected and counted over one hundred varieties of ferns, from the beautiful maidenhair, which carpets the island like grass, to the tall stately tree-ferns growing in gullies.[6]

There were special treats such as when they went picnicking with Ted, who took them with him in his motor-boat around Dunk and to neighbouring islands and islets in the course of his patrols and inspections as Honorary Ranger of the reserves. They saw sharks, giant rays, dugongs and turtles feeding in water so clear that the ocean floor showed the shadows of the boat with their heads over its side. Ted was full of information about the marvels of bird life, pointing out feathered residents such as the sulphur-crested white cockatoos which flew to the mainland each day for breakfast, lunch and supper.

While living on Dunk was an unforgettable experience for Elinor Hough and her children, as far as her husband was concerned it did not work out very well. The natives who had been in the settlement on the mainland opposite Dunk were now at a new settlement in Challenger Bay, Great Palm Island. The new superintendent was not as indulgent towards the Banfields as John Kenny had been, so they were often without native help. Ted looked to all male guests to pull their weight by assisting with the daily duties and general maintenance. Hough was not cut out for the discipline of the life here; they might be on a tropical island, but what should be done today could not be left until tomorrow. Ted and Bertha adhered to this, and that was why, unlike so many other islanders, they did not deteriorate.[7]

Ted was philosophical about Hough and tried to tell himself that in future he would limit the population strictly to Bertha, himself and Essie. He managed to resist most requests, but some years later there was one which so touched him that he could not persist in saying no.

Just before the outbreak of war, Ted had received a letter from a woman on a cattle station near Morven in Central Queensland, telling him that her crippled daughter Dorothy, a child of ten years to whom she had read the "Confessions" and who was so intensely interested in the story of the coral reef that her mother wondered if they came to the Island it would be possible to carry the child out to the reef to see the wonders for herself.

It pained Ted to refuse, but he had taken a stand and so he said no. Some ten years later there came a request from the girl herself, now a young woman and married. She wrote letters which captivated Ted because he sensed in the writer a talent for prose; and when she included a photograph of herself in the chair in which she was forced to live, he was so moved that he relented to the extent of writing back to say that he had a small hut vacant and that "if they cared to come and occupy that for 6 months they were at liberty to do so".[8]

Dorothy and Walter Cottrell "absolutely jumped at the offer and arrived with all their goods and chattels"[9] at the beginning of February 1923.

The hospitality of the island was also extended for a time to a soldier who had lost a leg in Palestine and who was interested in trying to make a living by growing nuts.

Between the departure of the Houghs and the arrival of the Cottrells there were of course many who would always be so welcome that life without their visits would have been greatly lacking — much as, from time to time, Ted and Bertha liked to have the island to themselves. The visits of Spenser Hopkins were always looked forward to and his departures regretted, whether he came alone or with his wife and children.

Young people, with whom Ted and Bertha continued to have such an affinity, were also very welcome guests, in particular Marjorie Green, one of the three gracious daughters of

The Beachcomber and Frank the Fisherman after gathering bananas, bringing them home in the *Yan-o-lee* ("I go this way"), a flattie built by Banfield.
(A.H. Chisholm Papers, courtesy of Mitchell Library.)

the "Big Man", and their lively cousin Isabel, daughter of David Green's brother Jack. Isabel became a great favourite. She worked at *The Bulletin* office in Townsville and was always willing and eager to undertake any secretarial work Ted might require. Whenever she visited the island she took it upon herself to give his typewriter a good clean and overhaul.

Another favourite guest was a visitor from England, Spenser's young sister Lillian, who was a very great help to the Banfields and a source of much delight to them. For her autograph book, which contained the signatures of an entire Australian Cricket Team, Ted typed the following on 12 September 1921:

> Charming in the parlor;
> Killing in the skillion —
>   That's Lillian.
>
> Hefty with the hoe,
> Making weeds look silly —
>   That's Lillie.
>
> Slipping, sliding, slithering,
> Down the smiling hill —
>   That's Lil.
>
> Lil, Lillie, Lillian,
> You're a girl in a million.
>
>   His
>   Beachcomber   X
>   Mark.

Opposite Ted's contribution, Bertha wrote:

> A little health, a little wealth,
> A little house and freedom;
> With some kind friends for certain ends,
> But — little cause to need 'em!!!

Another phase of the opening up of the north began after the Great War. Soldier settlers took up land on the coast opposite Dunk Island and some became good friends. One of them, Syd Harris, they had known since his babyhood in Townsville. There was an ever increasing cavalcade of pearlers, beche-de-mer gatherers, fishermen, tourists, yachtsmen and naval personnel in proas, sampans, luggers, launches, ketches and warships, including the survey vessel HMS *Fantome*.

Not all of these could be depended upon to accept the strictures of the reserves. At the same time there was an influx of shooters, egg-poachers, legal and illegal collectors of shells and coral, so that Ted had to increase his patrols and his vigilance, and found himself having to report more and more transgressions and outrages to the under secretary of the Department in Brisbane. What infuriated him was the attitude of the southern officials, either so dilatory in dealing with his complaints or ignoring them altogether. In the face of this, his despair at the failure of the far north to establish itself as a separate colony, and in turn as another state within the federal framework, became even deeper.

There was also the stream of government officials, scientists and state governors, all of whom were accorded the informal but courteous welcome that Robert — now Sir Robert — Philp had assured them many years ago they would receive.

That such a visit was impending was announced locally by Ted from the spit, from the new flagstaff there, when a commonwealth flag was raised. While to a certain extent this was a signal to the hoi polloi to kindly steer clear, at least until the flag came down, there were some who claimed it proved that Ted could be very hoity-toity when the occasion arose — and it has to be admitted that at times he did think himself a cut above the locals, whites as well as natives, with all of whom nevertheless he regarded himself as a kindred spirit, a fellow Beachcomber.

The governor of Queensland, Sir Matthew Nathan, paid a visit in June 1921, and his reception was in keeping with all that his staff had expected. Yet some two months later, when the governor-general of Australia arrived in HMAS *Sydney* — after his aide had sent a warning telegram ahead — it seemed that decorum had been thrown to the light breeze that made the day so beautifully temperate.

As His Excellency, Lord Forster, and Lady Forster, accompanied by their daughter Mrs Rachel Pitt-Rivers and Lady Digby and staff, reached the beach in the naval pinnace, an extremely odd collection of characters clad in seaweed, shells and coral, and with starfish medallions, appeared from the trees behind the beach opposite where the vice regal party landed. Ted was at their head, and his retinue included Spenser Hopkins, the oysterman George the Greek, and four or five other men who happened to be on the island at the time.[10]

In reporting the appearance of these motley members of the Ancient Order of Beachcombers, George Barrymore was of the opinion that while Ted Banfield had revelled in concocting the stunt, when it came to the point of having to carry it out in the face of His Majesty's representative in Australia, he was not all that sure of himself. Perhaps, as Bertha, who was out of sight in the trees, also feared, this time Ted really had gone too far with his leg-pulling.

Undaunted, he proceeded with the ceremony, unrolling a scroll and announcing that he and his colleagues were members of an exclusive brotherhood, devotees of the sun, the sea and the sand. If he were to dwell too long on the attractions of the Beachcomber's life, he might well lure His Excellency away from the path of duty and cause him to forsake his high office in order to be free to promenade a strip of the tropics.

While the governor-general appeared to give the address his most serious attention, the womenfolk were in fits of laughter, particularly Mrs Pitt-Rivers to whom the play-acting especially appealed; on her return to England, she was to become well-known on the London stage as Mary Hinton.[11] Ted was thus encouraged to continue, and he went on to present his distinguished visitor with an immaculate cowrie shell, and the address. With a grave air, Lord Forster accepted both and was thus proclaimed a Member of the Order.

A happy, relaxed afternoon ensued, with swimming, inspection of the island's show spots, a trip across to Purtaboi — yet even though the governor-general took his leave with much grace, Ted had a lingering concern that the levity had not entirely met with vice regal approval. He needn't have worried. Lord Forster was to declare that it had been one of the most unusual and delightful incidents in his term of office, and that the island was certainly one of the loveliest he had ever seen.

Word of this came to the Banfields from the author-naturalist, Charles Barrett, who stayed on Dunk about this time. His visit, first mooted in Melbourne in 1911, had been delayed by prolonged war service. Of the way of life of the islanders, Barrett wrote that it was "a compromise, perhaps; not too simple and not too far distant from the comfort that middle-class folk demand". Of the Beachcomber he wrote: "He ranks with the very few Australian authors whose books will be remembered at the end of this century."[12]

Meanwhile, in the face of increasing violations of the reserves, Ted had been taking a more militant attitude in his "Rural Homilies". He wrote of the "ruthless collectors", and those exploiters of plumage and bird skins who were pandering to the "barbarities of fashion". The situation had not improved since Walter Strickland's scathing comments on the same subject. In print Ted appealed not only to the good sense and honour of members of the public but also to the authorities. There was a law — compel its administration!

In 1921 that law was amended, but Ted was so angered at the changes, the inaccuracies, the inadequacies — and the plain injustices — that, in his seventieth year, the Honorary Ranger was to make what he believed was a dramatic decision. And this involved his friendship with a younger bird-lover whom he had met comparatively late in his life, Alec Chisholm.

Chapter 25
Romance and Reality

Alexander Hugh Chisholm claimed that he was first introduced to E.J. Banfield through the red pages of the Sydney *Bulletin* in which the reviewer wrote of one of Ted's books that it made him want to "go a-Dunking". Alec Chisholm read *The Confessions* and wrote of this book's effect on him: "How well I remember the glow imparted by those pages! . . . Here, on a little isle off the coast of northern Queensland, Romance and Reality met and were blended."[1]

The friendship between Chisholm and Banfield began in 1916 with a letter from Ted to Alec referring to the latter's bird notes in a periodical called *Emu*: "I am glad to find another kindred spirit — one who can look at a bird without wanting its skin and skeleton."[2]

Alec Chisholm was born in 1890 and started work as a journalist at the age of twenty-one on one of the newspapers Ted's father had helped to establish, *The Maryborough and Dunolly Advertiser*. In 1915 he joined *The Daily Mail* in Brisbane, and at the same time became involved in fauna protection and the editing of papers and magazines on natural history. The friendship between the two, based on the brotherhood of bird-study, grew through correspondence, but it was not until late in 1921 that they met in person when Chisholm came to stay.

At this stage Chisholm was a senior office holder in the Queensland Naturalists' Club, the Gould League of Bird-Lovers, and the Royal Australian Ornithologists' Union, and was co-editor of the Queensland *Naturalist*. He had also risen to become Leader of Staff of *The Daily Mail*, and through him Ted already had an outlet, a platform, as Chisholm used every opportunity to attack the ravagers of birds in the columns of the paper.

As they began "a-Dunking" together, Ted got on splendidly with the young, lean, blue-eyed naturalist who, like himself, was self-taught. Chisholm had also gone into the bush to bird-watch with volumes of the classics, including Shakespeare.

Bertha also took an immediate liking to their guest. Ted told her that Chisholm was one of the best informed men on natural history to come to the island since Sir Walter Strickland. She managed to avoid a shudder at the mention of that name. They had much to thank the baronet for, but she saw no similarity whatsoever between the two men, except that they were both fiercely opposed to the abuse of wild life.

As Ted showed Chisholm favourite and secret haunts of various species of birds, taking him around to the swiftlets cave, Chisholm carried his camera. He was a noted nature photographer and many of the finest snapshots of Dunk during the Beachcomber's occupation were taken during his ten days' stay. He knew that discoveries had been made here, dating back to 1848 when John MacGillivray, the naturalist on board HMS *Rattlesnake*, had found birds, a butterfly, a huge spider and a species of banana hitherto unknown to science, and had seen the shiny-leafed umbrella tree for the first time.[3]

Ted was shy about his own contributions to scientific discovery on Dunk. He always insisted that he was an observer: "I am not a professor with a mind like a warehouse, rich with the spoils of time, but a mere peddler, conscious of the janglings of an ill-sorted, ill-packed knapsack of unconsidered trifles". His discoveries were things he had more or less stumbled upon as an observer, but he was proud all the same. As he and Chisholm ranged the reefs, the beaches and the forest, Ted pointed out what he had found. He took his viewing-box from where it hung on the wall inside the boatshed, a square of glass set in the bottom of four sides of galvanized iron. It leaked, so water had to be shaken out of it frequently, but it still enabled them to obtain a clear steady view of a tiny spider crab that masqueraded as a spray of seaweed to elude its enemies at the time it was shedding its shell. In place of the carapace it fixed choice bits of weed to its back. It was called after Ted — *Zewa banfieldi*. In a pool Ted again used the viewing-box to help catch a glimpse of a tiny elusive and shadowy fish also called after him:

> Sought out by the sun,
> translucent fish revealed their presence
> by spectral shadows on the sand,
> and, traced by the shadows,
> became discernible,
> though but little the more substantial.[4]

On the beach, Ted introduced Chisholm to a discovery he had made "when the smoke of the belated steamer was a mere smudge in still air far to the south-west, and there was naught to do but wait the tidings, good or bad, from the sick and dis-comforted world", a grub which dug a shaft in the sand and emerged later as a plump, silvery grey moth.[5]

Up in the forest there was something that had not been recorded elsewhere in the world: "a diminutive orchid, the roots, tuber, leaf, and flower of which may be easily covered by the glass of a lady's watch". And then a living creature, a delicate, graceful fruit-eating rat, russet-brown in colour:

> The mother carries her young crouched on her haunches, cling-ing to her fur apparently with teeth as well as claws, and she manages to scuttle along fairly fast, in spite of her encum-brances. The first that I saw bearing away her family to a place of refuge was deemed to be troubled with some hideous defor-mity aft, but inspection at close quarters showed how she had converted herself into a novel perambulator.[6]

After Ted sent sample creatures to the Queensland Museum it was pronounced an extraordinary species and introduced to the scientific world under the title *Uromys banfieldi*.

As Ted wrote in *The Confessions*, "While the bird life of our island is plentiful and varied, mammalian is insignificant in number". There were two species of rat (following Ted's discovery of the second), a flying fox, two bats and the largest four-footed creature present, the echidna:

> An animal which possesses some of the features of the hedgehog of old England, and resembles in others that distinctly Australian paradox, the platypus . . . which in the production of its young combines the hatching of an egg as of a bird, with the suckling of a mammal, and which also has some of the characteristics of a reptile, cannot fail to be an interesting object to every student of the marvels of Nature.[7]

As Alec Chisholm knew, this creature was also called the "spiny ant-eater". He was eager to see its island haunts. Ted showed him these, and at the same time something of the feast of its favourite fare provided on Dunk:

> White ants, black ants, red ants,
> brown ants, grey ants, green ants;
> ants large, ants small;
> ants slothful, ants brisk;
> meat-eating ants, grain-eating ants,
> fruit-eating ants, nectar-imbibing ants;
> ants that fight, ants that run away;
> ants that live under coldest stone,
> ants that dwell among the tree-tops;
> silent ants, ants that literally "kick-up" a row;
> good ants, bad ants,
> ants that are merely so so —
> we have them all . . .[8]

In the second *Nee Mourna*, which Ted was thinking about

selling in order to be free to invest in a new boat with a less temperamental engine, they went to Kumboola, Timana, Bedarra, Clump Point and Tam O'Shanter Point. On the islands and islets of Ted's domain, some of the calico notices were weathered and torn, and he would normally have replaced them; but a new proclamation was imminent and fresh notices, most probably with revised wording, would be coming to hand.

On such excursions, when Ted allowed the boat to drift close inshore over a steeply-shelving beach, his guest experienced something of what Ted had written about in *Tropic Days*: "the

In the second *Nee Mourna*: officer from HMS *Fantome*, the Beachcomber in impish mood for camera, and A.H. Chisholm. (A.H. Chisholm Papers, courtesy of Mitchell Library.)

boat seems to float in an invisible element". They saw its shadow on the sea-floor. Other shapes and shadows, too:

with ghostly glide, a dull-skinned shark came into view with motion so steady and apparently effortless that it might have been a spectre. The pectoral fins swayed listlessly. The swirl of the tail was as tender as a caress. Passing the boat a few yards, it turned with a gracious sweep and nestled in its shade, and, though motionless, it was wide awake.

Light and shade, creatures big and small, captured in prose and poetry:

small sea-spiders sport under the lea of the boat,
each of the eight legs supported by a bubble.
With astonishing nimbleness,
the spider slips and glides over the surface
as a man in laborious snow-shoes over the snow.

Having basked in the sun
and frolicked with its kind,
the spider abandons its pads,
takes to its hairy bosom a bubble of air,
and dives below.
The shadows,
not the spiders alone,
gave pleasing entertainment.
Each vague shadow and eight bubble-shod feet
formed a broochlike ornament on the yellow sand —
a grey jewel surrounded by diamonds,
for every bubble acted as a lens
concentrating the light.[9]

The survey ship HMS *Fantome* was present during Chisholm's stay and he took some excellent photographs of the vessel in the bay and her officers ashore; also of the black flag which was erected on a patch cleared at the top of a high hill to act as a marker for the men carrying out the charting of nearby waters. Ted welcomed the *Fantome*'s presence — her engineers were always willing to have a go at curing the ills of the motor-boat's engine.

Chisholm's preconceived notions of the island life had come in for a jolt:

One expected to loiter, perhaps to laze, in the company of a kin-spirit who had ample time to stand and stare; but one found that to laze on Dunk Island meant to do so alone. The Beachcomber's step was brisk, his speech rapid (at times vehement), his enthusiasms as extensive and keen as those of any boy.[10]

That vehemence was currently being directed at the enemies of bird and other natural life and also at southern officials who were declining to alter the provisions for open and closed seasons, as applied to the nutmeg pigeons, in drafting the forthcoming new Act. Chisholm realized that Ted had found a "grand objective" after abandoning civilization, by first declaring the island a sanctuary and then having it officially proclaimed as such while he became its Honorary Ranger. He also became aware that the major event of Ted's occupation of the island had been the storm wind which had at first seemingly destroyed that sanctuary for all time, forcing him to have to consider leaving it. Ted admitted that it "crops up with irritating persistency" in his writings, but that the event was so real that it had "stamped itself so deeply on the face of the land that no glance is free from impressive reminders of its hasty coming, brief term, and boisterous disrespect towards the concerns and sentiments of human beings."[11]

In the evenings, after all the shared wonders of the day, Chisholm saw some of the sun's "transcendent gifts as a painter", about which Ted had written in *My Tropic Isle*, and, more recently, in an article "Tropic Glory": "Last evening we saw the very gates of heaven". Sunsets comparable in splendour with those Ted and Bertha had seen when the high-flying dust from the volcano Krakatoa had supplied the pigments for the brushes of the sun.[12]

The hills and peaks behind which the sun finally sank did not seem any great distance; in fact, the island seemed closely tethered to the mainland of Australia. At such times its remoteness was easy to forget, although a tragic incident was a reminder to the visiting naturalist of the real degree of the Banfields' isolation. After viewing a sunset from the bungalow verandah until "the scene burnt itself out in extravagant redness, leaving the Isle in a lurid gloom, and its inhabitants stiff-necked, but with a rare joy at heart",[13] Chisholm and his hosts learnt that there had been a fire of a different sort.

Syd Harris, the soldier settler whom Bertha and Ted had known since soon after he was born, had been reported missing. Searches by friends, neighbours and a policeman had failed to reveal any trace of him. Chisholm wrote of that soft tropic night:

> as we sat on the verandah of the single home of Dunk Island, three signal-fires broke out, one by one, on the mainland three miles away. Those were gripping signals. They marked definitely the death of a young soldier-pioneer, one who came to a tragic end near his lonely selection. One signal-fire was to indicate "All's well"; two, that help was needed; three, that the worst had occurred. I shall not soon forget the dismay that took possession of our small group on that remote tropic isle as the second and third signals glowed faintly across the channel.[14]

As it was discovered, Harris had lost his life when attempting to put out a bush fire that had got out of control when he had been burning off.

To Chisholm, the Banfields seemed to be in glowing health for a couple of their age, although he gathered that Bertha had been quite ill recently. By the time he left, a firm friendship had been cemented. As with Spenser Hopkins, Ted took a paternal interest, and he was to write: "Often since you were here I have pondered on your career and permitted myself to forecast probabilities with the result that I concluded your destiny was to occupy a much more important office than Leader of the Staff of a metropolitan journal." It was an astute prediction as Alec Chisholm was to go on to distinguish himself as an editor in Sydney and Melbourne, as editor of further journals on natural history, as editor-in-chief of the second edition of the *Australian Encyclopaedia* and as the author of many books.[15]

Ted hastened to enlist his support in a major cause when matters with the under secretary of the Department of Agriculture and Stock came to a head.

This was about the time Chisholm wrote under the heading "Traffic in Wild Birds" in his weekly column "Nature Notes" in

The Beachcomber, 1922,
aged seventy.
(A.H. Chisholm Papers,
courtesy of Mitchell
Library.)

Bertha Banfield, about
1922, aged about sixty-
four.
(A.H. Chisholm Papers,
courtesy of Mitchell
Library.)

The Beachcomber, 1922, with his last dog, Dalesman.
(A.H. Chisholm Papers, courtesy of Mitchell Library.)

the Saturday supplement of Brisbane's *The Daily Mail*. The extent of the traffic, and the degree of Chisholm's outrage, can be gauged from what he wrote after a passenger en route for England on the liner the *Largs Bay* had reported what had at first seemed to be a most unlikely thing to happen on the high sea:

> I thought the other night I heard a kookaburra, and again other birds, and have just made a horrible discovery. High up, right at the stern where passengers are not allowed to go, I looked up through the awning and there are heaps of beautiful birds — parrots, cockatoos, galahs and 12 dear old jackasses (looking very sad) and bronze-winged pigeons — and I thought I heard many little birds.

On investigation the passenger discovered "hundreds of emus and eagles, myriads of tropical birds with glorious colourings from Queensland and the Northern Territory . . . two thirds were expected to be dead before reaching England . . . there are also opossums and kangaroos in boxes scarcely able to move."[16]

That a storm with the under secretary had been brewing was all too evident from Ted's letter to Chisholm of 30 July 1922:

> Last mail brought a letter from E.G.E. Scriven asking for hints as to the closed seasons etc., to which I am responding, by reiterating, for about the fourth time, that unless Nutmegs are given a jubilee for about 3 seasons they will disappear at any rate from this part of the coast, Sanctuary or no Sanctuary. Every visitor or passer-by wants a shot at the big white birds. They are so easy to hit as they mass on the islets for nesting purposes. Even Lord Northcliffe indulged in the so-called sport of shooting nesting birds, little aware, I am sure, of the horror of it; and when a big steamer will anchor beside a small island and bombard the trustful mother birds what can be said by way of detriment of the little boats which play havoc on the easily accessible islets? I am writing to Scriven in anything but a good humour.[17]

The letter to the under secretary was in a packet of mail ready to be taken out next time the *Lass O'Gowrie* whistled. Ted spent the intervening days by running a pipe from his water supply to the vegetable garden to provide irrigation. Thus the endless improvements and improvisations for better living went on.

Because the steamer was not expected before daybreak, Ted was not keeping a vigil on the spit. When it whistled at two a.m., he responded with practised alarcrity, shedding his night attire and pulling on his clothes, adding a sweater as the night was quite chilly, and then rowing out to where the lights of the steamer rocked and blinked. As was usual at this hour the exchange of incoming and outgoing mail and packages was sleepy and brief, and presently Ted rowed back to the beach, where he fastened the dinghy to a shore anchor, then hurried up along the avenue of palm-tree sentinels to the bungalow where Bertha had turned up the lamps. She knew that Ted would want to scan through the mail, and she had a mug of warmed milk waiting for him. Long ago she had given up suggesting that he should come back to bed and leave the mail until the morning.

He quickly sorted out what could in fact wait, but anything of interest just had to be opened; this time there was a tubular package marked printed matter and with a Department of Agriculture and Stock label on it.

What emerged from the tube was a total surprise — a poster issued by the Department in connection with The Animals and Birds Act of 1921, with all the proclaimed sanctuaries listed on it.

Ted was incredulous. There was no mention of Dunk — nor of Bedarra, nor Timana. At first it seemed like some appalling bungle — until he saw "Rockingham Bay (the islands therein)" which, presumably, was meant to embrace Dunk, Bedarra, Timana and others.

"This is a deliberate slight!" Ted declared, going on to claim that certain officials were jealous of the fame brought to Dunk and its satellites through the writings of the Beachcomber and that they had set out calculatedly and maliciously to downgrade the island.

Bertha tried to reason that it must be some mistake and that it was not as deliberate as Ted believed, but he would not be calmed. Dunk was the *first* sanctuary of all. Had not he and Bertha between them declared it to be so? And made it their mission in life to provide a hermitage for all forms of bird life? Before any official steps whatsoever were taken? And was it not a fact that Dunk and other islands had become reserves due to Ted's approach to Robert Philp? Dunk had been gazetted as a sanctuary in its own name in its own right, but now it was being summarily parcelled in with all the islands of Rockingham Bay.

Ted was no longer able to appeal to the man to whom he had dedicated *The Confessions*. Sir Robert Philp had died only eight weeks ago, although he had been out of the mainstream of public life while devoting himself to family and business interests.

"For some time," Ted now announced, "I've had it in mind to bring public attention to official ignorance and conduct. But to do so, while still being officially an Honorary Ranger, would, in my view, be a breach of conduct. Therefore, so that I can take the steps necessary, I intend to resign."

Bertha nearly gave up her light hold on the hearing tube as she gasped, "Did you say resign?"

"I did. I'm sending my badge back south."

Bertha was aghast. How could he even *think* of doing anything of this nature when he had been so proud of the honorary office conferred upon him and gazetted like other important appointments?

"It's the only way," he told her, and went back to bed, refusing to discuss the matter further.

Bertha did not persist. She felt that he might well see the matter differently in the morning.

Ted was up and about at his usual early hour despite the summons from the steamer during the night and the upset it had delivered in the mail. He shaved in the bathroom and went down to the gully to pump up water from the stream into the tank; he chopped wood for the stove, kneaded the bread, then showered.

Hoping that he might now have second thoughts about resigning, Bertha made no reference to it. Perhaps he would forget about his outburst. But immediately after breakfast he told her that he was going to his office to write to the under secretary, resigning his honorary rangership of the sanctuary and returning his badge of office.

She could have wept. She, too, had been proud of that metal badge. She had looked upon it as a medal bestowed on Ted in recognition for that decision taken all those years ago to give up the hives and let the offending bee-eaters and wood-swallows go free. It was heart-breaking to think that he should find himself morally obliged to take this decision when, in exactly eight weeks, they would be celebrating a quarter of a century of occupation of the island. Worse still, the decision was being made on their wedding anniversary, their thirty-sixth.

Ted had not forgotten the date, as Bertha had feared he might. After drafting his letter, and to a certain extent getting some of the worst of his indignation off his mind, he came out of the office to announce that this, as on previous anniversaries, would be as far as possible a holiday — a day when he might potter, finishing the painting of the flattie, while Bertha attended to a few of the essential chores about the house, but marked by a little pilgrimage on foot to a pleasant spot where they would picnic on their own.

The next morning he was back in his office early.

After transcribing the drafted letter to the under secretary and packing the badge, Ted started a second letter, one to Alec Chisholm. It is unlikely that he was in the detached frame of mind he claimed to be in: "On mature consideration and without any sort of vexation of the spirit I have written to Mr Scriven the briefest of official notes resigning the office of Hon. Ranger of this sanctuary and tendering the badge thereof." His reason for this was to free his hands for a vigorous protest against the ignorance and misconceptions contained in the poster issued by the Department of Agriculture and Stock on The Animals and Birds Act of 1921.

Examine the list of Sanctuaries and you will notice that with Hinchinbrook are associated geographically Barnard islands,

Raine, Eva Islet, Agnes Islet, Channel Rock, Goold and Garden Islands. Well, the Barnard Group is about 30 miles away from Hinchinbrook, and Raine Island must be looked for somewhere not very far away from Thursday Island. What sense is there in this classification!

This Sanctuary is not specifically mentioned, being included, no doubt, in "Rockingham Bay (the islands therein)". Now, if you ask 100 people down South where Rockingham Bay is, 99 will probably laughingly profess ignorance. If you sought further information as to the whereabouts of the Family Group the answer would, also, very likely be negative: but, no doubt, few would blunder if asked the whereabouts of Dunk Island and other Islands or Islets of the Family Group?

After saying "You know that I don't care a straw for my own or anybody else's dignity", something that those who knew the Beachcomber may not have been altogether prepared to accept, he concluded with a justification for his attitude and action: "There are occasions when as Holy Writ tells one does well to be angry. Such is my mood."[18]

This was the sort of cause very close to Alec Chisholm's heart and he went to work on Ted's behalf behind the scenes, not only from his position of influence in the newspaper world but also as a senior office-holder in various wild life societies. The upshot was reported in *The Daily Mail*, 12 September 1922: "What naturalists regard as an important step in bird conservation was taken yesterday, with the official announcement that the nutmeg pigeons are to become totally protected."

In his "Nature Notes" on 30 September, under the heading "Saving the Pigeons", Chisholm acknowledged Ted's part in the campaign:

> Mr E.J. Banfield of Dunk Island, who has been championing the cause of the nutmeg pigeons, points out that the flock flights of these handsome birds constitute a feature of the North Coast that must not be obliterated. He makes a strong case against the alleged "sports" who fire into masses of the birds in the course of contests to fill sack bags with the beautiful creatures — this right in the middle of the breeding season! All good Australians in North Queensland will assist the authorities to save their country from incurring the stigma that rests on America over the fate of the passenger pigeons.[19]

After being officially informed that the Queensland cabinet had resolved to declare total protection to the nutmegs, and that the commissioner of police would be asked to instruct his officers to exercise strict supervision, Ted claimed victory. This justified his resignation as Honorary Ranger so as to free himself to be able to speak out. He maintained to himself and to Bertha that it had been essential for him to take such a drastic step to bring about forceful action at the highest official level.

Alec Chisholm meanwhile directed his war against ravagers in other directions — to those scavenging coral and birds' eggs

— and in a letter to Ted he asked for any details the Beachcomber might have of further current abuses.

Thinking of those creatures "Rolling and lurching along, gambolling like good-humoured, contented children", shy creatures with a strong affection for their young and love of the companionship of their fellows, Ted responded immediately:

> Yes, there is one other favourite beast of mine that you might take under your shield — the dugong. Like the nutmegs the harmless creatures are fast being exterminated by the Japs who have a practical monopoly of the Great Barrier Reef. No sooner does a lugger anchor in the Bay or anywhere in the neighbourhood than 3 or 4 dinghies will be chucked over-board for a raid. As you know, dugong are shy and slow breeders and since they are perpetually harried in shallow waters they like the pigeons will soon be numbered among the extincts.[20]

Ted continued to supply Chisholm with ammunition: "hordes of Italians recently sent to the sugar districts spend most of their time killing innocent and lovable birds". But their correspondence was starting to run out. A month later, Ted wrote to Chisholm to congratulate him on his engagement to be married, and added: "I once more record joyful satisfaction over your campaign against collectors." This was in fact the Beachcomber's last letter to him.[21]

Bertha had continued to deplore Ted's resignation. To her it remained an unnecessarily severe step to have taken. It was, of course, as she realized, partly based on his over-sensitivity. He could not entirely forget that in all the time he had acted as Honorary Ranger there had never been one word of encouragement or acknowledgment of his work from officials in the south.

Despite his resignation, Ted carried out all inspections and patrols as before; and while his letter of resignation was registered in Brisbane, it would appear that, like many preceding it, no action was taken. When new calico notices were issued in 1925, a letter was addressed to E.J. Banfield of Dunk Island, asking how many he required; but by this time he was stepping to the music of an altogether different drummer.[22]

Chapter 26

The Reading Room in Amsterdam

The living legend, the man who had been given possibly three and no more than six months to live when he was forty-five, now entered his seventieth year fitter, stronger and in some respects younger.

In March 1922 another visitor was made a member of the Ancient Order of Beachcombers, the Chicago millionaire who owned a floating palace called the *Speejacks* which was nearly thirty metres long and was the first motor-boat to go around the world. The Australian author Dale Collins was on board, and he wrote of Ted: "The first thing that struck you as he sprang nimbly aboard was that here was the youngest old man who had ever foiled time . . . a small, wiry chap burned nut-brown with the sun . . . and a chest like a gym instructor." Collins described Bertha as "small and plump and motherly". He was impressed by the open mutual affection shown by the couple: "They called each other 'Bertha' and 'Teddie' and in their eyes was outspoken love lasting through the long years, undisturbed, unshaken."[1]

About this time, Ted's diaries were studded with records of exquisite days. In May of that year, one such day was: "fine, clear, lovely, resplendent, and anything and everything else signifying perfection"; and a few weeks later: "A day to make a young man bold and an old man youthful, where beyond North Queensland is such invigorating, balmy, delicious weather."[2]

Nowadays he wrote only occasional articles, after giving up his "Rural Homilies" as such, but he was busy making plans and arrangements to be on the island for many full years to come. He decided that the second *Nee Mourna* with its chronic engine ailments was not only a vexation but also consumed so much petrol that it was too expensive to run, so he enlisted the help of Spenser Hopkins to find a suitable new boat. After seeing a Swedish engine highly recommended in a catalogue, he wrote to the maker, who claimed to know his books, and arranged to buy a five horsepower two-cylinder engine of extra good quality, to be shipped to Townsville.

The arrangements made with Spenser over the acquisition of half of Ted's land had assisted the Beachcomber in reconstructing his refuge after the "storm wind", and had given him and Bertha a sense of security. Even so, it was a matter of concern to their kind friend that as they grew older their isolation made them even more vulnerable. In Brammo Bay, Spenser had been on board a visiting warship when wireless messages were transmitted to Townsville — in fact, he had sent a message through himself — so he began investigating the pedal wirelesses that were coming into use between lonely inland cattle stations, and the possibility of obtaining one for the islanders.

In June of this year, HMS *Fantome* came in again and stayed for a fortnight, making tidal observations and carrying out a survey of Brammo Bay. Here, where surveys had been made from the earliest days of European occupation of Australia, Ted spent a most enjoyable and instructive time in the *Fantome's* launch with the cartographers as they took soundings and made measurements. From this emerged a chart of the bay, with "Mr Banfield's House" clearly marked. Ted was delighted when he was presented with a copy on calico.[3] The survey ship, although becoming obsolete, now carried a medical officer so that the crew members were protected from the dangers of sudden illness when their charting took them into lonely waters.

Ted still ribbed the naval gentlemen, and had some new evidence about James Cook and what he *nearly* did when he erected a mast on Possession Island and formally claimed the territory of New South Wales in the name of King George the Third. The navigator and his men were so busy saluting the English colours streaming out in the hot tropical breeze that they failed to take stock of where they stood. Had they done so, and kicked around a bit, it is possible that they might have discovered colours of a different kind. A quartz reef containing visible gold ran to the exact spot where Cook's flagstaff had been planted. The man who made this find — the explorer and surveyor, J.T. Embley — sank a shaft there and took out 2,480 ounces of gold (over 70 kilograms).[4]

"Now," Ted would say, "had Cook made this discovery, think of what would have happened. Before there was any chance to establish a penal colony in the south, there would have been a rush of diggers to the north from the other side of the world. That would have been the centre of settlement. We'd have had no problems of neglect, no need for a separationist movement — and my great-grandfather might well have founded a paper called, say, *The Cape York Advertiser*."

Later in the year, Ted managed to dispose of the troublesome motor-boat and began to look forward with increasing excitement to the arrival of his third *Nee Mourna* with its swish Swedish engine. He repaired the wooden tramway down the beach from the boatshed and got the trolley back on the rails in readiness to receive the new boat.

By this time the year 1923 had started, and Dorothy and Walter Cottrell had arrived for their stay of six months up in the hut. Cottrell happily assisted Ted in the work about the place. Despite his distress at finding himself morally obliged to resign the honorary rangership, Ted remained a contented and fulfilled man, and the excerpt from Thoreau's work which he had chosen as the closing paragraph to *The Confessions* held even greater significance for him: "If the day and the night are such that you greet them with joy, and life emits a fragrance like flowers and sweet-scented herbs, is more elastic, more starry, more immortal — that is your success."[5]

He had time to look back on his life, aided in this by the scents to which he had always been so acutely sensitive:

> Men of science tell us that the sense of smell possesses a kind of master key to the cells of the brain, in which are stored the treasures of memory. Other senses also unlock these cells, but that of smell throws all the doors wide open, and reveals a subtle plot, which entices us to rummage among those splendid hoards which become more precious the older we get.[6]

By day he still beachcombed among the islands and islets of his domain, on beaches where his feet were "dusted with glittering specks" of sand and where hot rocks glistened "with micaceous spangles":

> When one wanders among such scenes,
> where there is no sign of traffic
> save that of his own footprints,
> no sound
> save the confidential whispering of the sea,
> the thin screams of terns
> and the whimsical cackling of scrub-fowl
> in the jungle,
> he becomes a part of the realm of Nature,
> a trivial and insignificant item
> soon to disappear,
> but for a brief space supreme —
> the only part of teeming Nature
> capable of disinterested joy
> in all the other parts.

The sea will quickly smooth away
the last trace of his trespassing feet,
and will moan and gurgle in cool crevices
whither bottle-green crabs skurry
when the red-backed sea-eagle
soars vigilantly overhead.
Yet for a time he has been absorbed into the scene.
He possesses it and is possessed by it.[7]

Thus he continued to imprint his "pedal autographs", occasionally with Bertha's when they combined beachcombing and picnicking. Often there was a companion who left what might have been termed "paw autographs". Ted would have been lost without his dogs: "It seems to me that the man who walks through the wilderness of this world unaccompanied by dogs, who has not understood the mind of the dog, and who has not been the object of the self-denying devotion of a dog, misses a good deal of the art of living."[8]

Contemplating the hereafter with the company of all their dogs, he wrote:

> With what a composite pack shall I be surrounded! Indeed, it will be a pack, not a procession, for who would decree and insist upon any order of precedence among such a multitude of clamorous pets? Bull-terriers, retrievers, nondescripts — the dog-lover abhors the term mongrel — sheep dogs and cattle dogs, pointers, and, most beloved of all, Irish terriers. The pack would include two or three uncommon and somewhat foreign elements — a red Chow from Canton and a dingo from the silent places of the Star River.

Some died of old age, some were killed by ticks or snakes — Rowdy, Snuff, Paddy, Whirra, Irish, Lassie and Scoot, who, like his father Barry, was "melodiously voiced, and never a steamer nor a sailing boat went by night or day that he did not see and salute tunefully from uplifted muzzle". All these and more. His last, Dalesman, was still with him and using the restored "PUSH" gate at the back.[9]

By day he beachcombed by courtesy of that "imperious luminary", His Majesty the Sun, while by night he beachcombed by the light of the kerosene lamp, which threw the bright cone under which he explored the pages of those islands and islets he could hold between his two hands. Time and again he returned to those enchanted strands in the three volumes his father had given him nearly fifty years before. He kept finding treasures in Shakespeare's works. Indeed, in his diary he wrote: "Reading. How delightful and invigorating is Shakespeare after such writers as are popular today." He would share the spoils of such nocturnal expeditions with George Barrymore — "Dear old chum", "Dear Barry O'More", "Dear Old Slave of the Gas-Light" — by writing to tell him of more quotations he had "dug out of Shakespeare".[10]

❧ ❧ ❧

Two days after Dorothy and Walter Cottrell arrived on the island in early February 1923, David Green, his wife and three daughters left Townsville for a Grand Tour of Europe, expecting to be away a full year. In a farewell note, Dave Green said that he wished Ted were going in his place as he believed the Beachcomber would enjoy it more than he himself could.

Had Ted Banfield gone in David Green's stead, there is little doubt that he would have been in a situation where expert attention could have been obtained when his hour of greatest need arose.

From the morning of 31 May, Ted and Bertha had the "delicious Isle — this unkempt, unrestrained garden where all the centuries gaze upon perpetual summer" entirely to themselves. Essie was having the annual break which "set her up" and was not due back for a week. The Cottrells, ever hopeful of a miracle, had gone to Townsville to attend a faith healing mission. The itinerant fisherman Frank Henricksen had left for Innisfail. Ted was expecting the arrival of his third *Nee Mourna*, which Spenser Hopkins would be bringing up in a few days, but he was a little concerned as the weather outlook was not the best. In a letter to George Barrymore about this time he wrote: "I am up to my eyes in all sorts of jobs from dish-washing to carpentering", although against the dish-washing was written in a censorial hand: "Lies!!! BB". Ted was still finding outlets for his seemingly inexhaustible energy. However, in the diary there were a number of passing mentions that he had not been feeling well.[11]

Letters and postcards had arrived from the David Greens, all of whom, at this time, were in Amsterdam. On Friday 8 June, David and Mrs Green took their three daughters Marjorie, Ethel and Nancy to the reading rooms to attend to their mail, write up their diaries and browse through the English newspapers. *The Times* had arrived, and Ethel was turning the pages when a headline caught her eye.

"Look!" she cried.

Her parents and sisters crowded around, and this is what they read:

25 YEARS ON LONELY
ISLAND
DEATH OF MR. E.J.
BANFIELD

(From Our Own Correspondent)
Melbourne, June 7

Mr. E.J. Banfield, the naturalist and author of "The Confessions of a Beachcomber", and other books, has died at the age of 70 at Dunk Island, off the coast of Queensland, where he had been living alone with his wife for twenty-five years.

The crew of the steamer Innisfail, passing the island, saw a woman waving on the beach. A boat was landed and Mrs.

Banfield was found to be the only inhabitant on the island. Her husband was dead. The crew made a coffin out of ship's timber and the Chief Officer read the burial service.

Mrs. Banfield refused to leave the island, and the captain called for volunteers to stay with her. Every man offered, and the captain selected one to remain.[12]

An obituary followed in this, the newspaper which, in Ted Banfield's estimation, had no peer; the newspaper which had enabled him to experience something far beyond his wildest expectations by informing the world of the excellence of his books. Now it stated: "with his wife, he settled down to live the simplest of lives and indulge in his cherished pastime of observing the ways of birds, beasts, and fishes, and, while they remained, his black fellow men"; and that "He did not pretend to be a scientific naturalist, and he was emphatically not a collector; he was simply an observer of Nature."[13]

Very few of those who had marvelled at the extent of Ted Banfield's observations were to know that they had been carried out for the greater part of his life with but one eye. As George Barrymore said: "no man ever saw or appreciated what he saw with one eye, more than Banfield".[14]

Chapter 27
Last Leaves

Ted Banfield's last diary entry was on 31 May 1923; those that followed were made by Bertha:

June 1.   Ted very ill. Came in from barn about 4 o'clock suffering agony.
June 2.   Ted died about 12.45 pm today.
June 3.   Very high wind, rough seas.
June 4.   Mon. Last night wild westerly gale. Still all alone.
June 5.   Fine, clear and cold. Signalled to Innisfail coming from north about noon: at last when I had despaired of help she turned in. The Capt. came ashore with 12 or 14 crew and my Laddie was laid to rest. Never have I received so great kindness and consideration from those who were comparative strangers. A young sailor lad, Alick Milne stayed on shore until other friends should arrive.[1]

In a letter to Alec Chisholm, Bertha gave an account of her vigil:

He had suffered for three weeks from what he thought was a severe form of indigestion but the day before he died, it developed rapidly, causing him absolute agony for twenty hours . . . he spoke of trying to get sleep, and did so for about half-an-hour then his breathing ceased, there was not even a tremor. I had no idea that death could come so peacefully, indeed to me at the time it was beautiful and my one feeling was of intense thankfulness that he would suffer no more. As to my being alone, unless we could have had skilled medical — or as I believe surgical aid, no one could have helped me, and I would not have shared those last hours with any other, for all the world.[2]

The cause of death was put down to a ruptured stomach and peritonitis. How ironic that Ted should once have lightheartedly written: "every man, woman and child in Merry England . . . expects or dreads or hopes to have appendicitis, since King Edward the Peacemaker suffered, and renown came upon that disease."[3]

As the weather grew worse outside, there was less hope that someone — even one of those uninvited visitors who streamed into the bay when the sun shone — would call, except perhaps for shelter. No one came. Bertha carried on alone, placing each of the four legs of the bed in a tin of kerosene so that no ant could intrude upon the start of the Beachcomber's long sleep; "the sleep of eternity that no earthly din may disturb".[4]

In the face of fierce winds, she headed to the sand-spit where she managed to gather enough drift wood and debris to make three small stacks. At dusk she came back and waited until the swift tropic night had descended before setting the stacks alight, all three of them, thus signalling that help was needed and that the worst had happened.

As the sparks were blown away by the wind, she hoped that some mainland neighbour, in particular George Webb, might spot the three fires. The beating of the wind faintly penetrated her deafness, as if emanating from the drum, now muffled, of Ted's runaway Redcoat. But the fires burned themselves out unnoticed by anyone, and so she remained alone for three nights before the weather started to clear. She took a sheet to the spit in the hope that she might see some passing vessel to which she could wave. She could hardly have envisaged that it would come to this when Ted had visited Liverpool with his bewitching talk about tropical islands.

The *Innisfail* appeared from the north, but it very nearly did not stop. Mr A.H. Hardy of Townsville, then a young seaman, recalled:

> The Skipper was in a bit of a hurry, and we were steaming south on the inner passage because it was pretty rough. Mrs Banfield was spotted on the spit waving something white and the Skipper gave a couple of whistle blasts just to say goodday. But something seemed a bit odd, because if ever she was there, Banfield would be with her — and she was by herself. Then, after keeping waving, she seemed to fall — and we knew something was wrong. We were all there for the burial. The Skipper wanted Mrs Banfield to come back to Townsville with us, but she wouldn't, so a young chap Alick Milne stayed. Soon as we reached Townsville, Spenser Hopkins was notified, and he left to go up there by motor-boat — something a lot of people wouldn't do in that weather, because there was a big stretch of open sea with the islands well apart.[5]

The skipper was Captain Robertson, brother of the young woman who had come to Dunk to type up *The Confessions*.

During her wait, Bertha had milked a cow and chopped up coconuts to feed the fowls, all of which she knew by name. She was grateful to have the young volunteer seaman's help as she adhered to her daily routine, keeping to the clock as usual, and acting as if Ted might simply be away on the mainland for a few days.

George Webb came across the day after the burial. He had not been within seeing distance of the three fires when Bertha set them alight. The day following this, Spenser and Mrs Hopkins arrived in the new *Nee Mourna*, which Ted was never to see. Bertha thought it a lovely little boat and risked a run around Purtaboi with Spenser, who had got into the way of handling it with trial runs from Townsville out to Magnetic Island. Later on the day after this, the *Innisfail*, heading north again, brought Essie and the two Cottrells back from Townsville — also the first in the stream of letters of sympathy, from high men in high places, ordinary people Ted had befriended, helped or inspired, and from some to whom he was but legendary name.

One of the first condolences was a cablegram from the travelling Greens; it was six weeks before a letter explained how they had come to know of Ted's passing so soon. Among the letters she greatly valued was Alec Chisholm's, and it was to him she revealed something of her feelings and plans:

> We had been everything to each other for thirty-seven years and now I am alone, although friends have helped me generously in all possible ways, still the black wall seems to rise just in front of me at every turn. For the present — that is I fully expect until the end of the year, I will remain here, and hope to lease the Island. I have had half-a-dozen applications already, but will do nothing without a good deal of consideration. It should not go to any vandal who would destroy it in the first year.[6]

She went on writing up the diary, as she had done on the few occasions when Ted had been away without her, and so she recorded the return of Lillie Hopkins who was again to be of great help about the house and in the garden. Ted's brother Walter, now retired after having risen to be an inspector in the bank, came with his niece Audrey Strangward, a daughter of Ted's youngest sister, Eva. Bertha was to have their company and Walter's advice for a month. During their stay that of the Cottrells came to an end; the few months they spent on the island were to live on in the pages of the minor classic *The Singing Gold*, which Dorothy Cottrell was to write and have published (although Bertha was to have strong reservations about parts of it). Their departure was noted in the diary, as was another death, that of Ted's last dog Dalesman, from tick poisoning.

One of Bertha's main concerns was to have a cairn built over Ted's grave, and she discussed its shape with Spenser who had brought one of his men, Fraser, to lend a hand generally. She

The cairn over the Beachcomber's grave after the tablet was put in place. (A.H. Chisholm Papers, courtesy of Mitchell Library.)
Inset: Bertha's tablet set below Ted's. (Courtesy of Queensland Railway Department.)

was all too aware of the sort of cairn Ted favoured; his views had dominated when a memorial over Syd Harris's grave was designed. So it was decided that the cairn would be along much the same lines. Spenser and his man did all the work in its construction, which Bertha described to Alec Chisholm: "They brought the stones from near Coconut Bay. They built a sort of low wall of cement inside all round, then filled in that with smaller stones and cement to make a solid foundation for the larger stones which are *set* in the cement". On the grey granite tablet, at George Barrymore's suggestion, Ted's favourite Thoreau quotation was cut in simple lettering: "the grave is just beyond the garden fence, on the north side, from whence there is one of our loveliest views of sea, mainland and 'Purtaboi'."[7]

This was heavy work. After finishing it, Spenser and Fraser built a very strong crate for the shell cabinet and watched over the packing of its contents and saw it safely taken on board the steamer for shipment to the Queensland Museum, Brisbane.

With so much energy being expended it was as if Ted was somehow still present to set the pace. Lillie Hopkins (who later married the man of few words, George Webb) never stopped for a moment, gardening, mowing, trimming bushes and hedges; and if inside the house, dressmaking or baking cakes. She helped Bertha burn some old letters on the beach. Valuable records undoubtedly went up in smoke, there on the Beachcomber's promenade, his favourite strip of the tropics.

As for his books, Walter made a list of them before he left. Bertha asked a number of friends which they would like. Ted's three volumes of Shakespeare were chosen by George Barrymore; they eventually came into Alec Chisholm's possession when given to him by Barrymore's widow, Freda. Chisholm was also invited to make a choice, and shortly afterwards Bertha wrote to him on another matter: "I have been going carefully through his papers, and find in a box apart, quite an amount of material, some of it arranged evidently in chapters. It consists mainly of 'Rural Homilies' that at different times were published in the N.Q. Register."[8]

It was an exciting discovery, the possibility of a fourth Banfield book. Would Chisholm be prepared to look at this material and give his candid opinion? And if there was a book in it: "You are the only one, who like him has the two-fold knowledge of a journalist and a nature lover, and if it is possible I would prefer you to any other as the one who should edit his work."[9] In this choice, T.P. Adlam, who was based in Sydney, entirely agreed with her; Chisholm was the only man who could undertake such a task.

What writer would not have jumped at this opportunity? Chisholm wasted no time in thanking Bertha for thinking of him; as soon as he received the material, which he had no doubt would be the basis of a book, he would get to work on it. Isabel Green, who had arrived on the island and had been helping Bertha to continue to sort through Ted's papers, packed the material from the box and sent it to Brisbane.

Even before receiving it, Chisholm was so confident of what the find would yield that he decided to sound out a publisher. Ted had taken him into his confidence about his skirmishes with T. Fisher Unwin. Quite apart from this, Chisholm felt that a posthumous book by E.J. Banfield should be published in the country in which it was written, so he wrote to George Robertson of Angus and Robertson who answered by return post, saying his firm would be proud to publish anything of Banfield's.[10]

The material proved to be a rich repository of typed, printed and handwritten pieces arranged in much the same pattern that had governed the shape of Ted's previous books, especially *Tropic Days*. There were three main sections: the first philosophical and reminiscent as he celebrated his freedom and revelled in his domain; the second, the natives and their idiosyncrasies; the third, miscellanea. Most pieces had been published, although many had extensive emendations, and some were pen-scored almost out of their original state. In his introduction to the new work, Chisholm was to write that the title was not of E.J. Banfield's own choosing: "But the form of the work is largely of the author's making; an unfinished scrap of a preface, written while the great sea-storm was still beating in his mind, indicates that he regarded the story of the tempest of 1918 as worthy of chief place in any further book he might prepare."[11]

While the posthumous book was being prepared for publication, Fisher Unwin advised that because of popular demand *The Confessions* and *My Tropic Isle* (which by this time had appeared in Dutch as *Het Leven op Mion Tropisch Eiland*) were to be reprinted. Bertha and Spenser had not known that the publisher had acquired the copyrights of these two works in addition to that of *Tropic Days*, and only now realized that no royalties would be forthcoming. It was understandable that when Fisher Unwin wrote expressing the hope that there might be fresh material for publication in Ted's papers, they took some satisfaction in the knowledge that the fourth book was under way with another publisher.

Chisholm asked Bertha whether she had any fancy for the name of the new book. She replied by asking Chisholm what he thought, and later wrote: "I think it ought to have some connection with previous ones and with that thought in mind Spenser suggested 'The Last Confessions of a Beachcomber' and yet to neither of us did it seem just what we would like." The two thought about it again a few days later, and Bertha came up

Bertha, after Ted's death, with A.H. Chisholm's daughter Deirdre. (A.H. Chisholm papers, courtesy of Mitchell Library.)

with "Notes from Dunk Island"; but when Chisholm put forward "Last Leaves from Dunk Island" Bertha was sure it could not be improved upon: "so if you please we will decide upon that. It pleases me exceedingly and is I think out of the common as titles go, and I feel it is the sort of title *he* would have liked."[12]

When Chisholm mentioned in a letter that he had met a young journalist, formerly a medical student, Lewis Townsend, Bertha confirmed what he had been told about her future plans: "I hope all being well to make my home with his mother. I do not know that I shall be there all the time, but it will be my headquarters . . . I have known Mrs Townsend since she was 7 years of age; she was a most winning child, a particularly attractive girl, and developed into a fine woman, and has always been a real joy to me and Ted." Gladys Townsend, née Johnson, her sister Gwen and their mother had been friends since all coming out from England in the same ship. Mrs Townsend now lived at Amamoor, near Gympie, and it was to this address that Bertha consigned enough furniture for her needs when she left Dunk about the middle of August 1924. She remarked that she was entitled to a "walk-about" after "sitting down" in one spot for a quarter of a century; so while having her base near Brisbane, she stayed at Sydney, visited Melbourne and returned to Townsville for short breaks with old friends such as the Greens.[13]

Essie had left in January. Bertha told Chisholm: "I had felt for a very long time that it was not right for her to be working if only doing our cooking; at her age, she is 74 last month, she needs rest and now has a room with an old friend and will have the old age pension. I think, too, when my affairs are definitely settled, I will be able to help her a little." A small annual sum to supplement Essie's age pension was arranged.[14]

Last Leaves from Dunk Island was published in time for Christmas 1925. At the start of *My Tropic Isle*, Ted had written:

Can the record of such a narrow, compressed existence be anything but dull? Can one who is indifferent to the decrees of constituted society; who is aloof from popular prejudices; who cares not for the gaieties of the crowd or the vagaries of fashion; who does not dance or sing . . . or play cards or billiards, or attend garden parties; who has no political ambitions; who is not a painter, or a musician, or a man of science . . . who is a casual, a nonentity, a scout on the van of civilization dallying with the universal enemy, time — can such a one, so forlorn of popular attributes, so weak and watery in his tastes, have aught to recite harmonious to the ear of the world?[15]

Many apparently thought so. The reviews were as good as ever before, although it was nearly eighteen months later that Bertha realized just *how* good. At the Sydney office of Angus and Robertson she was left in a room with an album of cuttings. As she said in a letter to Alec Chisholm: "I was astonished at the number of notices, from all the States of Aus, N. Zealand, Tasmania, S. Africa, England, Scotland & even old Ireland". *The Australian*, Melbourne, stated that Ted "awoke one morning to the realization of fame. 'The Confessions of a Beachcomber' reached the heart of the world of letters"; he was a "prophet honoured in his own country" and he had "truth, beauty, poetry, philosophy and romance in his work". Comparisons with Thoreau and R.L. Stevenson were again inevitable. Regarding the former, Ted had none "of the egoism discernible in Thoreau"; and as for the latter, "Stevenson was his superior as a literary craftsman, but had not the vision to see deeply into the heart of nature which Banfield possessed." Of his work in general, *The Sydney Mail* stated: "no better, more human, more finely descriptive, or more enticing books have ever been written by an Australian of Australia, or indeed, by any writer of any portion of the earth's surface". There were in all nearly eighty of these reviews, and while they were from some of the world's leading voices, including *The Manchester Guardian* and *The Illustrated London News*, it would appear that on this occasion there was no mention in *The Times*.[16]

One of the longest reviews, in the Australian *Woman's Mirror*, carried a photograph of Bertha, to whom Alec Chisholm paid the following tribute: "It is scarcely conceivable that Banfield's books would ever have been written, or, indeed, that his life would ever have become so fragrant, without the companionship of the cultured, courageous, merry little woman who braved isolation on a lonely island for a quarter-century."

The Beachcomber's very last article, written in the style and vein of his "Rural Homilies", was found waiting on the desk in his office after his death. It appeared at the end of *Last Leaves*, after first being published in *The Townsville Daily Bulletin*, 25 June 1923, when it was described by the acting editor, George Barrymore, as embodying "the charm of style, the sweet charity, the playful humour, and merriment of the man".

Philosophical to the last, the Beachcomber had written: "Is not life, however, a patchwork of compromises?"[17]

Epilogue

Bertha paid at least three return visits to the sanctuary where Ted was laid to rest — summer visits in 1925, 1927 and 1930, when the white nutmeg pigeons were in residence and the sunbirds flashing their gold among the red hibiscus flowers.

While Spenser Hopkins relieved Bertha of the burden and worry of business affairs, anything of a literary nature was usually referred to Alec Chisholm. A letter received from one of the inmates of San Quentin Prison, California, for instance: believing Ted to be still alive, Prisoner No. 37422, one Joseph Moran, wrote: "After reading several commendatory articles about your 'Confessions of a Beachcomber', it was decided we must endeavour to read it. But as our library was without it, and we were comparatively penniless, we felt sure the author would not disregard to supply us with a copy."[1]

Ted would have been delighted and amused at such a request, so Bertha asked Chisholm if he could kindly arrange for a complimentary copy to be sent.

She left the leasing of the island to Spenser, and for a considerable time they had well-based hopes that Dunk would be taken over by a university department as a research centre. This was something that would certainly have met with Ted's whole-hearted approval. He had pushed for "the establishment of a college for the study of tropical agriculture in the North" for many years; as stated in one of his "Rural Homilies", it was "a theme often harped upon in this column". Unfortunately, the negotiations fell through, and it was not until May 1933 that the Butlers of Tully entered into a lease, their plan being to set up accommodation for tourists.[2]

Bertha died of a coronary thrombosis at St Kilda Private Hospital, Wynnum, Brisbane, on 6 August 1933, at the age of seventy-five. She was cremated at Rookwood, New South Wales, and her ashes were flown to Townsville. Spenser Hopkins took them to Dunk Island in the third *Nee Mourna*, making an open-boat journey in open sea which Bertha would undoubtedly have hesitated to undertake before her passing. Others came on the *Innisfail*. Spenser's wife and several of his children accompanied him and helped those who had come over from Mission Beach in their best Sunday clothes to collect golden orchids on Purtaboi and other flowers, such as Granny's Nightcaps, which they combined with crotons to make wreaths. A stone was removed from the cairn over the Beachcomber's grave and the ashes of the Lady of the Isle were poured into the hole. The stone was cemented back in place, and round and cross-shaped wreaths were placed all over the cairn.[3]

The inscription on the tablet, which was set below Ted's at a later date, was taken from the words of Ruth in the biblical quotation which "Cestus", George Barrymore, had used in his published tribute to Bertha:

"For *whither thou goest, I will go, and where thou lodgest, I will lodge:* Thy people shall be my people, and thy God my God; *where thou diest, will I die, and there will I be buried:* The Lord do so to me, and more also, if aught but death part thee and me."[4]

Barrymore went on to say that it was Bertha who had made life possible on the island; with her care and wisdom she had "buttressed, strengthened, and encouraged that sensitive, tensely-strung man"; and that while "Banfield was the very spirit of the Island, Mrs Banfield was the heart-beat, the very soul of their idyllic existence"; and that she was a woman who "with her husband, 'stepped to the music she heard' ".

To Spenser Hopkins, who already had acquired a half interest in Ted's Dunk Island land, Bertha left all her property there, on the understanding that the friend who had been like a son to her would pay a small monthly sum to Essie McDonough for her lifetime. That life did not have much longer to run; after having been one of the scouts on the van of civilization Essie died in June 1936, aged eighty-three, at the Eventide Home, Charters Towers.[5]

In the mid-1930s, Spenser Hopkins sold all but 41 of the 360 acres of land which the Banfields had owned. An Englishman, a wealthy former cavalry officer, Captain Robert Brassey, eventually took over the island, then gave it to his son, Hugo, a London insurance broker who was married to a kinswoman of Queen Mary, wife of the reigning monarch King George the Fifth, a German noblewoman from a castle near Munich, Baroness Christa Von Boderhausen.[6] She was to provide Dunk

The coconut avenue and the bungalow during Hugo Brassey's occupation of Dunk Island.
(Courtesy of Queensland Railway Department.)

with another legendary character by allegedly paying court to "His Majesty the Sun" in the way advocated by the Beachcomber, allowing its beneficial rays full access to her shapely anatomy as she promenaded the island's strands unclad and luxuriated in its waters.

During the Second World War, when Hugo Brassey returned to England to join the Royal Navy, the spirit of the Beachcomber must have been anxious. Ted Banfield had passed through the waters where the Battle of Trafalgar was fought; now Dunk Island, where secret radar equipment was installed near its highest point, Mount Koo-Tal-oo, was to play a part in another of history's decisive conflicts when the Battle of the Coral Sea was waged.

Hugo Brassey returned in 1945, but had to go to the family property in Ireland when his father died, and so Dunk Island passed into the hands of others, until today it is a world-class tropical holiday resort where painted wooden notices now state: "There is complete protection of all plant, animal and bird life on this National Park".

In his 1968 introduction to the paperback reprint of *The Confessions*, Alec Chishom wrote: "Possibly the Beachcomber sometimes cogitated concerning the fate of his little kingdom in years ahead".[7]

Ted Banfield had in fact done so, firstly sixty years earlier, when he wrote: "Personally, I like to dwell on the future of Dunk Island as not the least conspicuous item in a great insular national park, the area of which would embrace Hinchinbrook and all intermediate isles — a park not to be improved by formal walks or set in order to straight lines or lopped and trimmed according to the principles of horticultural art, but just a wilderness — its primitive features preserved; its excesses unrestrained; its waywardness unapologized for. In such a wilderness the generations to come might wander, noting every detail — except in regard to original population — as it was in Cook's day and for centuries before."[8]

In a later article, composed three years before his death, Ted again looked into the future, and what he set down was very much closer to what was to happen, even if at the time of writing he might have been musing on what to him was an impossibility. He pictured an invasion of tourists: beaches that "swarmed with reddening bathers"; the forest removed "to give way to golf links and cricket pitches and tennis courts".

While it has been claimed that in recent times the ghostly figure of the Beachcomber has been glimpsed in his old domain, as yet there is no record of any comment from him; nor has anyone spotted a runaway Redcoat, or heard the beat of his drum. All the same, while those who come to the island stroll rather than step, they usually find themselves doing so to a different sort of rhythm.

The Beachcomber's predictions come true. (Courtesy of TAA Resort on Dunk Island.)

Acknowledgments

As the first to tackle a biography of E.J. Banfield, I am in a sense an opening batsman. Should anyone else decide to follow on after me, by then more material — letters, writings, reminiscences and photographs — will undoubtedly have emerged. Nevertheless, I have had an enormous amount of assistance, and a book such as this is largely written by those people and institutions providing the material, and the organizations enabling the writer to obtain it. So many have been involved that I am concerned that I may leave out some acknowledgment.

I began this project with a good start: I'd had a copy of *The Confessions* at my side for many years; I had spent much time in North Queensland and had written about it; I had collaborated with John Heyer in the research and script of his awards-winning film *The Reef*, the definitive cinematic biography of Australia's Great Barrier Reef.

The Queensland Film Corporation, thanks to the enthusiasm of Chairman Allen Callaghan, assisted me in my initial research by supporting me in the writing of a treatment and then a draft script for a documentary feature film to be based on Banfield's books.

This research could not have been undertaken without the personal interest of Ralph Conley, the then Queensland Manager of Trans Australia Airlines, who arranged travel in Queensland, and to Sydney, Melbourne and Canberra, and accommodation on Dunk Island.

When I realized that there could well be enough material for a biography of Banfield, this required much more research and travel, and then time to write. For the opportunity to do all this, I am indebted to the Literature Board of the Australia Council for a One-Year Senior Fellowship in 1981.

There have been a number of most important sources of information and assistance which I must acknowledge with great thanks at the outset. The help and encouragement in so many ways from members of the family of Spenser Hopkins. In the order in which I met them: John Hopkins and his wife Peg, Joan Hopkins and her husband Harry, and Helen Dyer (née Hopkins), all of Townsville.

The Mitchell Library, Sydney, placed a treasure trove at my disposal by granting me first access to the uncatalogued papers of the late A.H. Chisholm (ML MSS. 3540). I am indebted to the library and members of the staff, especially Paul Brunton; and through him to Deirdre Chisholm for giving me permission to quote from certain of her father's writings.

My freedom to quote from the Chisholm Papers would have been severely restricted but for the very kind permission granted by Helen Green of Townsville and her brother David Green of Perth, Tasmania, the joint copyright holders of the unpublished writings of E.J. Banfield and his wife Bertha. I should mention here the assistance received in tracing the copyright holders from R.S. Walls, District Public Trustee, Townsville, and the Australian Copyright Council Limited.

The help of members of the Banfield family has been essential. I am most grateful to the late Lorna L. Banfield, E.J. Banfield's niece, whom I met in Ararat, Victoria, before her death at the age of ninety in March 1981, and to the continuing help and loan of photographs from her sisters Irene L. and Zoe Banfield. Also their nephew, the Reverend Tom Banfield of Dunolly, Victoria; E.J. Patton of Phillip Island, Victoria; and Mervyn Carroll when he was residing in Brisbane.

Among the highlights of my research have been the vivid recollections of others who knew the Banfields, in particular Marjorie Green of Townsville, daughter of Banfield's friend and editor, David Green. Also Walter Cottrell of Bowen; A.J. Hardy of Townsville, a member of the crew of the steamer which came to Mrs Banfield's aid following the death of her husband; the artist Noel Wood, long-time resident of Bedarra Island; Hugh Willmett formerly of Townsville; W.T. Johnston and his wife of Cairns.

When I was researching the film only, Emeritus Professor Colin Roderick of Townsville gave me most generously of his time, knowledge and advice, all of which assisted with the biography. Ron Burnett, Editor-in-Chief of the North Queensland Newspaper Company Limited, kindly arranged publicity for my quest for material. His colleague, James Manion, now manager of *The Townsville Daily Bulletin*, did not hesitate to share his research with me and to offer suggestions where further information might be found; he has kindly given me permission to quote from his excellent book *Paper Power in North Queensland*, a store of information in itself.

Much key information was obtained from the James Cook University, Townsville, thanks to Helen Mays, Reader Services Librarian; to Cheryl Frost and Ross Smith of the Department of English; and to the "Reef" poet, Mark O'Connor. Others in North Queensland to whom I am indebted are members of the staff of the Dunk Island Resort; the island resident and master weaver, Bruce Arthur; Dr Bruce Logan of Townsville for arranging an unforgettable vision of the early morning seascapes about which Banfield wrote; W.H. Phillips, Banfield Caravan Park, Cardwell; Sergeant Aitken of the Tully Police; Eileen Smith of Malanda; the Townsville Harbour Board.

In Brisbane, without the extensive facilities of the State Library of Queensland, the John Oxley Library and the Queensland State Archives, it would not have been possible to carry out so much primary and secondary research so close to home. I would like to thank the staffs and the State Librarian, S.L. Ryan, the John Oxley Librarian, Colin Sheehan, and the Reference Librarian, M.F. Lynch.

Also in Brisbane, I am indebted to the Queensland Museum, to the Director, Dr. A. Bartholomai, Roger Hardley and Dan Robinson; to L.T. Padman, Director of Boolarong Publications for providing a key photograph; to the Secretary, Premier's Department, for permission to publish and reproduce items held in the State Archives; to the Royal Geographical Society of Australasia, Queensland; to Dr Leonard J. Webb for much advice, especially on botanical matters and conservation; to Dr Rod McLeod, President of the Queensland Maritime Museum Association; to Dr Richard Wilson of the Department of English, University of Queensland, for his perceptive analysis of the first draft of this book and his constructive suggestions; to H. Matthews of Overseas Containers Limited, for his information about early coastal steamers; to the Queensland Railway Department for some unique photographs; and also for photographic material, to TAA Resort on Dunk Island.

In Sydney, I have received assistance from the Dixon Library; from History House; and from David McNicoll, Australian Consolidated Press.

In Canberra, thanks initially to the interest of Catherine Santamaria, Principal Librarian, Australian Reference, a mass of material was made available to me; I would like to thank members of the staff for their help. Also in Canberra, my thanks to the Australian Institute of Aboriginal Affairs.

At the La Trobe Library, Melbourne, invaluable material was made available to me. Also in Melbourne, I must thank the

Australian Conservation Foundation; and in Ararat, Victoria, the library which I visited with the late Lorna L. Banfield.

In the United Kingdom, I received some reminiscences of Dunk Island during the latter part of the occupation of the Banfields from the remarkable Lillian Webb (née Hopkins) of Winchester; I would also like to thank her niece, Jean Valechy of Southampton. I am grateful to publishers Ernest Benn Limited, London, for permission to reproduce material relating to Banfield's dealings with his publisher T. Fisher Unwin; to the British Museum (Natural History); to the Royal Geographical Society; to Captain John Weston, North Wales, of the P & O Cargo Division, for information about the Port of Liverpool.

If, after all this, I have omitted any acknowledgment I can but apologize.

Abbreviations

AHC	Alexander Hugh (Alec) Chisholm
BB	Bertha Banfield
EGB	Edward George Barrymore "Cestus"
EJB	Edmund James Banfield "Beachcomber"
ML	Mitchell Library, Sydney, NSW
NLA	National Library of Australia, Canberra, ACT
TFU	T. Fisher Unwin

Notes

Shortened references are given to those books listed in the bibliography.

Prologue

1. E.J. Banfield, *The Confessions*, pp. 17, 92.
2. E.J. Banfield, "The Gentle Art of Beachcombing", p. 226; *My Tropic Isle*, pp. 104-5.

Chapter 1: World of Change

1. J.W. Banfield, "Reminiscences".
2. Jabez Banfield's Indenture of Apprenticeship, 16 August 1833, MS 1860, NLA.
3. Jabez Banfield's testimonial from printer John Rose, 12 June 1852, MS 1860, NLA; marriage certificate Jabez and Sarah Banfield, MS 1835, NLA.
4. Testimonial from John Rose, and personal letter to Jabez Banfield from John Rose, MS 1860, NLA.
5. Lorna L. Banfield, *Colonists of the Early Fifties*.
6. J.W. Banfield, "Reminiscences".
7. Lorna L. Banfield, *Colonists of the Early Fifties*.
8. T.E. Biddle, "Transactions British Shipping".
9. MS 1860, NLA.

Chapter 2: Black and White Gold

1. W.B. Withers, *History of Ballarat*, pp. 26-27.
2. J.H. Heaton, *Australian Dictionary of Dates*, p. 124.
3. Withers, *History of Ballarat*, p. 26.
4. MS 1860, NLA.
5. Lorna L. Banfield, *Colonists of the Early Fifties*.
6. *The Illustrated London News*, 27 August 1859; T.E. Biddle, "Transactions British Shipping"; Heaton, *Australian Dictionary of Dates*.
7. *The Illustrated London News*, 27 August 1859.
8. Lorna L. Banfield, *Colonists of the Early Fifties*.
9. J.W. Banfield, "Reminiscences".
10. Lorna L. Banfield, *Shire of Ararat*.
11. *The Mount Ararat Advertiser*, 1 August 1857.
12. Invoice re purchase of *The Mount Ararat Advertiser*, MS 1860, NLA; La Trobe

Library, Melbourne. Later in 1861, Jabez Banfield took on Thomas Merfield; the partnership was dissolved in 1868. Lorna L. Banfield, *Colonists of the Early Fifties.*
13. Information from Lorna L. Banfield at Ararat, Victoria, 19 December 1979 (died 29 March 1981, aged ninety years).

Chapter 3: The Bone-Shaker

1. Lorna L. Banfield, "Early Ararat Advertiser Index".
2. Ibid.
3. Lorna L. Banfield, *Colonists of the Early Fifties.*
4. Ibid.
5. Charles Kingsley, *Hereward the Wake* (London: Macmillan & Co., 1873), chap. II.
6. Lorna L. Banfield, *Colonists of the Early Fifties.*
7. Ibid.
8. J.W. Banfield, "Reminiscences".
9. Lorna L. Banfield, *Colonists of the Early Fifties.*
10. Lorna L. Banfield, letter to author, 12 January 1981.
11. Lorna L. Banfield, "Early Ararat Advertiser Index".
12. Lorna L. Banfield, *Colonists of the Early Fifties.*
13. J.W. Banfield, "Reminiscences".
14. Una Pope-Hennessy, *Charles Dickens* (London, Chatto and Windus, 1945).
15. The question of whether Banfield lost his right eye or his left eye remains unresolved, although an eye specialist and an optometrist, presented with a variety of photographs of Banfield, were both of the opinion that his right eye must have been removed. This is supported by one of the entries in Banfield's diaries. However, in a letter to the author, 12 January 1981, Miss Lorna L. Banfield stated that he had lost his left eye.

Chapter 4: Quiet Desperation

1. Estimate of cost, plan of dwelling and price from builders, MS 1860, NLA.
2. Lorna L. Banfield, *Colonists of the Early Fifties.*
3. Ibid.
4. *The Ararat Advertiser*, 3 April 1885; Lorna L. Banfield, *Like the Ark.*
5. E.J. Banfield, *My Tropic Isle*, p. 50.
6. Henry David Thoreau, *Walden*, "Higher Laws", pp. 157-59.
7. Ibid., "Economy", p. 7 and "Conclusion", p. 241.

Chapter 5: A Drummer from Afar

1. Henry David Thoreau, *Walden*, "Reading", p. 80. "Gandhi was guided to free India by his [Thoreau's] influence", *Walden*, "Introduction" to the Harper & Row edition, 1965, by Harvey Curtis Webster, p. xii.
2. T.P. Adlam, "An Old Friend's Tribute".
3. E.J. Banfield, "Homeward Bound", 11 July 1884.
4. Adlam, "An Old Friend's Tribute".
5. E.J. Banfield, *Within the Barrier*, pp. 8–10; James Cook, *Journals.*
6. Banfield, *Within the Barrier*, p. 17.
7. Ibid., pp. 17-19.
8. R. Logan Jack to E.J. Banfield, 22 August 1917, A.H. Chisholm Papers.
9. J.H. Heaton, *Australian Dictionary of Dates*, p. 206.
10. Harry C. Perry, *The Memoirs of the Hon. Sir Robert Philp*, p. 123.
11. Adlam, "An Old Friend's Tribute".
12. Perry, *Memoirs of Sir Robert Philp*, p. 128.
13. Matthew Flinders, *A Voyage to Terra Australis*, p. 88.
14. *Who Was Who, 1916–28.*
15. Banfield, *Within the Barrier*, p. 28.
16. Ibid.
17. W. Saville Kent, *The Great Barrier Reef of Australia.*
18. E.J. Banfield, *My Tropic Isle*, p. 108.
19. E.J. Banfield, *Last Leaves*, p. 62. Banfield spelt Krakatoa as "Krackatoa"; another spelling is "Krakatua".

Chapter 6: Homeward Bound

1. E.J. Banfield, "Homeward Bound", 11 July 1884.
2. E.J. Banfield, *The Torres Straits Route*, Appendix, "Fleet of Steamers".
3. Ibid., pp. 5-6.
4. Banfield, "Homeward Bound", 11 July 1884.
5. Banfield, "Homeward Bound" II, 15 July 1884.
6. Ibid.
7. Ibid.
8. Ibid.
9. Henry David Thoreau, *Walden*, "Economy", p. 16.
10. Banfield, "Homeward Bound", 11 July 1884; Thoreau, *Walden*, "Solitude", p. 101.
11. Banfield, "Homeward Bound", 11 July 1884.
12. Ibid.
13. Banfield, "Homeward Bound" III, 18 July 1884.
14. Banfield, "Homeward Bound" IV, 22 July 1884.
15. Ibid.; "Homeward Bound" VI, 26 August 1884.
16. Banfield, "Homeward Bound" IV, 22 July 1884.
17. Banfield, "Homeward Bound" VI, 26 August 1884; VII, 2 September 1884.
18. Banfield, "Homeward Bound" VII, 2 September 1884.
19. Ibid.
20. Ibid.
21. Banfield, *The Torres Straits Route*, p. 4.

Chapter 7: Erratic Rovings

1. E.J. Banfield, "Erratic Rovings" I, 7 November 1884.
2. E.G. Barrymore, "Address to Townsville Literary Club".
3. Banfield, "Erratic Rovings" I, 7 November 1884.
4. Ibid.
5. Ibid.
6. Banfield, "Erratic Rovings" II, 18 November 1884.
7. Ibid.
8. Banfield, "Erratic Rovings" III, 2 December 1884.
9. Ibid.
10. Banfield, "Erratic Rovings" IV, 23 December 1884.

Chapter 8: Pedal Autographs

1. Bertha Banfield's Death Certificate, A/17124, Queensland State Archives.
2. Miss Irene L. Banfield, letter to author, 29 April 1981.
3. BB to AHC, 12 December 1932, A.H. Chisholm Papers.
4. BB to AHC, 3 April 1924, Chisholm Papers.
5. Information from Miss Marjorie Green in Townsville, 22 June 1981; Mrs Lillian Webb (née Hopkins), Winchester, Hants., England, letter to author, 6 March 1980.
6. BB to AHC, 6 July 1929, Chisholm Papers.
7. E.J. Banfield, "Erratic Rovings" III, 2 December 1884.

Chapter 9: Rob Krusoe

1. E.J. Banfield, *The Torres Straits Route*, p. 4.
2. *The Ararat Advertiser*, 1 January 1885; 3 April 1885.
3. Harry C. Perry, *The Memoirs of the Hon. Sir Robert Philp*, p. 125.
4. E.J. Banfield, *My Tropic Isle*, p. 29.
5. E.J. Banfield, *Last Leaves*, p. 216.
6. Geraldton became confused with a town of the same name in Western Australia, so it was changed to Innisfail. The town has the distinction of being the wettest place in Australia in terms of annual rainfall.
7. J.W. Fawcett, *A Narrative of a Terrible Cyclone and Flood in Townsville.*.
8. Perry, *Memoirs of Sir Robert Philp*, pp. 128-29.
9. Ibid., p. 130.
10. Ibid., pp. 140-143, 165.
11. Margriet R. Bonnin, "E.J. Banfield", *Australian Dictionary of Biography*; Mrs Lillian Webb, letter to author, 27 April 1981.

Chapter 10: First Whispers

1. E.J. Banfield, *Within the Barrier*, p. 2.
2. BB to AHC, 24 January 1928, A.H. Chisholm Papers.
3. E.J. Banfield, *My Tropic Isle*, p. 14.
4. Lorna L. Banfield, *Colonists of the Early Fifties*.
5. EJB to his father, 5 November 1890, MS 1860, NLA.
6. Ibid.
7. Ibid.; EJB to his brother Harry, 1 November 1897, MS 1860, NLA.
8. EJB to his father, 5 November 1890, MS 1860, NLA.
9. E.G. Barrymore ("Cestus"), "David Green", *The Northern Miner*, 27 November 1941 (Obituary).
10. E.J. Banfield, "Homeward Bound", 11 July 1884; "Erratic Rovings" I, 7 November 1884.
11. E.J. Banfield ("Rambler"), "Up North. Recreative Days".
12. Ibid.
13. Ibid.; Henry David Thoreau, *Walden*, "Solitude", p. 96.
14. Banfield, "Up North. Recreative Days".
15. Ibid.
16. Ibid.

Chapter 11: Runaway Redcoat

1. E.G. Barrymore, "Address to Townsville Literary Club".
2. "Abridged Dunk Island Diaries of E.J. Banfield".
3. J.W. Banfield, "Reminiscences".
4. Barrymore, "Address".
5. J.W. Fawcett, *A Narrative of a Terrible Cyclone*.
6. E.J. Banfield, *The Confessions*, p. 86.
7. The Family Islands were: Richards — Bedarra; Thorpe — Timana; Wheeler — Toolgar (Tool-ghar in revised chart by T.P. Adlam); Coombe — Coomboo; Bowden — Budjoo; Smith — Kurrabah; Hodson (later Hudson) — Koolah (also Coolah).
8. E.J. Banfield ("Beachcomber"), "Rural Homilies", "About Islands", *The North Queensland Register*, 11 June 1917.
9. E.J. Banfield, *Tropic Days*, p. 127.
10. E.J. Banfield, "Dunk Island. Its General Characteristics", p. 52.
11. Information from Miss Marjorie Green in Townsville, 7 August 1979; Banfield, *The Confessions*, p. 7; BB to AHC, 3 April, 1924, A.H. Chisholm Papers.
12. Banfield, *The Confessions*, pp. 108, 114.
13. Ibid., p. 108.
14. E.J. Banfield, *My Tropic Isle*, p. 51.
15. Ibid., p. 18.
16. Banfield, *The Confessions*, p. 10.

Chapter 12: Escape to Live

1. E.J. Banfield, *The Confessions*, pp. 10, 15.
2. E.J. Banfield, "Dunk Island. Its General Characteristics", p. 52.
3. BB to AHC, 3 April 1924, A.H. Chisholm Papers; E.G. Barrymore, "Address to Townsville Literary Club"; T.P. Adlam, "An Old Friend's Tribute".
4. Henry David Thoreau, *Walden*, "Conclusion", p. 237.
5. Banfield, *The Confessions*, pp. 11–12.
6. E.J. Banfield, *My Tropic Isle*, p. 21.
7. Ibid., p. 20.
8. Ibid., p. 46.
9. Ibid., p. 27.
10. Thoreau, *Walden*, "Economy", p. 48; Daniel Defoe, *Robinson Crusoe*, Journal: November 7.
11. Banfield, *The Confessions*, pp. 14, 122.
12. Ibid., pp. 9–10.
13. EJB to brother Harry, 1 November 1897, MS 1860, NLA.
14. Banfield, *The Confessions*, p. 4.

Chapter 13: Man of Many Parts

1. E.J. Banfield, *My Tropic Isle*, p. 41.
2. Ibid., p. 42.
3. Ibid., p. 43.
4. "Abridged Dunk Island Diaries of E.J. Banfield".
5. Ibid.
6. E.G. Barrymore, "Address to Townsville Literary Club"; E.J. Banfield, *The Confessions*, p. 14.
7. Banfield, *The Confessions*, p. 46.
8. Banfield, *My Tropic Isle*, p. 39.
9. "Abridged Diaries".
10. Banfield, *My Tropic Isle*, p. 47.
11. Ibid., p. 28, *The Confessions*, p. 53.
12. Banfield, *My Tropic Isle*, p. 24.
13. "Abridged Diaries".
14. Ibid.
15. E.J. Banfield, *Tropic Days*, p. 72.
16. E.J. Banfield, *Last Leaves*, pp. 222–23.
17. Ibid.
18. E.J. Banfield, "The Sensation of Drowning", A.H. Chisholm Papers.
19. Ibid.
20. Ibid.
21. Banfield, *My Tropic Isle*, pp. 77–78.
22. Lorna L. Banfield, *Colonists of the Early Fifties*.

Chapter 14: Sea-Girt Hermitage

1. "Abridged Dunk Island Diaries of E.J. Banfield".
2. File LAN/DF 2670 Farm No. 271 Ingham, Queensland State Archives.
3. "Abridged Diaries".
4. Will of Jabez Walter Banfield, 25 March 1893, Office of Registrar of Probates, Melbourne.
5. "Abridged Diaries".
6. *The North Queensland Telegraph*, 28 August 1885; James Manion, *Paper Power in North Queensland*.
7. Banfield's letter of 18 May 1901 to the Land Commissioner, Cairns, File LAN/DF 2670 Farm No. 271 Ingham, Queensland State Archives.
8. E.J. Banfield, *The Confessions*, pp. 47, 49.
9. Ibid., pp. 49, 50.
10. Ibid., pp. 50, 93.
11. Ibid., p. 51.
12. H.J. Massingham, "A Modern Crusoe".

Chapter 15: The Modest Castle

1. E.J. Banfield, *My Tropic Isle*, p. 23.
2. BB to AHC, 17 July 1924, A.H. Chisholm Papers.
3. "Abridged Dunk Island Diaries of E.J. Banfield".
4. Ibid.
5. Guy Murchie, *Song of the Sky*: "this elephant among winds has many names for his many haunts". There are moves to have Australian cyclones called hurricanes or typhoons.
6. E.J. Banfield, *The Confessions*, p. 129.
7. Information from John Hopkins in Townsville, 7 August 1979.
8. Banfield, *My Tropic Isle*, p. 44; *The Confessions*, p. 143.
9. E.J. Banfield, *The Confessions*, pp. 55, 59.
10. Ibid., pp. 57–59.
11. Ibid., p. 17; Banfield, *My Tropic Isle*, p. 70.
12. E.J. Banfield, *My Tropic Isle*, pp. 65, 67–68.
13. Banfield, *The Confessions*, pp. 9, 53; *My Tropic Isle*, p. 70.
14. Banfield, *The Confessions*, pp. 190, 192.
15. Information from Harry Hopkins, Townsville.
16. C.E. Montague, *A Writer's Notes on His Trade*, p. 9.

17. Harry C. Perry, *The Memoirs of the Hon. Sir Robert Philp*; BB to AHC, 3 April 1924, Chisholm Papers; E.J. Banfield ("Rob Krusoe"), "A Beachcombing Exploit", *The North Queensland Register*, Chisholm Papers (undated clipping); undated and untitled typescript, A.H. Chisholm Papers.
18. "A Beachcombing Exploit", Chisholm Papers (undated clipping).
19. *The North Queensland Register, Christmas Number*, 17 December 1906.

Chapter 16: A Lunatic on the Coast

1. G.H. Pritchard and E.J. Banfield, *Townsville Illustrated*.
2. E.J. Banfield, *Within the Barrier*, p. 37; Review, *The North Queensland Register*, 7 January 1907.
3. E.J. Banfield, *The Confessions*, part of first edition sub-title.
4. E.J. Banfield ("Beachcomber"), "Rural Homilies", "A Wanderer", *The North Queensland Register*, 8 September 1913.
5. E.G. Barrymore, "Address to Townsville Literary Club".
6. Banfield, "A Wanderer".
7. E.J. Banfield ("Beachcomber"), "Facts and Musings", *The North Queensland Register*, 16 April 1923.
8. Ibid.
9. Henry David Thoreau, *Walden*, "Conclusion", p. 245.
10. E.J. Banfield ("Beachcomber"), "Sportsmen, Men of Science, Collectors", *The North Queensland Register*, 3 November 1913.
11. Banfield, *The Confessions*, p. 130.
12. Ibid., pp. 137–38.
13. File No. AGS/N 352, Queensland State Archives.
14. BB to AHC, 3 April 1924, Chisholm Papers, "Abridged Dunk Island Diaries of E.J. Banfield".
15. Dunk Island map revised by T.P. Adlam; Contract for "The Confessions of a Beachcomber", Chisholm Papers.
16. Contract for "The Confessions".
17. Ibid.
18. "Abridged Diaries".
19. Banfield, "Facts and Musings".
20. Banfield, "A Wanderer".
21. Banfield, "Facts and Musings".
22. A.H. Chisholm Papers.

Chapter 17: Islands Ranger

1. E.J. Banfield, *The Confessions*, p. 334.
2. Ibid., p. 334–35.
3. BB to AHC, 21 December 1924, A.H. Chisholm Papers.
4. E.J. Banfield, *My Tropic Isle*, chap. XXI.
5. Banfield, *The Confessions*, p. 94.
6. Ibid., p. 127.
7. Ibid., p. 128.
8. "Abridged Dunk Island Diaries of E.J. Banfield".
9. Files No. N/351 and N/352, Queensland State Archives.
10. Ibid.
11. Ibid.
12. Ibid.
13. Ibid.
14. Banfield, *The Confessions*, pp. 31, 128; "Abridged Diaries".
15. Banfield, *The Confessions*, p. 60.
16. Banfield, *My Tropic Isle*, p. 152.
17. BB to AHC, 3 April 1924, Chisholm Papers.
18. E.J. Banfield, *Last Leaves*, p. 216.
19. "Abridged Diaries".

Chapter 18: No Hat Big Enough

1. T. Fisher Unwin Ltd.
2. E.J. Banfield, *My Tropic Isle*, pp. 200–201.
3. "Banfield Adventure", *The Daily Mail*, 21 November 1925.

4. *The Times*, 17 September 1908.
5. *The Daily Chronicle* review was quoted in *My Tropic Isle*, 1st ed., 1911; "Abridged Dunk Island Diaries of E.J. Banfield".
6. *The Confessions of a Beachcomber* was published in the United States of America by Appleyard, New York, 1909.
7. *The Times Literary Supplement*, 17 September 1908 (then part of the main paper).
8. Henry David Thoreau, *Walden*, "Economy", p. 3.
9. Banfield, *My Tropic Isle*, p. 14.
10 E.J. Banfield, *The Confessions*, pp. 20, 22.
11. Information from Miss Marjorie Green in Townsville, 22 June 1981.
12. Information from Noel Wood on Bedarra Island, 3 August 1979.
13. Information from John Hopkins in Townsville, 7 August 1979.
14. BB to AHC, 6 July 1929, A.H. Chisholm Papers.
15. "Abridged Diaries"; see chapter 3, note 15.
16. Banfield, *My Tropic Isle*, pp. 49, 50–51.
17. Ibid., pp. 56, 61.
18. "Abridged Diaries".
19. TFU to EJB, 26 August 1910; EJB to TFU, 20 June 1910, Chisholm Papers.
20. E.J. Banfield ("Beachcomber"), "Rural Homilies", "A Friend's letter", *The North Queensland Register*, 12 August 1918.
21. E.J. Banfield ("Beachcomber"), "The Age of Hurry", "Southern Scenes Revisited", *The North Queensland Register*, 19 June 1911; Thoreau, *Walden*, "Where I Lived", p. 68.
22. Banfield, "The Age of Hurry".
23. Ibid.
24. E.J. Banfield, "A Day in Sydney", "Southern Scenes Revisited", 17 April 1911.
25. E.J. Banfield, "Street Gardens", "Southern Scenes Revisited", 15 May 1911.
26. E.J. Banfield ("Beachcomber"), "With the Tourists", *The North Queensland Register*, 26 June 1911.
27. "Abridged Diaries".
28. *The Times Literary Supplement*, 21 September 1911.
29. *Nature* (28 December 1911); undated clipping found pasted in library copy of *My Tropic Isle*,
30. TFU to EJB, 15 January 1912, 13 April 1912, Chisholm Papers.
31. Banfield, *My Tropic Isle*, p. 299; TFU to EJB, 8 January 1912, Chisholm Papers.
32. E.G. Barrymore, "Address to Townsville Literary Club"; Banfield, *My Tropic Isle*, p. 77.
33. Banfield, *My Tropic Isle*, p. 79.

Chapter 19: The Pleasures of Authorship

1. BB to AHC, 7 September 1923, A.H. Chisholm Papers.
2. Messrs Russell, Cook & Co., Lincoln's Inn, handed over to C.J. Turner and Sons, Leadenhall. Chisholm Papers.
3. TFU to EJB, 26 August 1910, Chisholm Papers.
4. E.J. Banfield, *My Tropic Isle*, p. 129.
5. TFU to EJB, 24 September 1912, Chisholm Papers.
6. Ibid.; EJB to TFU, 13 November 1912, Chisholm Papers.
7. TFU to EJB, 31 December 1912, Chisholm Papers.
8. EJB to TFU, 18 February 1913, Chisholm Papers.
9. TFU to EJB, 11 April 1913, Chisholm Papers.
10. Banfield, *My Tropic Isle*, p. 156.
11. Reasoning, oft admire
   How Nature, wise and frugal, could commit
   Such dispositions with superfluous hand.
   My Tropic Isle, p. 152.
12. Banfield, *My Tropic Isle*, pp. 158–59.

Chapter 20: Lifelines

1. E.J. Banfield, "The Ideal Isle — A Rhapsody", A.H. Chisholm Papers; "Abridged Diaries" state it was sent by Banfield to E.G. Barrymore, 12 July 1920.
2. Daniel Defore, *Robinson Crusoe*, Journal, 30 September 1659; E.J. Banfield, *My Tropic Isle*, p. 29.
3. H.J. Massingham, "A Modern Crusoe".

4. *The Athenaeum*, 2 December 1908.
5. *The Times Literary Supplement*, 17 September 1908.
6. Information from James Manion in Townsville, 23 June 1981.
7. Lloyd's Registers; information from Miss Marjorie Green in Townsville, 7 August 1979.
8. "Abridged Dunk Island Diaries of E.J. Banfield"; shell cabinet sent to Queensland Museum following death of E.J. Banfield.
9. John Hopkins in letter to author, 11 August 1982; as in Longfellow's *Hiawatha*.
10. Information from Miss Marjorie Green.
11. BB to AHC, 30 December 1923, A.H. Chisholm Papers.
12. Banfield, *My Tropic Isle*, p. 34.
13. Ibid., pp. 248–49.
14. Information from Miss Marjorie Green.
15. "George Barrymore (A Westerner's Tribute)", *The North Queensland Register*, 4 March 1944 (Obituary).
16. James Manion, *Paper Power in North Queensland*, pp. 56–57.
17. Harry Gordon, "The Press, Power and the Story", *The Courier-Mail*, 30 October 1982. The David Green Memorial Award for Journalism commemorates one of North Queensland's most notable newspapermen.
18. E.G. Barrymore, "Address to Townsville Literary Club".
19. Banfield, *My Tropic Isle*, pp. 81–82.
20. Information from A.H. Hardy in Townsville, 21 June 1981.
21. E.J. Banfield ("Beachcomber"), "Rural Homilies", "The Storm Wind", *The North Queensland Register*, 8 April 1918.

Chapter 21: Original Inhabitants

1. E.J. Banfield, *The Confessions*, p. 42.
2. Ibid., p. 251.
3. Henry David Thoreau, *Walden*, "Where I Lived, and What I Lived For", p. 68.
4. Banfield, *The Confessions*, p. 39.
5. Ibid., p. 238.
6. Ibid., p. 307.
7. Ibid., pp. 270, 297, 298; E.J. Banfield ("Beachcomber"), "Rural Homilies", "Dynamiters", *The North Queensland Register*, A.H. Chisholm Papers, undated clipping, probably about 1908–9.
8. Banfield, *The Confessions*, pp. 301–2.
9. Ibid., p. 302.
10. Ibid., p. 271.
11. Ibid., pp. 255, 258, 259.
12. E.J. Banfield, *My Tropic Isle*, p. 74.
13. Ibid., p. 276.
14. Banfield, *The Confessions*, pp. 237–38.
15. Banfield, *My Tropic Isle*, p. 281–83.
16. Ibid., p. 284.
17. E.G. Barrymore, "Address to Townsville Literary Club".
18. E.J. Banfield, *Tropic Days*, p. 118.
19. Ibid., pp. 118-20.

Chapter 22: Home Front

1. E.G. Barrymore ("Cestus"), "The Beachcomber", *The North Queensland Register*, 11 June 1923; reproduced with slight changes by A.H. Chisholm in his introduction to *Last Leaves*, pp. xix–xx.
2. E.J. Banfield, *My Tropic Isle*, p. 59.
3. E.J. Banfield, *The Confessions*, pp. 24–25; E.J. Banfield ("Beachcomber"), "Rural Homilies", "About Islands", *The North Queensland Register*, 11 June 1917. Banfield also says in "About Islands": "The 1st Earl of Sandwich reinvented the sandwich — an historical delicacy from ancient Rome."
4. *Encyclopaedia Britannica*, 11th ed. (Cambridge: Cambridge University Press, 1911).
5. Map Room, British Museum, London.
6. Information from James Manion in Townsville, 23 June 1981.
7. E.J. Banfield ("Beachcomber"), "Rural Homilies — The Ruthless Collector", *The North Queensland Register*, A.H. Chisholm Papers (undated clipping, but referred to in "Abridged Diaries", 22 September 1912).

8.   E.J. Banfield, *Tropic Days*, p. 18.
9.   Ibid., p. 16.
10. BB to AHC, 3 April 1924, Chisholm Papers.
11. Banfield, *Tropic Days*, p. 15.
12. "Abridged Dunk Island Diaries of E.J. Banfield".
13. Banfield, *My Tropic Isle*, p. 31.
14. Banfield, *Tropic Days*, p. 52.
15. Banfield, *My Tropic Isle*, p. 169.
16. *The Queenslander* (weekly), 23 March 1918, dated-lined Townsville 14 March.

Chapter 23: The Clocks Have Stopped

1.   E.J. Banfield ("Beachcomber"), "The Tempest", *The North Queensland Register*, 18 March 1918.
2.   E.J. Banfield, *Last Leaves*, p. 18.
3.   Ibid., pp. 2–3.
4.   EJB to EGB, 12 March 1918, UNCAT MSS. 472, ML, Sydney.
5.   E.J. Banfield ("Beachcomber"), "Rural Homilies", "The Storm Wind", *The North Queensland Register*, 8 April 1918. In *Cardwell Shire Story*, Dorothy Jones states that at least five Aborigines were killed, one in a tidal surge, and that "many more of the Mission Aborigines were probably killed as they sheltered in all directions in the scrub" (p. 310).
6.   EJB to EGB, 19 March 1918, Barrymore Papers UNCAT MSS. 472, ML.
7.   Ibid.; EJB to AHC, 2 April 1922, A.H. Chisholm Papers.
8.   "Abridged Dunk Island Diaries of E.J. Banfield".
9.   E.J. Banfield, *My Tropic Isle*, pp. 68–69.
10. Banfield, *Last Leaves*, p. 8.
11. Information from Miss Marjorie Green in Townsville, 7 August 1979 and 22 June 1981.
12. *The Times Literary Supplement*, 9 May 1918; E.J. Banfield, *Tropic Days*, p. 40.
13. Banfield, *Last Leaves*, pp. 19, 153.
14. BB to AHC, 7 September 1923, Chisholm Papers.
15. From E.J. Banfield's letter of 23 July 1918 attached to A.H. Chisholm's copy of the first edition of *The Confessions*, ML.
16. Information from John Hopkins, Townsville.

Chapter 24: Ancient Order of Beachcombers

1.   E.J. Banfield, *My Tropic Isle*, pp. 191–92.
2.   Ibid., pp. 195–96.
3.   E.G. Barrymore ("Cestus"), "Dodd S. Clarke", *The North Queensland Register*, 29 July 1918; E.G. Barrymore, "Address to Townsville Literary Club".
4.   Barrymore, "Dodd S. Clarke".
5.   E.J. Banfield, *The Confessions*, p. 171; EJB to AHC, 14 November 1917, A.H. Chisholm Papers.
6.   *Walkabout*, 1 September 1953.
7.   Information from Miss Marjorie Green in Townsville, 22 June 1981.
8.   BB to AHC, 26 December 1929, Chisholm Papers.
9.   Ibid.
10. Lord Forster (1866–1936) was created First Baron of Lepe in 1919; he had been a politician and was sworn in as governor-general of Australia on 6 October 1920; his two sons were killed in the Great War. From *Australian Encyclopaedia*, 3rd ed. (Sydney: The Grolier Society of Australia Pty Ltd, 1977).
11. Ibid.
12. A.H. Chisholm, "Charles Leslie Barrett"; Charles Barrett, *Koonwarra*, pp. 171, 177.

Chapter 25: Romance and Reality

1.   A.H. Chisholm, Introduction to *Last Leaves*, p. xvii; A.H. Chisholm, Introduction to 1st Australian ed., *The Confessions* (1933).
2.   EJB to AHC, 17 July 1916, A.H. Chisholm Papers.
3.   John MacGillivray, *Narrative of the Voyage of HMS Rattlesnake*, pp. 85-86.
4.   E.J. Banfield, *Tropic Days*, pp. 38, 180; *My Tropic Isle*, p. 77.
5.   E.J. Banfield, *Last Leaves*, p. 137.

6. Banfield, *Tropic Days*, p. 24; *The Confessions*, p. 90.
7. E.J. Banfield, *The Confessions*, pp. 87, 88.
8. Ibid., p. 227.
9. Banfield, *Tropic Days*, pp. 71, 72, 84.
10. A.H. Chisholm, Introduction to *Last Leaves*, pp. xxi–xxii.
11. H.J. Massingham, "A Modern Crusoe"; Banfield, *Last Leaves*, p. 21.
12. Banfield, *My Tropic Isle*, p. 75, *Last Leaves*, p. 62.
13. Banfield, *Last Leaves*, p. 64.
14. A.H. Chisholm, "Fantome Mystery", *The Daily Telegraph*, 9 February 1923.
15. EJB to AHC, 2 October 1922, Chisholm Papers.
16. *The Daily Mail*, 29 July 1922.
17. EJB to AHC, 30 July 1922, Chisholm Papers.
18. EJB to AHC, 4 August 1922, Chisholm Papers.
19. Once seen in millions, the passenger pigeons became extinct in 1914.
20. Banfield, *The Confessions*, p. 164; EJB to AHC, 23 October 1922, Chisholm Papers.
21. EJB to AHC, 16 April 1923 and 8 May 1923, Chisholm Papers.
22. File No. AGS/J 330/870/1925, Queensland State Archives.

Chapter 26: The Reading Room in Amsterdam

1. Dale Collins, *Sea-tracks of the Speejacks Round the World*, pp. 39-41.
2. "Abridged Dunk Island Diaries of E.J. Banfield".
3. Lieut. W.I. Farquharson RN, "Calico Chart of Brammo Bay, Dunk Island", privately held.
4. R. Logan Jack, *Northmost Australia* vol. I, p. 88; vol. II, p. 660.
5. Henry David Thoreau, *Walden*, "Higher Laws", p. 162, quoted by Banfield in *The Confessions*, p. 336.
6. E.J. Banfield, "The Madagascar Rose", pp. 261–62.
7. E.J. Banfield, *Last Leaves*, pp. 53–54.
8. Ibid., p. 221.
9. Ibid., pp. 221, 226.
10. "Abridged Diaries"; EJB to EGB, 4 March 1921, Barrymore Papers.
11. E.J. Banfield, *My Tropic Isle*, p. 29; BB to AHC, 3 April 1924, and EJB to EGB, 29 May 1922, A.H. Chisholm Papers.
12. *The Times*, 8 June 1923; information from Miss Marjorie Green in Townsville, 22 June 1981.
13. *The Times*, 8 June 1923.
14. E.G. Barrymore, "Address".

Chapter 27: Last Leaves

1. "Abridged Dunk Island Diaries of E.J. Banfield".
2. BB to AHC, 23 September 1923, A.H. Chisholm Papers.
3. E.J. Banfield, *The Confessions*, p. 85; Death Certificate
4. Ibid., p. 175.
5. Information from A.H. Hardy in Townsville, 21 June 1981.
6. BB to AHC, 28 June 1923, Chisholm Papers.
7. BB to AHC, 3 April 1924, Chisholm Papers.
8. BB to AHC, 4 October 1923, Chisholm Papers.
9. Ibid.
10. George Robertson to AHC, 22 October 1923, Chisholm Papers.
11. A.H. Chisholm, Introduction to *Last Leaves*, p. xxiv.
12. BB to AHC, 3 April 1924, 28 May 1924, 1 June 1924, 13 July 1924, Chisholm Papers.
13. BB to AHC, 7 September 1923, Chisholm Papers; A.H. Chisholm, "The Lady of Dunk Island", *Argus*, 11 August 1933.
14. BB to AHC, 3 April 1924, Chisholm Papers; E.G. Barrymore ("Cestus"), "Essie", *The North Queensland Register*, 20 June 1936.
15. E.J. Banfield, *My Tropic Isle*, pp. 13–14.
16. Angus & Robertson Reviews, Book 18, pp. 142–53, ML.; BB to AHC, 17 May 1927, Chisholm Papers.
17. A.H. Chisholm edited the original article as it had appeared in *The Townsville Daily Bulletin*, 25 June 1923, for inclusion in *Last Leaves*.

Epilogue

1. Letter from Joseph Moran, 28 August 1924, A.H. Chisholm Papers.
2. BB to AHC, between 13 June 1926 and 6 July 1929; also Spenser Hopkins to BB, 9 June 1926, Chisholm Papers; E.J. Banfield, "Rural Homilies", "Tropical College", *The North Queensland Register*, 9 June 1913; BB to AHC 6 May 1933, Chisholm Papers.
3. Bertha Banfield's death certificate, File No. A/17124, Queensland State Archives; information from Miss Marjorie Green in Townsville, 7 August 1979; and from Helen Dyer in Townsville, 21 June 1981.
4. E.G. Barrymore ("Cestus"), "Mrs Banfield", *The North Queensland Register*, 12 August 1933; italics indicate the words used on the inscription on the tablet.
5. E.G. Barrymore ("Cestus"), "Essie", *The North Queensland Register*, 20 June 1936.
6. Valerie Albiston, "The Dunk Island Story", *The Cairns Post*, 1979; Dorothy Jones, *Cardwell Shire Story*; Joan Hope White, "Dunk Island", *The Sunday Mail*, 13 May 1936.
7. A.H. Chisholm, Introduction to 1968 ed., *The Confessions*, p. xi.
8. E.J. Banfield, "Dunk Island. Its General Characteristics", p. 64.
9. E.J. Banfield, "The Ideal Isle", "A Rhapsody", Chisholm Papers; Abridged Diaries" state it was sent by Banfield to E.G. Barrymore, 12 July 1920. In his Introduction to the 1968 abridged edition of *The Confessions*, Alec Chisholm wrote that when he returned to Dunk after some forty-six years and saw the resort there for the first time, he found the Isle "still a most endearing spot" with "an amiable balance between the 'wild' and the 'tame' ".

Bibliography

Published Sources

Adlam, Thomas Philip. "An Old Friend's Tribute". *The World's News*, Sydney, 23 June 1923.
_____. "In the Valley of Death". *The World's News*, Sydney, 15 August 1925.
Albiston, Valerie. "Where Shadows Linger". *The Sunday Mail Magazine*, Brisbane, 10 March 1974.
_____. "The Dunk Island Story". *The Cairns Post*, 1979.

Bailey, F. Manson. *Queensland Flora*. Brisbane: Diddams, Printers, 1899-1902.
Banfield, E.J. *The Confessions of a Beachcomber; Scenes and Incidents in the Career of an Unprofessional Beachcomber in Tropical Queensland*. 1st ed. London: T. Fisher Unwin Limited, 1908.
"The Modern Travel Series". 1st ed. 2nd imp. London: T. Fisher Unwin, 1910.
Sydney: Angus & Robertson Ltd, 1933 (abridged).
Australian Pocket Library. Sydney: Australian Publishing Co. Pty Ltd, [1945] (abridged).
Sydney: Angus & Robertson Ltd, 1968 and 1974 (abridged).
Melbourne: Lloyd O'Neil, 1974. Most of the quotes have been taken from this edition, the page numbers of which are identical with the first edition.
_____. "Dunk Island. Its General Characteristics". *Proceedings Royal Geographical Society of Australasia, Queensland* vol. xxiii (1908): 51-64. Read on 28 May 1908 by E.J.T. Barton in the absence of E.J. Banfield.
_____. "Erratic Rovings". *The Ararat and Pleasant Creek Advertiser* (reprinted from *The Townsville Daily Bulletin*). No. I, 7 November 1884. No. II, 18 November 1884. No. III, 2 December 1884. No. IV, 23 December 1884.

_____. "The Gentle Art of Beachcombing". *The Lone Hand* (1 January 1913): 226-32.

_____. "Homeward Bound". *The Ararat and Pleasant Creek Advertiser* (reprinted from *The Townsville Daily Bulletin*). 11 January 1884. No. II, 15 July 1884. No. III, 18 July 1884. No. IV, 22 July 1884. No. V, 19 August 1884. No. VI, 26 August 1884. No. VII, 2 September 1884.

_____. *Last Leaves from Dunk Island*. Ed. A.H. Chisholm. Sydney: Angus & Robertson Ltd, 1925.

_____. "The Madagascar Rose". *The Lone Hand* (1 September 1914): 261.

_____. *My Tropic Isle*. London: T. Fisher Unwin Ltd, 1911. 2nd ed. 1912. New York: Outing Publishing Company, 1912.

_____. "Rural Homilies". Mainly in *The North Queensland Register* with some in *The Townsville Daily Bulletin*. While Banfield's main newspaper articles were published under this title, his writings were prodigious in range of subject as well as in number of articles. They are far from fully catalogued and are a subject for much research on their own. Valuable research has already been carried out by the Department of English, James Cook University of North Queensland. Some 200 articles, mainly "Rural Homilies", have been traced between 1911 and 1921. Prior to 1911, Banfield had already been turning out "Rural Homilies"; "Fearsome Insects", for instance, appeared in *The North Queensland Register*, 24 February 1908. In his Preface to *My Tropic Isle*, 1911, Banfield wrote: "Much of the contents of this book was published in *The North Queensland Register*, under the title of 'Rural Homilies'." According to "The Abridged Dunk Island Diaries", Banfield"Began seriously new Book" on 27 March 1909. In the A.H. Chisholm Papers there are scores of undated clippings of articles from unnamed newspapers. Research in this area has been difficult because of the losses suffered by the North Queensland Newspaper Company Limited by fire on 17 October 1912, and by incomplete collections in libraries, with many issues in a fragile state. After giving up "Rural Homilies" as such in 1921, Banfield wrote occasional articles, a number under the title "Facts and Musings".

_____. "Southern Scenes Revisited". *The North Queensland Register*. At least 12 articles in this series were published between 17 April 1911 and 2 July 1911; "With the Tourists", 26 June 1911, although not described as "Southern Scenes Revisited", would also appear to be one of the series.

_____. *The Torres Straits Route from Queensland to England by the British-India Steam Navigation Company's Royal Mail Steamer "Cheybassa"*. Townsville: T. Willmett, 1885.

_____. *Tropic Days*. London: T. Fisher Unwin Ltd, 1918. New York: Brentano's, n.d.

_____. "Up North. Recreative Days". *The Ararat Advertiser*, 27 November 1891.

_____. *Within the Barrier: Tourists' Guide to the North Queensland Coast*

(cover title *Queensland, The Winter Paradise of Australia*).
Townsville: Messrs Willmett & Son, 1907.

Banfield, E.J., and Pritchard, G.H. *Townsville Illustrated*. Townsville:
Printed by T. Willmett & Sons, 1906.

Banfield, Lorna L. *Colonists of the Early Fifties: J.W. and S.A. Banfield*.
Produced by Tom Banfield, privately published.

———. *Green Pastures and Gold*. Canterbury, Victoria: Mullaya
———. Publications, 1974.

———. *Like the Ark: The Story of Ararat*. Melbourne: F.W. Cheshire,
1955.

———. *The Shire of Ararat; its settlement and development, 1864–1964*.
Ararat: Ararat Shire Council, 1964.

Banks, Joseph. *Endeavour Journals of Joseph Banks, 1768–1771*. Ed. J.C.
Beaglehole. 2 vols. Sydney: Angus & Robertson Ltd, 1962.

Barrett, Charles. "The Beachcomber". *The Weekly Times Annual*, 1921.
A.H. Chisholm Papers.

———. "Dunk Island Days". *Walkabout* (October 1935): 33–36.

———. *Koonwarra: A Naturalist's Adventures in Australia*. London:
Oxford University Press, 1938.

Barrymore, E.G. "Address to Townsville Literary Club". *The Townsville
Daily Bulletin*, 16 November 1934.

———. ("Cestus"). "Dodd S. Clarke". *The North Queensland Register*,
29 July 1918.

———. ("Cestus"). "The Beachcomber". *The North Queensland Register*,
11 June 1923.

———. ("Cestus"). "Mrs Banfield". *The North Queensland Register*,
12 August 1933.

———. ("Cestus"). "Essie". *The North Queensland Register*, 20 June 1936.

———. ("Cestus"). "David Green". *The Northern Miner*, 27 November
1941.

Barrymore, Freda. *Portrait of Tropic Isles and Coral Seas*. Produced con-
jointly by the Townsville City Council and the Townsville
Harbour Board. Townsville: T. Willmett & Sons (Pty) Ltd,
1933.

Bassett, Marjorie (Marnie). *Behind the Picture. "HMS Rattlesnake's
Australia–New Guinea Cruise, 1846–50"*. Melbourne: Oxford
University Press, 1966.

Bonnin, Margriet R. "Edmund James Banfield (1852–1923)". *Australian
Dictionary of Biography* vol. 7 (1979), pp. 165-66.

Brady, E.J. *Australia Unlimited*. Melbourne: George Robertson & Co.,
1912–14.

———. *The Land of the Sun*. London: Edward Arnold, 1924.
Book Review Digest. Minneapolis: The H.H. Wilson Company,
1909, 1912, 1919.

Carroll, Lewis (C.L. Dodgson). *The Adventures of Alice in Wonderland*,
1865; *Through the Looking-Glass*, 1871.

Chisholm, A.H. "Charles Leslie Barrett (1879–1959)". *Australian
Dictionary of Biography* vol. 7 (1979), p. 185.

———. "Charles Leslie Barrett". *Australian Encyclopaedia*. 3rd ed.
Sydney: The Grolier Society of Australia Pty Ltd, 1977.

———. "The Beachcomber Passes". *The Daily Mail*, 13 June 1923.

———. "Bird Seeking in Queensland, 1770–1922", read to the Royal

Australian Ornithologists' Union, 6 March 1922, reprinted in *The Queensland Naturalist*.

_____. "Fantome Memory". *The Daily Telegraph*, Sydney, 9 February 1923.

_____. "Introduction". *The Confessions of a Beachcomber*. Sydney: Angus & Robertson, 1933, 1968.

_____. "Introduction". *Last Leaves from Dunk Island*. Sydney: Angus & Robertson, 1925.

_____. *The Joy of Earth*. Sydney: Collins, 1969.

_____. *Mateship with Birds*. Melbourne: Whitcombe and Tombs, 1922.

_____. "Nature Notes". *The Daily Mail*, Brisbane, 30 September 1922.

Church, Richard. *Kent*. London: Robert Hale Limited, 1948.

Cilento, Sir Raphael. *Triumph in the Tropics*. Brisbane: Smith & Paterson Pty Ltd, 1959.

Collins, Dale. "The Man who Found Paradise on Earth". *The World Magazine*, 2 September 1923.

_____. *Sea-tracks of the Speejacks Round the World*. London: Wm. Heinemann Ltd, 1923.

Colson, Percy. *Melba*. London: Grayson & Grayson, 1932.

Cook, James. *The Journals of Captain James Cook on his Voyages of Discovery*. Ed. from the original MSS. by J.C. Beaglehole (and others). Cambridge: Cambridge University Press for the Hakluyt Society, 1955–74.

Cottrell, Dorothy. *The Singing Gold*. London: Hodder and Stoughton, 1928.

Defoe, Daniel. *Robinson Crusoe*, 1719.

Doran, C.R. "Separation Movements in North Queensland in the Nineteenth Century". *LINQ* Series 3 (1979): 85–99.

Endean, Robert. *Australia's Great Barrier Reef*. St Lucia: University of Queensland Press, 1982.

Farnfield, D. Jean. *Frontiersman: a Biography of George Elphinstone Dalrymple*. Melbourne: Oxford University Press, 1968.

Fawcett, J.W. *A Narrative of the Terrible Cyclone and Flood in Townsville, North Queensland, 25–28 January, 1896*. Townsville: R.H. Thomas, 1896.

Feeken, Erwin H.J. and Gerda E.E. *The Discovery and Exploration of Australia*. Essay by O.H.K. Spate. Melbourne: Nelson, 1970.

Fitchett, T.K. *The Vanished Fleet: Australian Coastal and Passenger Ships 1910–1960*. Adelaide: Rigby, 1976.

Fitzgerald, Ross. *From the Dreaming to 1915*. St Lucia: University of Queensland Press, 1982.

Flinders, Matthew. *A Voyage to Terra Australis*. Vols. I and II. London: G. and W. Nicol, 1814.

Gould, John F.R.S. *An Introduction to Birds of Australia*. London: Printed for the author, by Richard and John E. Taylor, Red Lion Court, Fleet Street, 1848.

_____. *Handbook to the Birds of Australia*. Vols. I and II. London: the author, 1862. Melbourne: Lansdowne Press, 1972.

Gregory, Dickson. *Australian Steamships: Past and Present*. London: The Richards Press, 1928.

Harting, J.E. *The Ornithology of Shakespeare*. Old Woking, Surrey: Unwin Bros, 1978.

Heaton, J.H. *Australian Dictionary of Dates and Men of the Times*. Sydney: George Robertson, 1879.

Heseltine, H.P. "The Confessions of a Beachcomber". *LINQ* vol. 9, no. 1 (1981): 35–52.

Holthouse, Hector. *Cyclone*. Adelaide: Rigby, 1971.

_____. *Illustrated History of Queensland*. Adelaide: Rigby, 1978.

_____. *Ships in the Coral*. Melbourne: Macmillan, 1976.

Hough, Elinor, M. "Coonanglebah". *Walkabout* (1 September 1953).

Howard Smith Limited. *Tourist Handbook of Australia*. Ed. Donald MacDonald, 1904.

_____. *The First 100 Years (1854–1954)*. Sydney: "The Harbour" Newspaper and Publishing Co. Ltd, 1954.

The Howard Smith Line. *Handbook of Information for Travellers on the Australian Coast*. Compil. and ed. Lachlan Beaton. Melbourne: Sands and McDougall, 1897.

Huxley, Thomas Henry. *Life and Letters*. Vols. I-III. London: Macmillan, 1913.

_____. *T.H. Huxley's Diary of the Voyage of HMS Rattlesnake*. Ed. from MSS. by Julia Huxley. London: Chatto and Windus, 1935.

Ingleton, Geoffrey C. *Charting a Continent*. Sydney: Angus & Robertson, 1944.

Jack, R. Logan, *Northmost Australia*. Vols I and II. London: Simpkin, Marshall, Hamilton, Kent & Co., 1921.

Jerrold, Walter. *Highways and Byways of Kent*. London: Macmillan and Co. Ltd, 1914.

Jones, Dorothy. *Cardwell Shire Story*. Brisbane: The Jacaranda Press, 1961.

_____. *Hurricane Lamps and Umbrellas*. Cairns: G.K. Bolton, 1973.

Jukes, J. Beete. *Narrative of the Surveying Voyage of HMS Fly commanded by Captain F.P. Blackwood RN . . . during the years 1824–46*. London: T. & W. Boone, 1847.

Kent, W. Saville. *The Great Barrier Reef of Australia*. London: W.H. Allen, 1893.

_____. *The Naturalist in Australia*. London: W.H. Allen, 1897.

King, Philip P. *Narrative of the Survey of the Intertropical and Western Coasts of Australia, performed between the years 1818 and 1822*. London: Murray, 1827.

Kingsley, Charles. *Hereward the Wake*. London: Macmillan and Co., 1873.

Lawson, Albury and Peter. *Townsville: an Early History*. Adelaide: Rigby, 1977.

Leach, J.A. *An Australian Bird Book; a complete guide to the identification of the Australian Species*. 8th ed. Rev. and ed. Charles Barrett. Melbourne: Whitcombe & Tombs, 1939.

Lubbock, Adelaide. *Owen Stanley, RN*. London: Heinemann, 1968.

MacGillivray, John. *Narrative of the Voyage of HMS Rattlesnake commanded by the Late Captain Owen Stanley, RN, FRS, during the years 1846–50*. London: T. & W. Boone, 1852.

Manion, James. *Paper Power in North Queensland; A History of Journalism in Townsville and Charters Towers*. Townsville: The North Queensland Newspaper Company Limited, 1982.

Manion, J., and Davis, Sonia. *Townsville Yesterday — in Pen and Picture*. Townsville: North Queensland Newspaper Company Limited, 1978.

Massingham, H.J. "A Modern Crusoe: How an Author Turned Away from Civilization". *Cassell's Weekly*, 15 August 1923.

Mayhew, Athol. *A Jorum of "Punch", with Those Who Helped Brew It*. London: Downey & Co., 1895.

McKellar, N.L. *From Derby Round to Burketown, The AUSN Story*. St Lucia: University of Queensland Press, 1977.

Monkman, Noel. *Escape to Adventure: Travels in North Queensland and on the Great Barrier Reef*. Sydney: Angus & Robertson, 1956.

Montague, C.E. *A Writer's Notes on his Trade*. London: Chatto and Windus, 1930. London: Penguin Books, 1949.

Murchie, Guy. *Song of the Sky*. London: Secker & Warburg, 1955.

Page, M.F. *Fitted for the Voyage: The Adelaide Steamship Company Limited, 1875–1975*. Adelaide: Rigby, 1975.

Park, Ruth. "The Delicious Isle". *Walkabout*, vol. 31, no. 1 (1965): 12–15.

Pemberton, Barry. *Australian Coastal Shipping*. Melbourne: Melbourne University Press, 1979.

Perry, Harry C. *The Memoirs of the Hon. Sir Robert Philp KCMG 1851–1922*. Brisbane: Watson, Ferguson & Co. Ltd, 1923.

Pope-Hennesey, Una. *Charles Dickens*. London: Chatto & Windus, 1945.

Singe, John. *Torres Straits*. St Lucia: University of Queensland Press, 1979.

Stokes, Captain J. Lort. *Discoveries in Australia: with an Account of Coasts and Rivers Explored and Surveyed During the Voyage of HMS Beagle in Years 1837–43*. London: Boone, 1846.

Taylor, H.J. *The History of Townsville Harbour 1864–1979*. Brisbane: Boolarong Publications, 1980.

Thoreau, Henry David. *Walden or, Life in the Woods*. 1856. New York: Harper and Row, 1965.

Traill, William Henry. *Historical Sketch of Queensland*. 1886. Sydney: Lansdowne Press, 1980.

White, Joan Hope. "Dunk Island". *The Sunday Mail*, 13 May 1936.

Withers, W.B. *History of Ballarat*. Ballarat Star, 1870.

Who Was Who, vol. II, 1916–28, vol. III, 1929–40. London: Adam & Charles Black, 1947.

Newspapers and Periodicals

Ararat Library, Ararat, Victoria: *The Ararat Advertiser*.

James Cook University Library, Townsville: *The North Queensland Register, Christmas Numbers*.

La Trobe Library Newspaper Collection, Melbourne: *The Ararat Advertiser; The Ararat and Pleasant Creek Advertiser; The Mount Ararat Advertiser*.

State Library of New South Wales: *The Daily Telegraph; The World's News*.

State Library of Queensland/John Oxley Library: *The Bowen Independent; The Cairns Post; The Daily Mail; The Sunday Mail; The Courier-Mail; The Illustrated London News; The Northern Miner; The North Queensland Register; The North Queensland Telegraph; The Queenslander; The Times; The Times Literary Supplement; The Townsville Daily Bulletin; Walkabout*.

Other Sources

"Abridged Dunk Island Diaries of E.J. Banfield, 1898–1923". Privately held.

Anderson, H. Photographic Collection. James Cook University Library, Townsville.

Angus & Robertson Reviews, ML.

Baines, Thomas. Sketches and Water-Colours. vols. I-IV. Royal Geographical Society, London.

Banfield Biographical Files. John Oxley Library, Brisbane.

Banfield, E.J. "The Confessions of a Beachcomber". Typescript. A 2532. ML.

———. "The Ideal Isle", "A Rhapsody". A.H. Chisholm Papers. ("Abridged Diaries" state it was sent by Banfield to E.G. Barrymore on 12 July 1920.)

———. "Last Leaves from Dunk Island". Proof sheets. Uncat. MS Set 257. ML.

———. "The Sensation of Drowning". A.H. Chisholm Papers. ML.

Banfield, J.W. "Reminiscences of an Incident at Dunolly Gold Rush and of coming to Australia in 1852". A.H. Chisholm Papers. MS 3540. ML. Also MS 1723. NLA.

Banfield, Lorna L. "Early Ararat Advertiser Index". October 1857–October 1863. La Trobe Library, Melbourne.

Barrymore Papers. Uncat. MSS 472. ML.

Biddle, T.E. "Transactions British Shipping Between Ports in the United Kingdom and Port of Melbourne". La Trobe Library, Melbourne.

Chisholm, A.H. Papers. MSS 3540. ML.

Dunk Island File. National Parks and Wild Life Services Library, Brisbane.

Forbes, George. "Anthony Horderns: Historical Sketch, 1824–1921". ML.

National Library of Australia, Canberra. MS 1723; MS 1835; MS 1860; MS 2225.

The North Queensland Register Card Index. Department of English, James Cook University, Townsville.

Queensland State Archives: A/17124; AGS/Farm No 271 Ingham LAN/DF 2670; AGS/N 351 and 352; AGS/J 330/870/1925.

Sheriff, M.A. "Some NQ Creative Writing and Belles Lettres", BA (Hons.) Discourse 1970. Department of English, James Cook University, Townsville.

Index

Index